Thomas Nagel

Philosophy Now

Series Editor: John Shand

This is a fresh and vital series of new introductions to today's most read, discussed and important philosophers. Combining rigorous analysis with authoritative exposition, each book gives a clear, comprehensive and enthralling access to the ideas of those philosophers who have made a truly fundamental and original contribution to the subject. Together the volumes comprise a remarkable gallery of the thinkers who have been at the forefront of philosophical ideas.

Published

David Armstrong
Stephen Mumford

Robert Brandom
Jeremy Wanderer

Donald Davidson
Marc Joseph

Nelson Goodman
Daniel Cohnitz & Marcus Rossberg

Saul Kripke
G. W. Fitch

David Lewis
Daniel Nolan

John McDowell
Tim Thornton

Thomas Nagel
Alan Thomas

Hilary Putnam
Maximilian de Gaynesford

John Rawls
Catherine Audard

Wilfrid Sellars
Willem A. deVries

Peter Strawson
Clifford Brown

Bernard Williams
Mark P. Jenkins

Thomas Nagel

Alan Thomas

McGill-Queen's University Press
Montreal & Kingston · Ithaca

ISBN: 978-0-7735-3559-6 (hardcover)
ISBN: 978-0-7735-3560-2 (paperback)

Legal deposit first quarter 2009
Bibliothèque nationale du Québec

Published simultaneously outside North America
by Acumen Publishing Limited

McGill-Queen's University Press acknowledges the financial support of the Government of Canada through the Book Publishing Development Program (BPIDP) for its activities.

Library and Archives Canada Cataloguing in Publication

Thomas, Alan, 1964-
Thomas Nagel / Alan Thomas.

(Philosophy now)
Includes bibliographical references and index.
ISBN 978-0-7735-3559-6 (bound).--ISBN 978-0-7735-3560-2 (pbk.)

1. Nagel, Thomas, 1937-. I. Title. II. Series.

B945.N334T46 2009 191 C2008-907560-9

Printed by the MPG Books Group in the UK

Contents

Preface

The aim of this book is systematically to exposit and to criticize some of the central themes of Thomas Nagel's philosophy, primarily for the benefit of a reader coming to Nagel's work for the first time. The good news, both from my point of view and that of the student of Nagel's work, is that he is an outstandingly clear writer. I have not felt that I have had much work to do in explaining his central ideas. The bad news from my point of view is that Nagel is a very wide-ranging philosopher who has made important contributions to nearly all of the central areas of philosophy. In a book of this restricted length I have not been able comprehensively to cover all of the issues that he discusses. My overall approach, in the light of both Nagel's clarity and comprehensiveness, has been to focus on the overall structure of his philosophy and the philosophical context in which it was developed. Fortunately, Nagel's work lends itself to this approach owing to the structural importance throughout his work of a central dichotomy between the subjective and the objective. I have aimed to bring out underlying themes and to come to some overall evaluation of his approach within the limited scope available to me. Inevitably I have prioritized an analysis of underlying structure as opposed to comprehensive coverage. Such important Nagelian topics as, to take just two examples, his panpsychism or his account of the good life and the moral life are omitted in this book. That is regrettable, but some difficult choices had to be made.

Practically, in deciding how to organize this book, it seemed to me sensible to follow the structure of Nagel's *The View from Nowhere* (*VN*). While Nagel has published, at the time of writing, eight books and has co-authored a ninth, *The View from Nowhere* is the book that provides the most comprehensive presentation of his central ideas. I have, therefore, broadly followed the order in which Nagel presents his topics in that book. I have, however, taken over *only* the structure of *The View from Nowhere*. Where Nagel has since updated his views I discuss them in their most recent form. I have drawn on Nagel's more recent systematic presentation of his views, *The Last Word* (*LW*), to supplement themes from *The View from Nowhere*. In particular, *The Last Word* does a great deal more to fill out the details of Nagel's rationalist epistemology that is put to use, but only sparingly discussed, in *The View from Nowhere*.

I have further departed from this basic plan of following the structure of *The View from Nowhere* in two respects. First, I have inserted, as Chapter 4, an account of Nagel's brilliant monograph *The Possibility of Altruism* (*PA*), published in 1970.[1] That short work focused solely on the idea of reasons for action. It precedes the discussions of Nagel's application of his ideal of practical objectivity to the issues of freedom, autonomy and the correct form of a normative ethical theory. Secondly, *The View from Nowhere* concludes its discussion of ethics by noting the need explicitly to extend the argument into political theory. At that stage Nagel did not pursue the argument further. He did so, however, in his following monograph, *Equality and Partiality* (*EP*), which was revised from the Locke lectures he gave at the University of Oxford. I have therefore appended an account of this work at the end of my discussion.

As I have already noted, Nagel is an outstandingly clear writer and fine prose stylist whose work needs little exposition. His clarity, however, does not mean that he is not sometimes difficult to understand. While he can explain vertiginously difficult ideas with great ease, sometimes his presentation lacks a context that makes his underlying train of thought clear. I have, therefore, tried to contextualize some of his discussions and to cross-relate them to each other in order to bring out the underlying unity of his approach where that has been appropriate. I have also, in places, discussed the work of philosophers whom Nagel has either influenced, or who have influenced him, or (more usually) where the influence has been mutual. This includes the work of Thompson Clarke, Saul Kripke, Colin McGinn, A. W. Moore, Derek Parfit, Samuel Scheffler, John Rawls and Bernard Williams. Again, limitations of scope have meant that I have not been able to pursue the kind of independent lines of thought that some of these philosophers have developed from their interpretation of Nagel as I would have liked to do.[2]

It did not seem to me appropriate to abstain from criticism of Nagel's views as well as interpretation. Nor did it seem appropriate merely to catalogue a list of the criticisms that have been made of Nagel in the many different areas of philosophy to which he has contributed. The criticisms that I have presented here are, as it were, from an interested point of view – my own – and over the course of the entire book it should be clear that these criticisms have a unity of their own. But I have been mindful of the fact that this is a book about Thomas Nagel's views, not mine. I have also acknowledged where my criticisms of Nagel are influenced by the work of others.

I have found the systematic study of Nagel's work very rewarding: he is among the most consistently original, profound and wide-ranging of contemporary philosophers. At a time when narrow specialization is the norm, he has made important contributions throughout philosophy. His work is notable for its depth and sophistication and it is the key to several areas of intense contemporary philosophical interest. A study of Nagel is virtually a complete course in contemporary philosophy. I hope that this book will help you in your reading of Nagel and that you will derive as much profit from this study as I certainly have.

This book has been written over a lengthy period of time. I have been grateful throughout this time to my editor, Steven Gerrard, for his patience and his constant understanding and support. Max de Gaynesford and another referee both provided invaluable critical feedback on the manuscript that greatly improved the final product. I was taught philosophy by four people who take Nagel's work very seriously, namely, the late Bernard Williams, the late Mark Sacks, Adrian Moore and Naomi Eilan. Their influence is, I think, evident throughout this book. It will also be clear that I have found Jonathan Dancy's critical notice of *The View from Nowhere* on its first publication particularly helpful. For a short piece, Dancy's notice is long on wisdom and it provides one of the central ideas that I use in my interpretation of Nagel's work. Special thanks are due as ever to my partner, Kathryn Brown, who has been a constant source of help and practical advice. She has read the manuscript several times and has made numerous philosophical and stylistic improvements. This book is dedicated to her.

Abbreviations

Full publication details for each of the following works by Thomas Nagel are given in the Bibliography.

C&E	*Concealment and Exposure* (2002)
EP	*Equality and Partiality* (1991)
LO	"The Limits of Objectivity" (1980)
LW	*The Last Word* (1997)
MQ	*Mortal Questions* (1979)
PA	*The Possibility of Altruism* (1970)
PN	"The Psychophysical Nexus" (2000)
SO	"Subjective and Objective" (1979)
VN	*The View from Nowhere* (1986)

Chapter 1

Subjective and objective

This chapter will begin to characterize the central dichotomy that gives Thomas Nagel's work its unified character, namely, the dichotomy of the subjective versus the objective. It will describe Nagel's conception of the aims of philosophy, introduce some concepts necessary to understand the idea of a representation from a point of view, explain the idea of the radically perspectival and discuss whether Nagel is committed to the controversial idea of a perspectival fact. This material will provide the framework for the discussions in the remainder of this book.

Nagel's aims

What is the point of philosophizing? Nagel's view is that the point is to live reflectively in the light of the truth (*VN*: 1–5). That sounds like a description of any philosopher's aims. However, Nagel's view is distinctive in that (like Kant and Wittgenstein) he believes that there is an aspect of our nature that leads us away from this ideal. According to Nagel we have an inner drive towards philosophical error. That drive is caused by our internally conflicted human nature. The effect that this inner division has on our attempts to philosophize is described as follows:

> What really happens in the pursuit of objectivity is that a certain element of oneself, the impersonal or objective self, which can escape from the specific contingencies of one's creaturely point of view, is allowed to predominate. Withdrawing into this element one detaches from the rest and develops an impersonal conception

> of the world and, so far as possible, of the elements of self from which one has detached. That creates the new problem of reintegration ... One has to *be* the creature whom one has subjected to detached examination, and one has in one's entirety to *live* in the world that has been revealed to an extremely distilled fraction of oneself. (*VN*: 9)

This passage already begins to connect Nagel's view of our divided nature with the fundamental theme of his philosophy as a whole: the dichotomy between a subjective and an objective point of view on particular topics.

The conflict that Nagel describes here between a part and the whole of the self is one that leads us into philosophical error in the following way: one part of us, the rational part, naturally seeks a unified view of the world. Our capacity to reason in an objective way suggests that ideal to us. That is because of the connection between the idea of unity and an intuitive conception of objective understanding (*VN*: 4). But Nagel thinks that this ideal cannot, in fact, be attained when we try to attain a unified worldview. Attempts to realize it lead us into philosophical error. This tension between our impulse to seek an objective view and its frequent unattainability runs throughout Nagel's philosophical work in both a positive and a negative way: "The transcendent impulse is both a creative and a destructive force" (*VN*: 4).

What is this connection between reason and unity? The impulse to adopt a unified worldview arises in this way: we have an intuitive idea of what it is to understand something objectively. The intuition is that if something can be understood objectively, then it is maximally accessible to a range of different points of view. This idea of representing the world from a particular point of view leads naturally to the idea of a *perspective*.[1] The connection between the two ideas is that occupying different points of view on one and the same reality will have the consequence that representations of that reality will be, in various ways, perspectival.

The idea of perspective is at home in our thought about artistic representation, but it also plays a role in our ordinary thinking about our place in a world that is not of our making. Each of us, as an agent or thinker, moves through or thinks about a real world that is independent of our will and our thought. One natural way to conceive of what we are doing is to conceive of our representations of the world, in our experience and thinking, as various different perspectives on a single objective reality. The metaphor of perspective and this intuitive realism about the world seem intrinsically tied together.

Furthermore, the world in which we find ourselves is a shared world with other subjects of experience just like you or me. Just as you strip away perspective to think of the world for anyone, so do other people; they have this thought about the world that contains *you*. Objectivity seems to consist in overcoming perspective: in stripping it away to find a conception that is maximally perspective free. The underlying thought is that there is a conception of the world that is perspective free because the world itself is a unified and substantial whole. The metaphor of perspective invites this thought because of its connection to realism: perspectives have to be perspectives *on* something, indeed, something beyond all perspectives. Perspectives are, we intuitively think, someone's "angle" or "take" on a subject matter, where the subject matter itself is not perspectival. (Or, in a variation of that last thought, not *as* perspectival.)

These ideas will be examined more closely in this chapter and the next. But, at present, I simply want to flag up the role played in this argument by the idea of an underlying unity and its connection to our faculty of reason. A world made up solely of perspectives (if we could make sense of that idea) would, we think, be a fractured, multiple, reality. That is not our intuitive understanding of what we mean by the real. Reality is unified and substantial.[2] Our methods of understanding it, our ways of being objective, are dependent on this feature. It seems that we should seek a maximally unified worldview. But that, Nagel argues, is an aspect of us that leads us into philosophical error.

The world may well be a single, substantial thing that underpins our many representations of it. Nagel thinks that it is. But he also thinks that our ways of understanding it are not. A unified worldview is not a legitimate aspiration. When we take the method of thinking objectively that has succeeded so well in understanding the physical world, particularly through modern science, and try to extend its scope, we repeatedly fail. The impulse to apply this model everywhere conflicts, then, with our overall aim of living reflectively in the light of the truth:

> The right attitude in philosophy is to accept aims that we can achieve only fractionally and imperfectly, and cannot be sure of achieving even to that extent. It means in particular not abandoning the pursuit of truth, even though if you want the truth rather than merely something to say, you will have a good deal less to say. (*VN*: 9)

According to Nagel there is a tension deeply rooted in our nature. On the one hand, our capacity for reason leads us to seek a naturally unified view of the world. On the other hand, our overall goal of truthfulness gives us insight into the fact that this is not always appropriate. We can go further in diagnosing what goes wrong: the impulse to a single overall worldview leads us into error if it causes us to apply a single model of objectivity to all our problems in philosophy.

Nagel thinks that we are very often guilty of a particular kind of intellectual mistake, namely, false objectification (*VN*: 4). We apply an objective method of understanding to a subject matter that does not tolerate it and that can only be distorted by such a treatment. Our underlying impulse is to a unified way of understanding the world and hence, we think, to a single worldview. But that is simply unattainable. One reaction we can have to this situation is that of denial and bad faith. We can pretend to ourselves that we have succeeded when we have not. Nagel thinks that we engage in three characteristic forms of evasion: *reduction*, *elimination* and *annexation* (SO: 210–11).

What might be examples of false objectifications that take each of these three forms? An example that will be discussed at length in Chapter 3 is understanding mentality. Each of us is a subject of experience: we undergo experiences of the world and of the inner reality of consciousness in the form of auralized utterances and imagistic thinking (Siewert 1998: 65–73). But how does one think about experiences in general terms? The very idea of experience seems elusive: you might say, as a first attempt to capture what we mean, that experiences reveal the world to a point of view. We certainly have a general concept of the mind such that the single instance of being a thinking subject that we are acquainted with in our own case is not restricted to us. Other people are subjects of experience just as we are. But to think of them as such is to think of each of *them* as occupying a perspective on the world. Their experiences are the revealing of the world to their perspective, just as your experiences are the revealing of the world to you. But how can we think objectively about this kind of case, if to think objectively is to strip away all notions of perspective? The very idea seems self-defeating. Nagel thinks that too many contemporary philosophers of mind try to convince themselves that we can extend a restricted form of objective understanding to the mental. In so doing, such philosophers of mind end up with a position that reduces mentality to something else, eliminates it entirely or annexes it and replaces it with an objective surrogate.

However, Nagel thinks that these intellectual evasions ought to be avoided. The impulse to truthfulness should overcome them. But what is to be done when a philosopher persists in applying inappropriately objectified methods to a subject matter that does not tolerate it? Nagel thinks that we need to be returned to the reality of our own experience. That is one way in which Nagel could be described as a phenomenologically oriented philosopher who emphasizes careful descriptions of our experience as an antidote to falsely objectifying theories. Time and again, when confronted with a philosophical theory of some phenomenon that falsely objectifies it, Nagel offers as a response a description of how our ordinary experience has been misrepresented in that theory.

A great deal of Nagel's work in philosophy consists in the criticism of the falsely objectifying views of other philosophers. This is particularly true, as Chapter 3 will demonstrate, in the philosophy of mind. But it would be a mistake to conclude from this that the overall point of his work is critical. It will be clear throughout this book that Nagel very often finds himself in the position of defending views that run against contemporary trends. He describes it as "a deliberately reactionary work" (*VN*: 9). It is, in particular, a reaction against the combination of idealism (in his view an undervaluing of objectivity) and scientism (an overvaluing of objectivity) that he finds characteristic of much of the work of his contemporaries (*VN*: 5). The philosophical idealist, in this context, is a person who believes that reality is made up of mental things, or grasped using forms of understanding that are contributed by our own minds.[3] A scientistic attitude, by contrast, is the attitude of those over-impressed by the success of modern natural science and who seek to generalize its methods to all areas of enquiry. However, the overall point of Nagel's criticism of others is that it serves the overall ideal of mapping out the extent to which our natural impulse to objectify can be realized in particular areas of thought and language. The fundamental aim of Nagel's philosophical work is summarized in the following passage:

> This book is about a single problem: how to combine the perspective of a particular person inside the world with an objective view of that same world, the person and his viewpoint included ... If one could say how the internal and external standpoints are related, how each of them can be developed and modified in order to take the other into account, and how in conjunction they are to govern the thought and action of each person it would amount to

> a world view ... I want to describe a way of looking at the world and living in it that is suitable for complex beings without a naturally unified standpoint ... Instead of a unified world view, we get the interplay of these two uneasily related types of conception and the essentially incompletable effort to reconcile them.
>
> (*VN*: 3–4)

In understanding how Nagel believes we ought best to set about realizing this aim, some further understanding of the key ideas that he uses is necessary. Central to these are the ideas of a perspective, a point of view, and representation in general. In order fully to appreciate Nagel's view, however, those ideas require more detailed analysis, and I shall now turn to them.

Representation and perspective

I have already, in the brief exposition of some of Nagel's views about our intuitive understanding of objectivity, mentioned the idea of a perspective. The aim of this section is to explain this idea and to put it to philosophical use. I think it is more helpful to think of Nagel's contrast between the subjective and the objective using the idea of perspectivalness and of representations being from a point of view (or from no point of view). The reason for this terminological choice is that while the idea of the "subjective" remains relatively stable throughout Nagel's work, referring to a person's pre-reflective commitments (whether theoretical or practical), the idea of the "objective" is relatively diverse. It does not retain a core sense across Nagel's reflections on metaphysics, the philosophy of mind and value theory (where the latter includes political philosophy). In the interests of clarity I shall opt for the terminology of the perspectival and the non-perspectival (or absolute) rather than that of the subjective versus the objective where possible. In this section I shall clarify this terminology and explain how I am going to use it.

Our linguistic actions are many and various, but one thing that we do is describe the world. Describing is an activity, but that activity seems to exploit a feature of language, namely that we can produce true indicative sentences about the world. These sentences are in the right form to be assessed as true or false. They express mental states like belief and knowledge when they are embedded in the speech act of asserting. Simplifying somewhat, I shall call the common element to both the expressed thought and the sentence a *representation*.

This representation has two aspects. In one aspect it relates to the world, and we assess it as true or false. But it also plays a role in the thoughts of a thinker. A further fact that we need to be able to explain is that, for example, you can take one reasonable attitude to the representation "Tully was a great Roman orator" and a different reasonable attitude to the representation "Cicero was a great Roman orator". That is because you do not know that the names "Tully" and "Cicero" refer to the same person (Frege 1948). To capture this idea that one and the same representation can be the object of different reasonable attitudes by the same thinker, we need to introduce the idea of the way in which the representation is grasped by a thinker. I shall call this aspect of representations its psychological *type* (Moore 1997: 10). The reason we need to introduce this supplementary idea is to make sense of the language-user and her rational attitudes. To interpret speakers as consistent in their attitudes in this kind of way seems to be intrinsic to understanding them as rational thinkers and speakers at all.

Are these all the ideas we need to think about representations? Arguably we need at least two more for the purposes of expositing Nagel's views. The first is the feature of indexicality. There are some words in English, such as "I", "here" and "now", for which there are entries in the dictionary. But it seems that in order to extract any representation from a use of these words on a particular occasion (picked out as something that we can assess as true or false) we need another element: we have to refer to context. "I am here, now", said by Alan Thomas in Vancouver on 1 January 2008 expresses a truth-evaluable representation different from the same sentence, "I am here, now", uttered by George Bush in Washington D.C. on 1 February 2008. By context, in this case, we mean simply a presupposed context of utterance, a specific time and a local place.

One view is that we can always replace such indexical sentences with their non-indexical counterparts without loss of a truth-evaluable content. You can always substitute a descriptive expression for the indexical one in a way that might affect the psychological type of the utterance (the role that it plays in the thinking of the speaker particularly in the control of action), but does not change its evaluation vis-à-vis the world. If that is true, it shows that indexicals are a suggestive analogy for a more philosophically interesting idea, namely, that of representations from a point of view. But they are only an analogy. We need to understand this further idea of representation from a point of view in order to understand linguistic representation in all its generality.

Consider the claim that the colours of objects are simply a reflection of the human point of view and that objects are not "really" coloured. One natural way to motivate that thought would be via an analogy with indexical uses of language (McGinn 1983). The idea is that in evaluating claims about whether objects are coloured or not, one needs to take into account not simply a presupposed context of utterance, but a more general idea. Colour discourse is from the human *point of view*. There is, therefore, a suppressed parameter in our talk about the colours of objects that it is a philosophical task to bring out and to highlight.

The basis of the analogy between contexts of utterance and points of view is that in order to evaluate the truths of statements about the colours of objects we may need, for certain purposes, to refer to a presupposition of what is said. In this case, the presupposition is that all such judgements are from a human point of view and dependent on our particular sensory capacities. But the presupposed context is not a context of utterance, such as a particular time and place, but a presupposed point of view: in this example, nothing less than the human standpoint.

We are now in a position to explain what a perspectival representation is: it is a representation from such a point of view. A non-perspectival or absolute representation would be one that does not depend on such a presupposed point of view. Henceforth, I shall restrict the words "perspective" and "perspectival" to representations produced from a point of view and the latter phrase, "point of view", to the standpoint from which representations are produced.[4]

However, we can also now see the basis of the *disanalogy* between indexical representations and perspectival representations. The former are always replaceable by non-indexical counterparts, with some loss of how the representation can be used or thought about, but no loss in how it can be evaluated vis-à-vis the world as true or false. Does the class of perspectival representations also have this feature; are they always replaceable by that which A. W. Moore has usefully called an "external counterpart" (1987b: 5)? The answer for this class of representations is "it depends". It depends on the details of the particular case. Furthermore, determining whether the members of a class of perspectival representations have external counterparts is a highly contested and controversial philosophical issue.

A good example is how we think of time and tense. We can think of time in two ways. Events can be seen as standing in a set of relations that determine an order in which, one might say, they "always" stand. The relation between the Battle of Hastings and the Battle of Waterloo is a relation that holds no matter how the events are described. Or we could talk about events using the distinctively tensed language of "before" and "after", which would be relations in which events could stand to each other at different times. One way of thinking about this contrast is that there is a perspectival way of thinking and speaking about time, and a non-perspectival way of thinking and speaking about time. The question is which is the more basic. One prominent argument is that if we are going to talk about time's flow and progression we have to accept the idea of an inherently perspectival temporal fact, corresponding to the tensed way we think and speak of time. However, this claim is controversial: it is one of the most centrally contested issues in the philosophy of time (Prior 1976; Mellor 1998).

My aim is not to contribute to this debate but to draw a moral from it. That is that there is no working out whether perspectival representations have an external counterpart independently of the arguments for and against this claim for each particular topic. But we can identify in general what grounds the difference between indexicals and perspectival judgements. Contexts of utterance are replaceable by descriptions, but not all perspectival representations can be rewritten in terms of an external counterpart that dispenses with perspective. Why is that? If we cannot formulate such an external counterpart that is because the presupposed point of view is entering into the *content* of the representation.

In the remainder of this chapter I shall show how these ideas are used to formulate some of Nagel's distinctive claims about our place in the world. But in order fully to capture his views a further development of these ideas is necessary. It has been established that both indexical and perspectival representations involve a linguistic item and a presupposed context or point of view functioning together to generate a truth-evaluable representation. But I mentioned above the idea of a psychological type: how a representation was grasped in thought. A natural way to think about this is in terms of how the thinker conceives of the thought: a structured way of grasping the thought that captures its role in the inferences that the thinker is immediately disposed to make. This idea of a structured way of grasping what is thought that reflects patterns of inference seems to draw on the idea of a thought component, or a concept.

Suppose that some points of view and some sets of concepts come together as a package deal so that you cannot understand one without the other. An example might be thinking about the mind. Each of us occupies a point of view on the world; perhaps it is better to say that each of us *is* a point of view on the world. Is this a privileged way of understanding mentality in the sense that it is only from this point of view that one can acquire the relevant set of concepts needed to think about mentality? Nagel thinks so, as Chapter 3 will demonstrate.

That puts the ideas encountered so far in a new combination: following another helpful phrase Moore has introduced, this would be an instance of the *radically perspectival* (1997: 15). In the case of a radically perspectival area of thought or language, a point of view and a proprietary set of concepts are so interconnected that you cannot understand the subject matter without both. To take up the point of view *is* to acquire the set of concepts necessary accurately to characterize the subject matter from the perspective of the thinker. Representations from that point of view then use those concepts. Nagel thinks that the clearest example of this phenomenon is when our subject matter is the perspective of a thinker. But that is an example of a more general pattern where a presupposed point of view, and the concepts made available to that point of view, are so inextricably linked that we cannot hope to understand one without the other.

Forcing us to recognize instances of the radically perspectival is one of Nagel's most distinctive contributions to philosophy. It is important because it is essential to understanding how he interprets the contrast between the subjective and the objective and explains why he believes we need to enrich our ideas of what it is to understand something objectively. Explaining how and why this is so – and whether recognizing this brings with it the problematic idea of a perspectival fact – is the focus of the remainder of this chapter. The idea of the radically perspectival itself, however, is a key interpretative idea that I shall use throughout this book to explain some of Nagel's most distinctive claims.

The subjective–objective contrast in general

With this preliminary terminology in place it is possible to set out some of Nagel's distinctive views about realism and objectivity. I shall consider these views, first, in the context of their most basic application: understanding our place in the world. We are located in the world as thinkers, perceivers and actors, but the issues that arise from our ability to act in the world will be deferred to Chapters 4–6. The opening three chapters will focus on what it is to think objectively about what is the case and the nature of the thinker, not how one might change what is in the world by acting on it.

As I have noted, the term "subjective", throughout all Nagel's work, means the pre-reflective, personal commitments of a particular person. "Pre-reflective" does not mean unreflective or uncritical. It simply means those commitments that the person has not, as yet, subjected to a particular kind of critical examination. We have a capacity to be objective and the form that this takes is detachment. We "step back" in thought from our commitments and reflect on their perspectival character. They are, at the beginning of this process, all perspectival in the minimal sense that they are representations *for you* (hence all, in this minimal sense, "subjective"). The question now is whether there is further reflective insight to be gained by detaching from that perspectival representation in a certain way. Can we helpfully think of it *as* perspectival? Can we place ourselves, the perspectival representation and objective world in a relation such that we can see the perspective for what it is, namely, a perspectival "take" on a non-perspectival reality?

Nagel thinks that the answer will vary, in a topic-specific way. Philosophers have been overly impressed by a single central paradigm that is central to our understanding of the realist claims of science. A key episode in the development of scientific understanding is the detachment from the contingencies of our human make-up in the formulation of a distinction between the primary and the secondary qualities of objects. For Nagel this represents a watershed in the development of our views about objectivity: the true physical account of nature will be in formal, mathematicized terms and therefore accessible to a wider class of thinkers than merely human thinkers (*VN*: 14). Secondary qualities, however, will not form part of this account. Tied in to the specific perceptual sensibilities of particular classes of thinker, they have simply turned out to be something that we can abstract away in thinking about the true theory of physical reality.

That is the basis for one, intellectually compelling, model of seeking a more objective understanding. This model of physical objectivity is both importantly true in its place and the source of many philosophical errors when it is mistakenly generalized. Its central feature is that when we think about the way in which colour judgements are perspectival and implicate a point of view on the world, that element can be treated in a distinctive way. Thinking about the kind of perspectivalness involved in judgements about colour represents a paradigm of that which, in Mark Sacks's helpful phrase, we can call "perspectival ascent" (1989: 95). When we reflect on the perspectival character of such judgements, the method of perspectival ascent allows us to transcend and renounce the element of perspective in such judgements. The "appearances" here are, as Nagel puts it, "relegated to the mind" (*VN*: 14). They receive a locally *debunking* explanation. Appearances in such a case are "mere appearances"; Nagel seems to treat them as similar to the delusive. If you are deluded into thinking that there is a cat on the lawn when, in fact, you discover on closer examination that it was a trick of the light, you simply reinterpret the initial appearances as delusive. They caused you to form a false belief. But with the false belief abandoned those initial appearances are simply discarded. They have been debunked by the correct explanation ("there was nothing there – it was just a trick of the light"). The original appearances are abandoned as wholly erroneous.

But equally importantly for Nagel's overall philosophy, this is just one paradigm of seeking a more objective understanding. In a perceptive critical notice of *The View from Nowhere*, Jonathan Dancy noted what he took, critically, to be an equivocation between two quite distinct accounts of objectivity in Nagel's work (Dancy 1988: 2, 7). Dancy thought that various mistakes could be traced to Nagel's attempt to run these two accounts side by side in that book.[5] I shall argue that, on the contrary, appealing to these two accounts of what it is to treat a subject matter objectively is essential to understanding Nagel's philosophical aims and that there is no inconsistency in proceeding as he does. However, Dancy's identification, and analysis, of these two accounts is an important interpretative insight into Nagel's work.

I shall slightly adapt the terms that Dancy uses to describe them. I shall call the first paradigm of physical objectification a "Cartesian" model of objectification instead of Dancy's term "absolute". In this case, a gain in objectivity involves taking a relatively subjective representation and acknowledging that it can be replaced by a more objective successor representation. As a result of this process of perspectival ascent, the original representation is lost: it is renounced and replaced. Perspectival ascent centrally involves debunking explanations.

By contrast, in a "Hegelian" model of objectification (here I stick with Dancy's terminology), a gain in objectivity involves taking a relatively subjective representation and acknowledging that it can be placed in a wider, non-debunking, explanatory context. This kind of gain in objectivity seems to leave behind the metaphor of perspectival "ascent", replacing ascent with contextualization and explanation. In this model the objective point of view becomes permissive: it tolerates the continuing existence of a range of subjective representations by contextualizing them. Interestingly, as the arguments of Chapters 4 and 6 will show, this understanding of two forms of relation to the objective standpoint was originally a development of Nagel's view of objectivity in ethics that he transferred, to considerable effect, to his metaphysics.

If this account of Hegelian objectification seems very abstract, Nagel means two more precise things by it, both of which appeal to the idea of explanation. The more satisfactory form of Hegelian objectification is when the subjective receives a non-debunking explanation from a more objective class of representations. A less intellectually satisfying form of Hegelian objectification transcends the subjective and asserts *that* it can be explained, without telling us *why* it can be so explained.

In the former case, a non-debunking form of Hegelian objectification means that we are left with the more objective and the subjective representation side by side, as it were, with the assurance that the former has transcended the latter, but has not renounced it.[6] What we have achieved by this is a deepened understanding (Dancy 1988: 12). There is something inherently unsatisfactory about the second kind of case because of our natural impulse to a unified worldview. But this kind of case asks us to reflect on our intellectual ambitions and urges us to be more modest.

These distinctions are very important because one of Nagel's most distinctive contributions to contemporary philosophy is to argue that our impulse to a unified worldview blinds us to the existence of that which, in the previous section, I called the "radically perspectival". Those were cases where point of view, set of concepts and associated representations were so closely tied together that all three need to be interpreted together. The connection between that idea and these two models of objectification is that, of their very nature, areas of thought and language that exhibit radical perspectivalness *can only receive a Hegelian form of objectification.*

Why is that? It is because if one applied the alternative, Cartesian, model then this application would be a clear example of simply changing the subject in an unhelpful way. Some examples will help (with the caveat that they will receive further discussion and clarification later when I discuss the individual topic concerned). Nagel's central example is the nature of the judging subject when we reflexively turn our objectifying impulse on the subject himself or herself. As Chapter 3 will show in detail, in the case of characterizing thinkers we need to take seriously the idea that while mentality is a basic feature of reality, when we try to think about it objectively we face an insuperable problem. That is that we think of the mind in ineliminably perspectival terms. The formulation I gave earlier was that we are points of view on the world: that to which the world is disclosed. Mentality is perspectival through and through. It is a clear instance of the radically perspectival. To be a thinker is to think and act from a standpoint, in which one acquires and uses mental concepts in such a way that representations from that standpoint are perspectival. You cannot understand these three ideas independently from each other. What would happen if one applied the model of Cartesian perspectival ascent to such representations?

Nagel's verdict is that to try to think non-perspectivally about the mind is a paradigm of false objectification:

> The subjective features of conscious mental processes – as opposed to their physical causes and effects – cannot be captured by the purified form of thought suitable for dealing with the physical world that underlies the appearances. Not only raw feels but also intentional mental states – however objective their content – must be capable of manifesting themselves in subjective form to be in the mind at all. The reductionist program that dominates current work in the philosophy of mind is completely misguided, because it is based on the groundless assumption that a particular conception of objective reality is exhaustive of what there is. (*VN*: 15–16)

While contemporary philosophy of mind is full of such falsely objectifying theories, supplying an objective surrogate for the mind, or reducing it or eliminating it entirely, Nagel's rival diagnosis is that we need to break the hold on us of a single model of objectification. What is required is a Hegelian model of objectification in which we try to think more objectively about the mind but in creative ways.

Nagel concludes that all that is available to us when we try to place the mind in nature, in the current state of our understanding, is the second pattern of Hegelian objectification. One can only surmise that future scientific developments will offer us an understanding of a substance that underlies both the physical and the mental aspects of mentality. This follows his second pattern for Hegelian objectification because this form of objective placing of the putatively subjective claims that while the mental and the physical do stand in an intelligible explanatory relationship we are not yet in a position to say what that relationship is.

One can conclude from the foregoing that there is a central tension in Nagel's philosophy as a whole. The impulse to truthfulness and to respecting the phenomenology of our experience will incline him to acknowledge all three forms of objectification. Each has their place. But there are special philosophical assumptions that make the primary–secondary distinction a paradigm for Nagel of a gain in objectivity. It is not simply that the objective standpoint is all controlling in that any subjective representation must at least be tolerated by it. (That constraint is met by both general forms of objectification, namely, Cartesian and Hegelian.) It is, rather, that Nagel is a rationalist and foundationalist about knowledge and justification. His philosophical ancestors are avowedly Plato, Descartes and Frege (*LW*: 9, 22–4, 37). Nagel believes that we have a capacity to reason in such a way that we can achieve self-transcendence. That is reflected in the modern cultural achievement of natural science, and, at the heart of the achievement of science, there is its capacity to mathematicize nature. Mathematical physics treats nature in an objectively quantifiable way and leaves behind the merely perspectival secondary qualities that are a species-wide illusion. This Cartesian form of perspectival ascent is a very important paradigm for Nagel.

But his phenomenological instincts force him to the realization that this kind of objectification is limited. Applied too widely it leads to false objectification in many domains. However, the priority given to the Cartesian model is reflected in one very distinctive aspect of Nagel's philosophy as a whole: he tends to represent our human condition as an inherent limitation. If self-transcendence is possible, then, if it is something we fail to achieve elsewhere, some of those failures can be blamed on the fact that the human point of view is itself a constitutive source of error or illusion. His critics, on the other hand, view this as finding tragedy in that which could not have been otherwise. I shall now offer a more detailed exposition of each of these different patterns for thinking objectively about specific topics. The Cartesian and Hegelian models are significantly different from each other in a way that ramifies throughout Nagel's treatment of different topics examined in this book. I shall now examine these models in more detail. I shall, however, begin with Nagel's account of the primary versus secondary quality distinction as it is clearly deeply influential in how he conceives of his first model of Cartesian objectivity.

Nagel on secondary qualities

When he wants to illustrate what he means by Cartesian objectification, there is a topic to which Nagel repeatedly returns for his main example. That is the distinction drawn in the early modern development of natural science between the primary qualities of objects (such as solidity, shape and size) and secondary qualities (such as colours, odours and tastes). Nagel associates this distinction with a key episode in the development of modern natural science (*C&E*: 188). He describes how he conceives of this distinction in a crucial passage in *The View from Nowhere* worth quoting at length:

> The first step is to see that our perceptions are caused by the actions of things on us, through their effects on our bodies, which are themselves part of the physical world. The next step is to realize that since the same physical properties that cause perceptions in us through our bodies also produce different effects on other physical things and can exist without causing any perceptions at all, their true nature must be detachable from their perceptual appearance and need not resemble it. The third step is to try to form a conception of that true nature independent of its appearance either to us or to other types of perceivers. This means not only not thinking of the physical world from our own particular point of view, but not thinking of it from a more general human perceptual point of view either: not thinking of how it looks, feels, smells, tastes, or sounds. These secondary qualities then drop out of our picture of the external world, and the underlying primary qualities such as shape, size, weight, and motion are thought of structurally. (*VN*: 14)

There are two issues to be clarified here: exactly what Nagel thinks this important historical transition implies for the status of the secondary and also how he conceives of primary qualities. I shall describe each of these in turn.

Reviewing Colin McGinn's *The Subjective View* (in turn a development of some key themes from Nagel), Nagel agreed with McGinn's claim that the status of secondary properties as secondary is an *a priori* matter (McGinn 1983: ch. 7; Nagel 1983b). The distinction between primary and secondary qualities is usually discussed in the context of the work of John Locke, itself a philosophical articulation of an experimental discovery made by Robert Boyle (Curley 1972). But Nagel, like McGinn, does not believe that the status of the secondary is discovered experimentally. It is *a priori*: a truth grounded in the nature of our concepts and representations. *A priori* truths can be known logically independently from any truths about experience as they are grounded in how we represent the world via our concepts. They are an exercise of our capacity of reason operating independently of experience. As they are grounded in representations, rather than reality, so they can be known in this special *a priori* way.

However, Nagel differs from McGinn in that the latter takes, for example, colour properties to be non-intrinsic, relational features identical to the dispositions of objects to cause experiences in us. Nagel argues, on the contrary, that a secondary quality such as colour is what he calls a "disposition in reality": "Redness might be ... the property that anything (actual or possible) has if and only if it is such that it would look red to us in the actual world – the world as it actually is" (Nagel 1983b: 1283). In a later discussion he clarifies his view of secondary qualities further. You cannot pick out this disposition without using a concept grounded in experiences of a certain kind: "When you look at a lemon and it looks yellow to you, there is no way of correctly describing your mental state without talking about color as a property which, if it exists, is a property of physical objects. The lemon looks to you *to be yellow*" (*C&E*: 192). But Nagel thinks that conceding the truth of that is perfectly compatible with treating our experiences of colours as "a natural illusion shared by all humans with normal sight ... naturally produced in us in a systematic way by reflected light" and with obvious usefulness as a way of classifying things simply by looking at them (*ibid.*).

An equally important aspect of Nagel's treatment of the primary versus secondary quality distinction, however, is his understanding of primary qualities. His view is the Galilean one that the book of nature is written in the language of mathematics, a famous observation made in Galileo's *The Assayer* (1623; *C&E*: 188). Nagel's version of the claim is as follows:

> Our senses provide the evidence from which we start, but the detached character of this understanding is such that we could possess it even if we had none of our present senses, so long

> as we were rational and could understand the mathematical and formal properties of the objective conception of the physical world. (*VN*: 14)

This view of primary qualities gives Nagel the content of his "bleached-out physical conception of objectivity" (*VN*: 15). With its intellectual origins uncovered, I shall now analyse this Cartesian model of objectification and its complementary Hegelian model in more detail.

The paradigm of Cartesian perspectival ascent

As the previous section has indicated, it would be naive to pretend that the development of modern science had not supplied Nagel with a paradigm that allows us to fix our ideas of Cartesian perspectival ascent. The treatment of secondary qualities in modern physics is, for Nagel, the paradigm of Cartesian objectification. Its uncompromising form of perspectival ascent has several key features that play an important role in explaining the nature of a more objective understanding. I shall describe these seven aspects in turn.[7]

These aspects are: (a) scale; (b) a connection between perspective and realism; (c) intersubjective accessibility; (d) the connection between perspectival ascent, accessibility and the thinker's capacities; (e) the constitutive role of human nature; (f) the connection between being more objective and the contrast between the true and the false; and (g) whether objectification has a terminus.

The first aspect is scale. Nagel mentions occasionally, although he does not place much emphasis on this, the fact that a person is a comparatively small part of a "big world" (*VN*: 5, 19). While that is undeniably true, it is a truism that really works to motivate the connection between objective understanding and realism. Scale simply thematizes the issue of transcendence of the individual subject by a larger reality of which he or she is merely a part.

More important is the second aspect, namely, the connection between objective understanding and realism. It is because of a prior commitment to realism that we understand the metaphor of perspective in representation as we do. Perspectival ascent is inherently tied to treating the element of perspective in a representation as precisely that: a perspectival element that can be transcended and renounced by formulating an "external counterpart" for that representation. In forming a conception of oneself as located in a world not of one's own making one thereby also locates one's perspectival "take" on that world in a way that eliminates it.

The third aspect is intersubjective accessibility. This is one of Nagel's most important ideas as, while we quite naturally connect realism with intersubjectivity, we usually do so by thinking in terms of *human* subjects. Something that is objectively the case is accessible to more than one person. However, Nagel means something more radical than that. He believes that we can think of our own cognitive powers as separable. While they are jointly applied to our experience, we can imagine what it would be like to apply them separately. So by "intersubjective" Nagel does not mean different human subjects, but different classes of thinker picked out by different sets of cognitive capacities. Again, it would be naive to ignore the role of the paradigm of perspectival ascent in modern physical science in Nagel's thinking here: that model suggests that a purely rational intelligence that thinks formally in terms of structure could have a complete physical understanding of the world even if its capacity for perceptual experience and sensation were very different from ours. Such an intelligence would simply need to understand advanced mathematics.

This leads to the fourth aspect, namely, the connection between perspectival ascent, accessibility and the thinker's capacities. That which substantiates the idea of multiple perspectives is the idea of different classes of thinker who are picked out in terms of different ranges of cognitive capacities. Those capacities are correlated with different sets of concepts. Nagel's intuition is that our colour concepts, for example, have as a condition of their possession that they are fixed by paradigm cases of colour judgement *for us*. The world is coloured from only a human point of view. A natural way to explain this is that colour judgement draws on intellectual capacities and correlated sets of concepts that are distinctive of us. Our ability to make mathematical judgements draws on intellectual capacities and correlated sets of concepts that are *less* distinctive of us. We can, therefore, conceive of other rational intelligences that would interpret the world using the same physically objective concepts, principles and theories as us, but via some very different perceptual sensibility (but not none at all; Nagel 1983a). The point of this detour into science fiction is not to worry about extraterrestrial makers of colour judgements, but to give us insight into what we are doing when we make these judgements ourselves.

The fifth aspect is the connection between this account of perspectival ascent and human nature. Nagel's language clearly implies (although nothing in the model of Cartesian objectification does so) that in so far as the contingencies of our human nature determine the perspectivalness of a class of judgements, that seems to involve us in a deep-seated, constitutive form of error. I have in mind passages such as this: "The old view then comes to be regarded as an appearance, more subjective than the new view, and correctable or confirmable by reference to it" (*VN*: 4). This passage and others like it go beyond identifying the perspectival component in judgements that can receive a Cartesian treatment as traceable to our human nature.[8] They do so in a way that directly ties them to the idea of appearances as delusive. This sort of error, however, would be a constitutive error, one that we could not avoid unless we could avoid the human standpoint itself (which, clearly, we cannot!).

This aspect of the process is connected to the sixth aspect of connecting being more objective to the contrast between the true and the false. The reason for a more objective view in the Cartesian model is that we want the truth and do not want to rest content with the mere appearances that are inherently untrustworthy. What ought to drive us forward is the idea that a more objective conception in Cartesian terms is simply truer than the preceding, more perspectival and hence more tainted conception.

This, in turn, leads to the final aspect of Cartesian ascent as the word "truer" might make one pause. We do use the word "more true to life" or "truer" in this comparative way, but it seems to depend on a more basic use in which things are true or false without qualification. If that is so, and we are to understand Cartesian objectification as the overcoming of error, then there is a clear sense in which the process of perspectival ascent *terminates* when we reach the truth. Cartesian objectification, then, has a fixed endpoint.

As Dancy insightfully points out, that means that some of Nagel's remarks about how "subjective" is properly to be contrasted with "more objective", not "objective" *per se*, are not entirely accurate: "We may think of reality as a set of concentric spheres, progressively revealed as we detach gradually from the contingencies of the self" (*VN*: 5). Dancy notes that this image of "concentric circles" fits the pattern of Hegelian objectification. However, it does not square with how Nagel motivates his account of Cartesian objectification: "Absolute objectification, by its very nature, does not tend to build a broader conception around a narrower one, but rather to banish to the realm of appearance parts of what were previously taken to be reality" (Dancy 1988: 4). When it succeeds in stripping away perspective and terminating in a maximally perspective free view of the world, the Cartesian process of being more objective about a subject matter comes to an end. That which brings it to an end is the truth: the overcoming of error by successive steps of removing appearance and discerning the underlying reality.

This has further implications for Nagel's claim that the subjective versus objective contrast is "really a matter of degree" (*VN*: 5). That remains true of both Cartesian and Hegelian objectification, but it has a different sense in the two cases. "More objective" in the Cartesian case means "truer, closer to the real and containing less error". In the Hegelian case it means something more like "more explanatory or insightful".

I have described each of these seven features of Cartesian objectification in what may seem exhaustive detail because collectively they contrast, in an interesting way, with the features of Nagel's contrasting model of Hegelian objectification. I shall now describe this alternative model to make this distinction clear.

Limitations of the Cartesian paradigm and the second model of objectification

Probably the most important claim in Nagel's work is that focus on a single paradigm of what it is to think objectively is mistaken. That is not to say that the Cartesian model of perspectival ascent is not importantly true in the appropriate context, namely, defending scientific realism. But it is a serious error to apply it elsewhere. Why?

The answer is that not all perspectives can be eliminated without distortion of the subject matter conceived of from that perspective. When an individual reflects in a critically detached way, not every topic is more insightfully understood from a more objective standpoint. That is why Nagel introduces a second model of objectification for those topics that seem to involve perspective more deeply than the case of physical objectivity.

This second model has the following aspects: (a) once again, Nagel appeals to scale in the sense of localness as the motivation to reflect objectively; (b) it involves not reflection in the sense of detachment, but reflection in the sense of disengagement; (c) it is linear and indefinite; (d) it contextualizes and does not replace the "subjective" and its successors; (e) it appeals to the idea of explanation in two ways that are distinct from the use that Cartesian objectification makes of that idea; and (f) it aims to deepen our understanding. I shall describe each of these points in turn and in each case flag up the major difference with Cartesian objectification.

First, the impulse to reflection is once again grounded in our scale, as is clear from an example of a topic for which Hegelian objectification is the appropriate model: "I want to think of mind, like matter, as a general feature of the world. In each case we are acquainted with certain instances in our small spatiotemporal neighborhood (though in the case of matter, not only with those instances)" (*VN*: 19).

Secondly, as I have noted, Nagel often argues that critical reflection involves detachment, a stepping back in thought. But that image seems more appropriate for Cartesian objectification. For the Hegelian model the issue seems better expressed in terms of a reflective disengagement from a previously engaged perspective. We have to balance continued commitment to a set of "subjective" beliefs with a more disengaged insight into those very same commitments. That is a subtly different way of thinking about increased reflectiveness, but it does not seem to involve complete detachment from the subjective. That reflection here does not involve detachment is connected to the fact that in this model we do not renounce the subjective because it is intrinsically erroneous, as in the Cartesian model. Instead, we retain our commitment to our subjective starting-point even as reflection transforms it.

Thirdly, this model of objectification exhibits both linearity and indefiniteness. The impulse to Hegelian objectification has the same basis in our rational nature as Cartesian objectification: we have an inner drive to be objective. But our goal in this case seems to be to gain more insight into our "subjective" commitments. At each stage of reflection it seems we could be even more objective. Therefore, the kind of progression in this model is linear, with one stage succeeding another, but not one that comes to a natural end. It could be continued indefinitely: for each stage of reflective insight we can imagine a further stage. This process seems indefinite. Cartesian objectification, by contrast, has a natural terminus.

Fourthly, when Hegelian objectification is applied to a subject matter we place it in a wider context that deepens our understanding of it. One could not, therefore, go back to the previous more subjective stage without irony. You cannot leave behind or forget the insight achieved at the more reflective level. But the previous subjective level is not renounced or discarded. It is preserved, but set in a new context. That is a very important difference from Cartesian objectification and the latter's treatment of our human point of view as a constitutive source of error that has to be overcome and renounced.

Fifthly, Cartesian objectification uses the idea of explanation in a debunking way. As in the example I have given of delusive perceptual appearance, the more objective view debunks the appearances at the subjective level such that the putative evidence they supplied can be discarded. Hegelian objectification has a more flexible notion of explanation in which placing a subjective phenomenon in a more objective context allows us to explain it in a more satisfactory way *without* debunking it: the explanation no longer classifies the subjective as the *erroneous*.

Furthermore, as I have already noted, Nagel has an even more flexible notion of explanation that motivates his subdivision of Hegelian objectification into two kinds. The first, more intellectually satisfying version involves explaining the relatively subjective in terms of the relatively more objective where one can state the explanation. The second, less satisfying (but still true) claim is that we know that the more subjective can be explained in terms of the relatively more objective without our being able to give the explanation or to state exactly how. (Nagel claims this is true for the relation between the mental and the physical in late works such as "The Psychophysical Nexus" [PN]).

Finally, our motivation at each level of the Hegelian model is not to proceed to the next level because it is truer and discards falsehood. Our impulse to be even more objective is based on a desire for ever deeper understanding. That seems to function as a distinct goal from objective enquiry than the desire for a maximally non-perspectival truth that is the terminus of Cartesian objectification. Nagel is clearly committed to two different models of objectification with two distinct goals for enquiry: the reduction of truth by perspectival ascent that strips away constitutive sources of error and the distinct goal of seeking a deeper understanding.

Each of these two models is philosophically contestable. Even more controversial is Nagel's clear commitment to running them side by side for distinct topics in a way that he views as consistent. I shall refer to these two models throughout my exposition of Nagel's views in this book. However, I shall conclude this chapter with an examination of the most controversial aspect of Nagel's philosophy as whole. Nagel is obviously motivated to postulate two distinct models of objectivity because Cartesian objectification has a damaging hold over our thinking. Its undoubted success as a way of understanding the physical world has given it an intellectual prestige that is in one way deserved: the success of modern science is a great cultural achievement. However, in other respects this prestige leads philosophers to extend this model beyond its proper bounds in a scientistic way. For essentially perspective-involving topics, particularly the philosophy of mind, we need to enrich our options and add a Hegelian model of objectification.

That is called for, in particular, because of the existence of what I have called radically perspectival topics in which point of view, concepts and perspectival representations are all bound up with each other. It is in order to explain these topics that Nagel develops the most distinctive aspects of his philosophy. But does this distinctive claim also commit him to an unacceptable cost? The suspicion that it does is bound up with a deeper concern that the two models of objectification are inconsistent. But the precise form in which the concern can be expressed is that were Nagel to acknowledge the existence of perspectival facts, then he would fracture the world into a multiplicity of interpretative perspectives. That would abandon the intuitive notion of realism from which we began: that the world is substantial and unitary. Whether Nagel is committed to the idea of a perspectival fracturing of reality into multiple perspectives is the subject of the next section.

From perspectives on the facts to perspectival facts?

Nagel's most distinctive philosophical claim is an acknowledgement of radical perspectivalness for some specific topics to which we are tempted inappropriately to apply the model of Cartesian objectification. Our natural impulse is to seek a unified worldview, but the largest single obstacle to such unity is the existence of such radical perspectivalness. If Nagel is right that a major obstacle to a unified worldview is the fact that difference in subject matter calls for different kinds of understanding, then he has highlighted something very important for philosophy. But we might reasonably think of philosophical reflection in terms of gains and losses. Nagel is offering us a reflective insight into a central philosophical problem. But does this insight come at an unacceptable cost? To evaluate this question we need to examine more closely the idea of the radically perspectival and its implications.

One prominent line of concern about his work is that Nagel does incur too high a cost for his insights. This concern could be described as follows. Nagel thinks that a mature natural science like physics should be taken at face value. Its mathematicized treatment of nature is a successful form of objective understanding that strips away all perspectival elements to reach a maximally perspective-free conception of reality. Nagel also tells us, however, that there are different forms of understanding besides the fully objectivized understanding of physics. To avoid false objectification we need to accept various other, more perspectival conceptions. That is particularly so when we are faced with the radically perspectival. The critic alleges that there is, however, a serious problem with this apparently sensible claim. The problem is that physics is a *complete* description of what there is. Everything that there is is fundamentally physical. Where in the world, then, are the other features of reality picked out by Nagel's different forms of perspectival understanding?

The critic alleges that Nagel's answer is that these features can only be located in their own distinctive areas of reality. Corresponding to perspectival forms of understanding, we have perspectival forms of reality. Reality is not, then, for Nagel, unitary and complete. Physical reality is, but that is not the only reality. There are various, overlaid, perspectival realities. Nagel is ineluctably committed to the idea of a *perspectival fact*. For reasons that I shall go into further below, this critic finds the whole idea of a perspectival fact unacceptable (and we shall see that he or she is right to do so). So we can apply to Nagel's insights the argument known as a *reductio ad absurdum*. His claims lead to the idea of a perspectival fact and the fracturing of what we took to be a single reality into multiple interpretative perspectives. That idea is absurd so at least one of Nagel's assumptions must be false.

I think that this line of criticism is entirely mistaken. It is the task of this section to disentangle the various threads that make up this argument. It is helpful to exposit this critical argument now as it involves several basic misunderstandings of Nagel's position. The three issues that need to be addressed are: does Nagel run together ways of understanding the world with how the world is; does he misunderstand the completeness of physics; and is he committed to the idea of a perspectival fact and, if so, is that idea defensible?

I do not think that Nagel does confuse considerations about how best to understand the world with ontological issues about what there is. Consider, first, this passage from "The Limits of Objectivity" (LO): "Perhaps no conception of objectivity adequate to the mind can exist, in which case we shall have to choose between *abandoning the assumption that everything real has an objective character and abandoning the assumption that the mind is real*" (LO: 83, emphasis added). Note our choices in this paragraph. We can either treat our subject matter objectively (in this case, the subject matter is the mind) or we have to deny that it is real. All claims that something is real have to be related to an objective understanding of them. It is clearly implied, if not stated, that there is no default position of the "subjectively real". Indeed, the two notions of reality and objective understanding are inherently connected: "We assume some connection, even if not a very tight one, between what is real and what can be objectively understood" (LO: 81). Not only is Nagel not committed to the "subjectively real", but he also explains why that notion is misguided. His point is that the kind of objectivity we find in a mature natural science, such as physics, is not the only form of objectivity. Objective understanding has to be developed in tandem with an accurate characterization of that which we are trying to explain: "Here it is essential, as it is in regard to other matters, not to identify objectivity with the *physical conception* of objectivity. We have to think of objectivity as something general enough to admit of different interpretations for different subjects of enquiry" (LO: 82). In the case of perspectival discourses, such as mental discourse, the issue is whether: "there can be an understanding of them independent of the specific point of view to which they appear, which *nevertheless keeps their perspectival character*" (LO: 83, emphasis added). These quotations show very clearly that Nagel's concern is with the different ways in which we can think objectively about different subject matters, developing an objectifying account that is "topic sensitive" to different issues. He is not doing ontology: dividing the world into the objectively real and the subjectively real.

I see no convincing evidence that Nagel equivocates between claims about how we must understand the world and claims about the world. Nagel repeatedly states that the terms "subjective" and "objective" are predicates of understanding: "Objectivity is a method of understanding. It is beliefs and knowledge that are objective in the primary sense. Only derivatively do we call objective the truths that can be understood in this way" (LO: 77; *VN* 4). These terms are predicated of ways in which we think about and understand the world. The phrases "subjective reality" and "objective reality" would both be illegitimate cross-classifications of ways of talking about understanding the world and ways of talking about the world. The words "real" and "fact" simply have no philosophically defensible qualification (Percival 1994).

Is Nagel being entirely accurate about his own views here? After all, he did refer above to the constraint that "raw feels" and intentional states had to be understood as manifested in the mind: is this not a clear sense of the phrase "subjectively real"? I agree it is a common use of the word "subjective" throughout Nagel's writing, but in the present context it is not relevant to the concern about whether or not Nagel is committed to the idea of a perspectival fact. There is an innocuous sense in which mental facts are "subjective" or "perspectival" facts but this is the same sense in which, for example, facts about trees could be called "arboreal facts". Facts about subjectivity are simply facts like any other kind of fact (Rosen 1984: 287–8).

These points help with the next question: has Nagel misunderstood the completeness of physics? No, he has not. Physics is a complete account of what there is, using its own proprietary concepts, theories and laws. Nagel's critics conflate the claims of physics and the claims of *physicalism*. The latter is a philosophical commentary on the status of physics. It takes physics as a paradigm of objective understanding and tries to extend it to all areas of thought and language. Physics is a theory of the physical world. Physicalism is a metaphysical theory that puts physics to philosophical use. Crucially, physicalism extends an account that uses the concepts of physics to what is involved in formulating and accepting theories (the theories of physics included). Physics is asked to supply the terms in which we can think about such ideas as representation, intentionality, theory acceptance, good reasons, communities of appraisal or knowledge. It is asked to do this by physicalism, but this is not, Nagel believes, an appropriate task for physics. These vaulting ambitions of physicalism, Nagel thinks, are misguided. The theories to which they give rise are falsely objectifying. Furthermore, Nagel turns the tables: the physicalist takes a form of understanding and makes it criterial for what is real. In doing so, he or she is no better than the philosophical idealist who claims that reality is mental. I shall discuss these claims in more detail in Chapter 2.

Physicalism is a prime example for Nagel of a falsely objectifying view. It blinds us to the correct conclusion that physics represents one highly developed form of an objective understanding of the world. But there have to be other forms of objective understanding, too, each of which is developed in a way that is appropriate to its subject matter.

If the foregoing is correct, then Nagel is not committed to adding a special subjective reality to the world to accommodate those perspective-involving ways of conceiving of it that resist objective understanding. That simply makes no sense. We find no application for the idea of objective understanding in any of its forms (physical objectivity or otherwise) unless we are dealing with something real:

> So although there is a connection between objectivity and reality – only the supposition that we and our appearances are parts of a larger reality makes it reasonable to seek understanding by stepping back from the appearances in this way – still not all reality is objective, for not everything is *better understood* the more objectively it is viewed.
>
> (LO: 78, emphasis added; see also *VN*: 4)

I think there is a further conclusion to be drawn: we also do not have to interpret Nagel as committed to another idea that is sometimes attributed to him in order to criticize him. That is the idea of a perspectival fact.

What is this idea supposed to be, why would it be a problem if Nagel were committed to it and on what basis is this ascription made? In ordinary speech we often refer to facts without theorizing what they are at all. In philosophy attempts have been made to regiment this idea to use it to explain truth as correspondence to the facts. It is difficult to find a notion of a fact robust enough to carry out this task (B. Williams 2002: 64–5). For present purposes it suffices to say that the idea of a perspectival fact would be the idea of a fact that made a perspectival representation true. If we think that facts can all be integrated into a single, substantial and unitary conception of the world, then if perspective is placed not simply in the representation of the facts but in the facts themselves, then this commitment is going to have to be revised. The result would be the kind of "perspectivism", sometimes incorrectly attributed to Friedrich Nietzsche, in which all we have are multiple interpretative perspectives that have simply dispensed with the idea that they are perspectives *on* anything independent of those perspectives (*ibid.*: 16–17; Clark 1990).

Many acute readers of Nagel think that something similar is going on in his work. If he is committed to an acknowledgement of radically perspectival representations, is he not thereby also committed to the idea of a perspectival fact? This suspicion has been expressed by Christopher Peacocke in the course of an otherwise sympathetic appraisal of Nagel's metaphysical views:

> It is natural to identify what is understandable from a given standpoint with what can be thought about using concepts available to any being capable of adopting that standpoint ... This is the phenomenon of certain concepts being available only to those who stand in certain relations to the world ... On this reading, a greater or lesser degree of objectivity has in the first instance to do with ways of conceiving of the world. It is a further step to suppose that differences in mode of conception correspond to differences in reality, a step corresponding to the difference between sense and reference ... But in his general, abstract discussion of the objective/subjective polarity Nagel moves directly *from forms of understanding to differences in reality*.
>
> (1989: 67–8, emphasis added)

How troubling is the slide from how we conceive of the world to the world itself? Not troubling if the idea of a perspectival fact is itself defensible.[9] However, several philosophers have argued that the idea is not simply a false one but an incoherent one, and their arguments are very convincing. Bernard Williams (1978: 295–6), Hugh Mellor (1989, 1991b, 1992–3) and A. W. Moore (1997: 50) have all argued along similar lines. Here is a representative expression of their concern in an argument from Williams:

> In taking [how things are from A's point of view], and putting it into the world as something we can conceive of as there, we are in effect trying to abstract from *how it is for A*, the *how it is*, and leave it as a fact on its own, which however has the mysterious property that it is available only to A.
>
> (1978: 295; cited by Moore 1997: 41)

But simply to state this putative argument for the existence of perspectival facts is to show why it is self-defeating. That which you sought to explain has been lost, or the problem has merely been deferred. The philosophical problem was to explain a *prima facie* case of special epistemic access to the facts: now we have instead special facts. Not only does this violate the idea of a fact, but *it has not explained what needed explaining*. What is it about this special class of facts that explains how one has special access to them? That was the question that needed answering, and postulating a class of special perspectival facts with this feature does not explain this feature. It presupposes it. Our problem is simply pushed one step back and it remains unsolved.

The idea of a perspectival fact, as opposed to a perspectival representation of the facts, is hopeless. Williams, Moore and Mellor each pick up on precisely the point that the features of ways of thinking and speaking that make us want to introduce a special kind of perspectival fact are better explained in a different way. We have a distinctive way of knowing a perfectly mundane fact. But if that is the feature we want to explain, taking perspective out of our access to the facts and attaching it to the facts leaves our original problem untouched. Furthermore, it leaves us with both a philosophically hybrid and problematic entity: a part of the world with one's special access to it glued on to it. Furthermore, postulating perspectival facts threatens the intuitive idea from which our reflections on realism began, namely, that our common-sense realism is a belief in a world that is substantial, unitary and independent of us.

If the idea of a perspectival fact is, as the German physicist Wolfgang Pauli was fond of saying, "not even wrong", then it is going to be troubling if Nagel is committed to it.[10] However, once again we have Nagel's explicit statement that the predicates "subjective" and "objective" apply to understanding and knowledge, not to the *objects* of that understanding or knowledge. Nagel wants us to recognize the problems posed by areas of thought and language that are perspectival, sometimes radically perspectival. He wants us to enrich the forms of objective understanding. Nagel believes that we can achieve the goal of realizing the ideal of objectivity to the greatest extent that we reasonably can while leaving the ideas of truth and fact untouched. I think that he is correct, but the final verdict can be deferred until the end of this book when one is in a position to judge whether Nagel illuminates the wide-ranging topics he discusses without needing to be committed to the self-defeating idea of a perspectival fact. One of my aims in this book is to exposit Nagel's view without any appeal to this idea.

Chapter 2

Understanding, knowledge and reason

This chapter discusses four interrelated topics. I shall first characterize Nagel's distinctive treatment of the issue of realism in more depth. As Chapter 1 established, Nagel believes that scientific understanding is capable of supplying that which Williams called an "absolute conception" of the world, namely, a conception of the world that is maximally independent of our distinctively human perspective (*VN*: 15; B. Williams 1978: 64–8). In the first section, "Cartesian absoluteness", I shall describe this view in order to establish how Nagel positions himself between two kinds of critic: those who undervalue objectivity and those who overvalue it (*VN*: 5). This discussion is intended to set the stage for three corollaries of Nagel's realism, each of which is of considerable interest in its own right.

The first corollary that Nagel derives from his realism is a well-known critique of what he took to be a strong tendency towards philosophical idealism in contemporary philosophy. I shall focus, in particular, on his critique of the views of Ludwig Wittgenstein and Donald Davidson. The focus of this discussion is understanding: how, in general, thought can so much as be about an objective world.

The second corollary that Nagel derives from his realism is a distinctive treatment of knowledge and scepticism. How is objective knowledge possible if we are finite and contingent creatures, products of a contingent evolutionary history, who simply find ourselves in a world not of our own making? The section "Knowledge and the shadow of scepticism" discusses the role that Nagel's two models of objectivity described in Chapter 1, the Cartesian and the Hegelian, play in formulating his claim that there is a close connection between his view of objectivity and the irrefutability of scepticism.

The third corollary of Nagel's realism that I shall discuss in this chapter is realism about the norms of rationality themselves. The section "Realism about reason" concludes the chapter with an examination of Nagel's realism about reason. Epistemology receives a comparatively brief treatment in *The View from Nowhere*, but the more general idea of how we ought to guided by reason receives an extended consideration in Nagel's *The Last Word*. Nagel defends a strong version of the claim that certain basic ways of thinking are inescapable for us. That is because any attempt to think without them, or to question them, only presupposes their validity.

Cartesian absoluteness

I described the basic elements of Nagel's realism in the previous chapter. We are over impressed by a Cartesian model of objectification and tend mistakenly to generalize its application. However, that model *is* appropriate as an account of a modern, mathematicized, mature physical science. In its proper place, this model of objectivity is correct and it is very important that it is correct. The objective standing of science has, however, come under attack both within philosophy and in science studies.[1] Nagel wants to defend this objective standing from both those who would deny it and those who would discredit it by extending the Cartesian model of objectivity beyond its proper bounds. The key passage for understanding his treatment of these themes in *The View from Nowhere*, and in Nagel's subsequent work, is this one:

> I shall offer a defense and also a critique of objectivity. Both are necessary in the present intellectual climate, for objectivity is both underrated and overrated, sometimes by the same persons. It is underrated by those who don't regard it as a method of understanding the world as it is in itself. It is overrated by those who believe it can provide a complete view of the world on its own, replacing the subjective views from which it has developed. These errors are connected: they both stem from an insufficiently robust sense of reality and of its independence of any particular form of human understanding. (*VN*: 5)

This represents an area of Nagel's work that converges with that of Bernard Williams, marking a great deal of mutual influence. Nagel refers approvingly to Williams's claim that it is appropriate for us to seek an "absolute conception" of the world (*VN*: 15).[2] First introduced in his expository study of Descartes's philosophy, Williams believed that it was appropriate, via physical science, to seek such a conception. An absolute conception of the world is one that is "maximally independent of our perspective and its peculiarities" (B. Williams 1978: 65). Modern science has made the prospects for a view of this kind compelling. We can, from within the many and varied ways in which we represent the world, distinguish those ways of doing so that are less dependent on our peculiarities as thinkers. It is paradigmatically a conception of reality that modern mathematicized physics expresses and it is not from any point of view in particular. Both Nagel and Williams claim that physics can supply an absolute conception of this kind.

There is clearly an ambiguity in the idea of the absolute conception of the world construed as "maximally independent of our perspective and its peculiarities"; does "maximally" here mean "completely"? A full consideration of this issue lies beyond the scope of this book. It is nothing less than the question of whether the Cartesian model of objectivity described in Chapter 1 is more fundamental than the rival Hegelian conception or vice versa. In my view the word "maximally" in the phrase "maximally independent of our perspective" need not be construed as "completely" (Thomas 2006b: 135–44). The aim is not a point of view that is from no point of view, which is clearly a self-defeating idea, but a point of view from nowhere *in particular*.[3] It is the latter idea that captures what we intuitively mean by thinking objectively. Our spatial and visual metaphors of perspective and point of view are inherently realist, as was argued in Chapter 1. We use them because we conceive of people as located in a world that exists *anyway*.[4] I concede that both Nagel and Williams want to develop this thought a step further. The process of perspectival ascent seeks a view from nowhere in particular that is more explanatory than the perspectival views it either replaces or contextualizes. My point is simply that we do not have to see this process as iterated so as to generate the idea of a maximally perspective-free view where "maximally" means "completely".

Could one not argue from the mere existence of perspectival ascent to the possibility of such a perspective-free view? I think that any such argument would be a mistake. It would be an instance of that which Elizabeth Anscombe called the "chain fallacy" (1957: 34; 1967: 15–16). That would be the faulty inference from the truth of the claim that "all chains have an end" to the faulty conclusion that "there is an end to all chains". By analogy, if for every perspectival view we can conceive of one that is less perspectival, it does not follow that we can conceive of a view guaranteed to have the following feature: no other view can be less perspectival than *it*. That is a property that it would be *guaranteed* to have if it were the maximal, completely non-perspectival view. Nagel is explicit that he is concerned with the comparative forms "more or less subjective" and "more or less objective". Neither he nor Williams need be interpreted as committed to reading "maximally independent of our perspective" as "completely independent of our perspective".

It is important to exonerate Nagel and Williams from the claim that they have implicitly misunderstood science in the course of their "scientistic" enthusiasm for it. Hilary Putnam has argued that modern physics has the feature of observer-relativity in a way that shows its ineliminable dependence on the human point of view (1992). Putnam believes that this hidden dependence shows that the human point of view cannot be evaded in the way that Nagel and Williams presuppose. That objection overlooks the point that the absolute conception is explained in terms of our distinctive peculiarities as judgers. "Perspectival" in this account does not simply mean "relational" (B. Williams 1991).

To illustrate this, suppose we conduct the thought experiment of a dialogue with Martians in order to work out for ourselves which of our cognitive capacities are distinctively ours (*ibid.*). Suppose we decide that, owing to the very different conditions of human and Martian life, we have to treat human and Martian ethics as highly perspectival and incommensurable. However, we would not say the same for Martian physics. If Martian physics is like human physics in being a form of rational enquiry into the fundamental structure of the world, then in the relevant sense it is less perspectival and more absolute than Martian ethics. But Martian physics can still be observer-dependent: these are simply two different issues that cut across each other. If physics is observer-relative, so be it, but that does not make it perspectival in the sense at issue. It can still be absolute. Martian physics will be observer-dependent, too, just like our physics. Nagel explicitly discusses observer-relativity in *The View from Nowhere* in a way that does not suggest that he views its mere existence as posing any problem for the possibility of an absolute conception of the world (*VN*: 16, 76).

One important difference between Nagel's and Williams's defence of the idea of an absolute conception is that, in his early presentations of the idea, Williams left himself open to some misunderstandings in a way that Nagel does not.[5] Because of Williams's focus on explanation, it seemed to some of his critics, notably once again Putnam, that Williams envisaged an absolute conception of the world as ideally reflexive. What I mean by this use of the word "reflexive" is that the absolute conception would supply not just its own content but also a wider physicalist account of its own generation and acceptance. This point is worth developing as it has a direct bearing on why Nagel is not, similarly, committed to physicalism although he is committed to the possibility of an absolute conception. Nagel is, in fact, a critic of physicalism.

Putnam argues that those committed to an absolute conception have to accept the surprising consequence that the ideal set of concepts and categories vindicated by the maximally perspective-free theory must then be used to explain how such a view is, itself, possible using only those concepts (1992: 98). That would certainly be a very ambitious set of reductions of one discipline to another. We think about how we represent the world using concepts such as knowledge, rational appraisal, communities of enquiry, canons of rational practice and all the other highly perspectival concepts we need to reflect on knowledge and its acquisition. Those concepts do not look reducible to the concepts of physics. However, Putnam argues that this consequence does follow. If the most plausible candidate for supplying the content of an absolute conception is physics, then if that same conception gives an account of its own generation and acceptance, this set of reductions would have to follow. An absolute conception of the world will have to give an account of those social, psychological and normative concepts needed to explain what it is successfully to theorize in physics *using only physics*.

To make this requirement plausible a philosopher will have to devise criteria for marking concepts as physicalistically acceptable. Such concepts will feature in a physicalistically acceptable account of psychological and linguistic representation. Many contemporary philosophers view their research programmes in precisely these terms (Field 1972, 1981; Papineau 1993). For Nagel, views of this kind represent the overrating of objectivity "by those who believe it can provide a complete view of the world on its own, replacing the subjective views from which it has developed" (*VN*: 5).

Are Nagel and Williams committed to that which Putnam claims is the physicalist consequence of their views? It seems to me that they are not. Putnam has not correctly represented the aspiration to form an absolute conception of the world.[6] What Putnam's anti-reductionist argument proves is not that the absolute conception is false because representation requires normativity, interpretation and irreducibly normative concepts. What Putnam shows is that *representations about representations* have all these features. But Nagel and Williams never denied *that*.

In Putnam's brilliant book *Reason, Truth and History* (1981) he argued that the concepts of truth, warranted acceptability and reasonableness were all deeply intertwined with our ethical values in a way summarized by his chapter title "The Place of Facts in a World of Values". For Putnam, all conceptualization and representation is tradition-based, active, draws on interpretation and commits us to representations that are irreducibly perspectival. Furthermore, that point of view is inescapably shaped by our ethical and rational values taken all of a piece. But, as Moore has pointed out, there are two arguments here. The first successfully establishes that in thinking about how we produce representations we need to draw on our values and proves that all representations *about* representations are from a point of view. However, the success of that argument in no way supports a second argument that the absolute conception is impossible. It does not follow, of all our representations, that none of *them* are from no point of view in particular (Moore 1997: 87–9). However, it is the latter claim that is important to those like Nagel and Williams who defend the possibility of an absolute conception of the world. That is all to which they are committed.

In thinking about how physical science produces truth we need all kinds of concepts in order to explain how it succeeds. Such concepts include the concepts of knowledge, rationality, constitutive standards of scientific appraisal and so on. These are not, themselves, concepts of physics. But they do not have to be. It is physics that produces representations from no point of view in particular. It is not the explanation of physics and its success in producing true representations that does so. Of course, any explanation of the truth of the absolute conception of the world and a further explanation of its generation and acceptance have to be mutually consistent. But that is a comparatively weak requirement. Knowledge that is non-physical, or that does not use the proprietary concepts of physics or an extended set of physicalistically acceptable concepts, is not un-physical or spooky.

This is important because it allows one to make sense of the fact that Nagel is both a realist and a critic of physicalism. In this context, the physicalist plays the role of the person whom Nagel calls the "objectivist". There is a very seductive misconception here that needs to be described: how can Nagel aspire to an absolute conception of the world, just as the physicalist does, and yet be a critic of physicalism in his philosophy of mind and in metaphysics? An ostensible criticism of Nagel is that this set of commitments does not add up. The kind of uncompromising realism reflected by a commitment to an absolute conception is a commitment to seeing an ideal physical theory of the world as able reflexively to explain its own generation and acceptance in its own terms (Putnam 1992). Physicalism, being complete, has to be able to explain itself. Furthermore, it must do so using only those concepts that it vindicates directly from its own point of view.

This tempting misconception arises in this way: the correct form of the aspiration to absoluteness is to argue that a mature physical science could represent a conception of the world maximally independent, but not completely independent, of our perspective and its peculiarities. That is the content of the representations of physics. But Nagel's counter-argument is that the truth of physics is not the truth of physicalism. It is a mistake to run together those two issues.

Physicalism, better called "objectivism" in this context, is a philosophical commentary on the status of physics. It is not itself a scientific view, but a philosophical view. It makes a mistake about Nagel's and Williams's position that exactly mirrors that of Putnam (and others).[7] It takes the truth represented by an absolute conception of the world, the content of which is supplied by physics, to mandate the further requirement that representations of the representations of physics be true in a physicalistically acceptable way, too. The key assumption that the physicalist highlights is that a physicalist view of the world has to be complete. The requirement that physics explain everything, including itself, is taken to follow from the claim that physicalism is a complete account of everything.

But it is not what *Nagel* means by "complete". It is this objectivist requirement that forces the view that if one aspires to absoluteness, then a reductive physicalist programme about language, mind and representation follows inevitably as we seek to explain the relevant sense in which physics is complete. The physicalist/objectivist's completeness claim means that, of course, the absolute conception has to explain itself: it has to explain everything. However, on Nagel's view, it is no part of the claim that physics can be absolute to make that further completeness claim. Moore puts the point very elegantly in a discussion of Williams that is worth quoting here because it applies equally to this crucial aspect of Nagel's view:

> In order to give a full account of how two items of knowledge from incompatible points of view cohere, it is necessary to go beyond the resources of the absolute conception ... [it] can supply part of the account, certainly. *In particular, it can indicate what makes the items of knowledge both true; that is of its very essence.* But it cannot indicate, on its own, *how either of them is made true* ... To give a full account of *that* requires exercise of such concepts as the concepts of knowledge and the concepts of content, neither of which can be exercised except from some psychosocial point of view. (Moore 2007: 35, first emphasis added)[8]

Nagel regards the physicalist as in the grip of an objectivist illusion. He or she, like an idealist, thinks that one way of conceiving of the world is privileged. The world is identified with what is, from Nagel's perspective, simply one way of understanding it. The way that physical science understands the world is very important, and that importance needs to be defended. However, that does not mean that this way of understanding the world is to be given a privileged status in this sense: that the method of understanding that it uses can be used to explain everything else. That leads only to the false objectification of topics that cannot be objectified in such a way. Nagel argues that it is deeply ironic that the physicalist is subject to exactly the same objectivist illusion as that which motivates the idealist. In philosophy, an idealist is a person who holds a view about the ultimate nature of reality. The idealist believes that reality is entirely mental or constitutively dependent on the mental. Nagel thinks that both the physicalist and the idealist suffer from "an insufficiently robust sense of reality" (*VN*: 5).

The distinctions that I have drawn in this section explain why it is consistent for Nagel to hold the following three views: first, that a legitimate interpretation of what it is to be realist about some areas of thought and language, paradigmatically physics, involves absolute representations; secondly, that contemporary philosophical physicalism is a mistaken form of objectivism that represents a misguided attempt to reduce reality to one of our conceptions of it; thirdly, that one can consistently be an anti-reductionist when the physicalist offers a "physicalistically acceptable" (for Nagel, falsely objectifying) reduction of aspects of language and mind that simply do not sustain it. The latter point will prove particularly important in the next chapter in the appreciation of Nagel's distinction between physicalism and objectivism in the philosophy of mind.[9] Nagel comments that "I want not to abandon the idea of objectivity entirely but rather to suggest that the physical is not its only possible interpretation" (*VN*: 17).

Constraints on understanding

The previous section further characterized Nagel's realism. He believes that it follows from the truth of that realism that there is a secure basis for a critique of some countervailing tendencies in contemporary philosophy. Nagel complains that:

> There is a significant strain of idealism in contemporary philosophy, according to which what there is and how things are cannot go beyond what we could in principle think about. This view inherits the crude appeal of logical positivism even though that particular version of idealism is out of date. (*VN*: 9)

In Nagel's view, contemporary idealists, although they would certainly refuse to accept this description of their own work, cut the world down to our size in an anthropocentric way that is tantamount to philosophical idealism. Controversially, in *The View from Nowhere*, Nagel argues that the leading source of contemporary idealism is the complementary work on meaning, truth and interpretation of Wittgenstein and Davidson.[10] Chapter 6 of *The View from Nowhere* contains a much-discussed critique of their views.

From Nagel's perspective, the interpretative arguments used by Wittgenstein and Davidson appeal to contingent features of our human make-up in order to establish conditions on understanding. They are, therefore, implicitly committed to idealism. That is because the contingent origin of those features in our human make-up is transformed into the contingent basis for a set of interpretative criteria. Those criteria identify the real with what we can *interpret* to be real. Taken together, Nagel thinks that Wittgenstein's and Davidson's views represent one form of misguided idealism that reduces reality to one of our ways of conceiving of it. They both deploy a "broadly epistemological test of reality" (*VN*: 91).

I shall describe both sets of arguments in turn beginning with Wittgenstein. Wittgenstein's work (1961, 2001), both early and late, was concerned with conditions of sense. The specific set of claims with which Nagel is particularly concerned involves the grounding of conditions of sense on agreements in judgements. No one, Nagel included, believes that Wittgenstein reduced the notion of objectivity to issues of inter-subjective agreement directly: you do not discover what is objectively true of the world by conducting an opinion poll (*VN*: 105). Working in the transcendental tradition, the kinds of agreement involved in Wittgenstein's and Davidson's work are agreements in that which Wittgenstein called a "form of life". They are transcendental agreements, not any actual agreement between a specific group of concept-users. However, Nagel argues that these agreements work, indirectly, to compromise our intuitive notion of objectivity. They do so in a way that justifies calling Wittgenstein's work a contemporary source for idealism (see also B. Williams 1981b). The distinction between transcendental agreements and actual agreements makes problematic what we mean by "us" when we say that such agreements constitute the bounds of sense for us:

> His [Wittgenstein's] later views on the conditions of meaning seem to imply that nothing can make sense which purports to reach beyond the outer bounds of human experience and life, for it is only within a community of actual or possible users of the language that there can exist that possibility of agreement in its application which is a condition of the existence of rules, and of the distinction between getting it right and getting it wrong.
> (*VN*: 105)

Nagel argues that this requirement is incompatible with his own claim that we can use our concepts of existence and reality to form the idea of a conception of the world of which we could not even, with our limited cognitive powers, conceive. He argues, in contrast to this putatively idealistic view in Wittgenstein and Davidson, that the idea of reality outstrips our contingent capacities to conceive the world (*VN*: 103–4).

Nagel sees a direct analogy between the views of the later Wittgenstein and those of Davidson in this focus on sense-constituting agreements. I, too, will treat both of their views together in assessing Nagel's critique. To complement Nagel's admirably concise summary of Wittgenstein's view I must explain some of the distinctive features of Davidson's approach. The full scope of Davidson's project cannot be described here: briefly, he suggests that the traditional aims of metaphysical enquiry are best realized by investigating language from an interpretative perspective (Davidson 1984b,e).[11] From this perspective we interpret all of the rational action, including the linguistic actions, of some target group. That interpretative perspective is one that follows from Davidson's "bold step" of replacing the idea of a theory of meaning for a natural language with that of developing a fully extensional truth theory as the core of a theory of meaning (Davidson 1984b).

Anyone trying to interpret linguistic behaviour faces the problem known as the "hermeneutic circle". If one knew what the group to be interpreted believed, then one could triangulate between those beliefs and the objective world to determine what that group meant. Similarly, if one knew what they meant, then one could interpret what they believed (again, locating the group and their behaviour in an objective world). But how does one break into this hermeneutic circle of meaning and belief? Davidson's solution is to hold beliefs fixed and "solve" this equation for meaning. But he carries out this project in a surprising way.

Davidson (*ibid.*) claims that a particular account of a model theory for a formal language, as developed by Alfred Tarski, can be put to use in an empirical theory of the semantics of a particular language. However, given that Tarski's interest was in truth, he assumed the idea of sameness of meaning. Given that Davidson is interested in using a truth theory to achieve what a meaning theory sought to achieve, he cannot make this assumption. That is why he appeals to interpretation. A *radical* interpreter offers an interpretation of the speakers of a language in the light of constitutive *a priori* constraints, such as that their beliefs must be mostly true and that the subjects must be assumed to be rational (Davidson 1984c). That is how Davidson holds beliefs fixed and "solves" for meaning by using the interpretative device of devising a truth theory for the language to be interpreted.

That is an incomplete description of Davidson's aims, but it does illustrate why he is interested in the idea of incommensurability and, by implication, the connection between agreement and truth (Davidson 1984d). The traditional claim of incommensurability involved taking two worldviews and arguing that there was a dimension across which they were not commensurable (comparable). That dimension was, standardly, what each group believed to be true. Given the importance, for Davidson, in every interpretative encounter of the single objective world that forms one of the points of "triangulation" when you interpret another person or group, his diagnosis of the source of putative cases of incommensurability has to be the following.

Given one shared and objective world, if two groups have incommensurable worldviews that is because they grasp different meanings. Conceptual relativism must be true. The concepts of each group, as linguistically expressed, must function like an interpretative grid such that we can see the same, pre-interpreted content being articulated into different repertoires of truths. To use Putnam's apt metaphor, each group is cutting up some amorphous stuff, "the world", using a different conceptual cookie-cutter. What this overall picture implies is that different groups, with different interpretative grids, have different sets of truths that are not mutually translatable. Davidson cannot accept that conclusion because of his assumptions about the relation between truth and meaning: there cannot be any untranslatable truths.

That is the motivation for his famous argument not that there is merely one conceptual scheme (because, as he points out "even monotheists have religion"), but that the very distinction between an unorganized, pre-conceptualized "content" and an interpretative grid or "conceptual scheme" makes no sense (Davidson 1984d: 183). The *a priori* constraints of Davidson's method of radical interpretation include his well-known principle of charity, according to which we ought, in our interpretation of another group, to minimize inexplicable disagreement. That is compatible with a great deal of *de facto* disagreement. However, with explanations of that disagreement in place, the effect of the principle of charity is to make the beliefs of the interpreted group come out as mostly true. There will be no residual conceptual relativity of any interest, certainly not enough to sustain the traditional scheme–content distinction. We need simply to abandon that idea. *A priori* constraints, grounded in the nature of interpretation, tell us that any group of language-users that are interpretable by us must have beliefs that are mostly true.

Nagel objects very strongly to this line of argument (*VN*: 95–9). Our intuitive commitment to realism tells us that we are contingent, finite creatures with a particular evolutionary history. Our general knowledge of the world tells us that there are a number of different species in the world, some concept-using and some not. Some types of concept-users are much more proficient with concepts than others. Even among human concept-users competence varies widely. Yet Davidson seems to take our status as human concept-users as criterial for the real. That seems to Nagel a very implausible form of anthropocentric hubris: we cut the world down to size by identifying the real with what we can interpret.

Nagel's criticism works via an argument by analogy: we do not think it is possible to explain very difficult and advanced concepts to people with the mental age of a nine-year-old (*VN*: 95). Suppose there are people among us who stand to us as we stand to the nine-year-olds. Such people can say of us, as we say of the nine-year-olds, that as a matter of contingent fact we are unable to grasp the concepts needed to understand the world. That shows that we can imagine people who hold a conception of the world that we cannot understand owing to our contingent limitations.

That only gets Nagel halfway to his conclusion. Simply by following a chain of successive groups of interpreters, each of whom is more conceptually proficient than the group before, one can exploit the intransitivity of interpretation to yield the idea of a possible group whose interpretative powers are discontinuous with our own. But that is not enough to sustain Nagel's stronger conclusion. Nagel wants to defend the idea of reality as outstripping *all* possible conceptions of it. He needs to break the connection between possible conception and the real. He has not proved this by arguing that there can be conceptions that have developed by a series of intransitive steps from our own. That is a vulnerability in Nagel's argument.

In order to come to an overall evaluation of Nagel's composite critique of Wittgenstein and Davidson I want to focus on precisely this point. Susan Hurley focused on this aspect of Nagel's argument in a very insightful paper (1992). Hurley argued that it is not possible to help oneself to those arguments from the conditions of mutual intelligibility that rule out solipsism, as Nagel does in *The Possiblity of Altruism* and *The View from Nowhere*, while also allowing the existence of conceptual relativism. Nagel needs to choose: if his critique of Wittgenstein and Davidson succeeds, then an important positive assumption of his own views will be undercut.

Hurley makes an important distinction between the kind of possibility involved in possessing a *capacity* and the kind of possibility involved in having an *ability*. One can have the capacity to do something (her example is to speak Chinese) without being able to do so (because you have not taken the time and trouble to learn). In the context of conditions for understanding other groups of people, the relevant notion is that of intelligibility. When we find people intelligible we do more than conclude that they have minds in a way that is opaque to us. We seek interpretative insight into those minds. Hurley argues that this idea of intelligibility follows the logic of a capacity, not an ability. A group of concept-users can be intelligible to another group if the latter could (in the capacity sense), with appropriate time and effort, and subject to contingent background conditions, come to be able to understand them. Furthermore, in this process the identity of the interpreting group is not held fixed: the changes involved in coming to be able to interpret the first group might bring about significant changes in who "we" were in the first place.[12]

Hurley believes that these points undermine Nagel's claim that forming a constitutive link between possessing a mind and being interpretable as having a mind is a hubristic intellectual imperialism. Such an intellectual imperialism would reduce all minds to minds that we can understand here and now. She notes that Nagel argues in the specific case of Wittgenstein's idealism that:

> As a desperate measure one might argue that Wittgenstein's claim about rules, if true, does not have such restrictive consequences as it is often thought to have. The possibility of agreement in judgements is a very broad condition that can be met in many ways. (*VN*: 105)

Hurley's aim is to defend this "desperate measure", but as a valid and acceptable defence of Davidson and, by implication, of Wittgenstein. The kind of constitutive connection between having a mind and being interpreted as such, that rules out solipsism (a view Nagel accepts), plus Hurley's distinctive understanding of what intelligibility is (explained in terms of to a capacity to understand, not the ability to understand), yields a consequence that Nagel ought to accept. That consequence is that we can prove that "all possible minds are minds". A corollary of this claim is that:

> Davidson cannot sensibly be supposed to hold that if other minds inhabit a very different physical environment from our own, we must somehow magically share their beliefs about their physical environment, with which we are not in contact. Rather, the point about overlap in attitudes being a necessary condition for interpretability must be liberalized and conditionalized; it's that either we do or *we would*, under the right conditions, share many beliefs; we are to include the beliefs *we would have were we* in the different environment, with appropriately different perceptual abilities, etc. (S. Hurley 1992: 100; see also Eilan 2001: 179)

The phrases that Hurley emphasizes in this passage show how loose the connection is between the *a priori* conditions on interpretation when "liberalized and conditionalized" and what there can be interpreted to be. They do not seem to be tight enough to justify Nagel's charge of idealism. This is not the place to assess all the details of Hurley's ingenious argument: its point is to show that there is no anthropocentric hubris involved in the constitutive claim that connects being a mental subject to being interpreted as such.[13] On the contrary, a Davidsonian view accepts that there can be many different ways of living a mental life including ones that are far beyond our current *abilities* to verify that they exist.[14]

Hurley concludes that Nagel represents Davidson and Wittgenstein as suggesting a one-way reduction of what there is to what we can understand there to be. A better reading is that both urge a two-way interdependence between what there is and what we can understand there to be, such that the result is neither realism nor idealism. Construed in this way, their joint concern is with an issue prior to knowledge and to truth. Wittgenstein and Davidson are concerned with the broader issue of representation and what Kant called the issue of "objective validity".[15] The relevant question is: how can it so much as be the case that we can have thoughts that represent an objective reality? In working out their very different answers to these questions neither Wittgenstein nor Davidson is committed to any anthropocentric hubris, as Nagel seems to fear is the case. That is because they are not attempting to reduce reality to how we can possibly represent it, but rather trying to explain how intentional representation is so much as possible. It is part of Davidson's view that, to use Putnam's cookie-cutter metaphor, the idea of the world as some indeterminate stuff waiting to be cut into parts by our concepts is not fully intelligible. However, in explaining why this is so, mind and world prove to be, as Hurley put it, "constitutively interdependent" (1992: 98).

In *The Last Word* Nagel returns, briefly, to a discussion of Davidson's method of radical interpretation. While brief, the discussion seems far more sympathetic to Davidson's views. Indeed, Nagel defends very similar conclusions to Davidson's own (but relativized to fundamental forms of rational thinking):

> Though Davidson's result [his attack on the idea of alternative conceptual schemes] emerges from the conditions of interpretation, it is not merely a matter of having to see other minds in terms of my own – which sounds much too subjective. Rather, it is the actual content of certain thoughts about the world and forms of reasoning that sets the conditions of interpretation: Nothing could qualify as thought which did not meet those conditions.
> (*LW*: 32 n.11)

I think this is an important shift of emphasis. *The View from Nowhere* offered the "too subjective" interpretation of Davidson's method of radical interpretation. However, that interpretation has been corrected in Nagel's more recent work. Hurley has shown how Nagel's overall position can be revised so as to avoid the following inconsistency: first, that Nagel believes that conditions on interpretation can be used to rule out solipsism (a claim central to *The Possibility of Altruism*); secondly, that those very same conditions have to be rejected because they are inconsistent with Nagel's uncompromising realism. Nagel's treatment of Wittgenstein's and Davidson's putative idealism does, indeed, seem to have changed between *The View from Nowhere* and *The Last Word*.

Knowledge and the shadow of scepticism

These very abstract questions about understanding and intentionality in general lead naturally to what follows when one has established that thoughts can represent the world. Do they do so successfully? Is knowledge not simply possible, but attainable? Nagel's consideration of these issues, once again, represents a counter-reaction to the work of many of his contemporaries. In particular, he views the responses to scepticism exemplified by the work of Wittgenstein, Peter Strawson and J. L. Austin as deeply unsatisfactory.[16] The nature of Nagel's dissatisfaction is similar to that exemplified by his discussion of interpretation and understanding. He believes that our capacity to reason gives us a limited degree of self-transcendence. His understanding of Cartesian objectivity leads him to conclude that our human point of view is a limitation that we need to overcome and that it can be a constitutive source of error in how we represent the world.

Nagel connects this issue to the assessment of philosophical scepticism about the external world. The philosophical sceptic seeks an overall assessment of the totality of our knowledge from a detached, reflective standpoint. In order to make this task realistic, the sceptic construes it as applied to very general classes of belief. He or she then exploits gaps between our ostensible claims to know and the canonical forms of evidence for those claims. This makes sceptical arguments forms of argument from the *under-determination* of conclusions by evidence (Ayer 1956; see also DeRose 1995; M. Williams 2001: 75–8).

To take a single representative example, a sceptic about our knowledge of the external world argues that we can be subject to visual delusions. In such a case we would form false beliefs on the same evidential basis that we exploit when we are successful in achieving perceptual knowledge. But what this shows, the sceptic continues, is that our knowledge of material objects in the external world is indirect. We are directly acquainted with a different epistemic class, namely, beliefs about sensory experience. The sceptic then considers a list of candidate rational principles for connecting these experiential beliefs to perceptual knowledge such as deductive, inductive, abductive or criterial principles. Finding no such candidate principle plausible as a means of connecting beliefs about experience to knowledge of the external world, the sceptic concludes that we possess no perceptual knowledge at all (Ayer 1956).

The style of philosophy with which Nagel became acquainted at the University of Oxford in the 1960s developed various responses to this sceptical line of argument. In so far as Wittgenstein, and those he has influenced, try to return the sceptic to our ordinary or everyday experience, and to accuse the sceptic of violating the ordinary sense of the word "know", Nagel finds all such views to be complacent. He believes that philosophical scepticism arises simply and naturally from our intuitive commitment to realism. It is, strictly speaking, irrefutable.

According to Nagel, the sceptic does not misuse words or arbitrarily impose standards for knowing that are inappropriate in an everyday context. High standards for knowledge are implicit in our ordinary use of the concept. The sceptic simply uncovers these implicit standards and shows how poorly we live up to them when ordinary claims to know are placed under the spotlight of reflective examination (Thomas 2006b: 170–79). Influenced by Berkeley philosopher Thompson Clarke, Nagel forms part of a group of epistemologists whom Michael Williams has called the "New Sceptics" or "New Humeans". He says of their composite views that:

> It represents a powerful reaction to post-Wittgensteinian (or "ordinary language") and neo-pragmatist tendencies to *dismiss* traditional philosophical problems, particularly sceptical problems, as not really problems at all … The New Sceptics, or New Humeans, are unconvinced. The fact is that we seem to understand the sceptic very well, certainly well enough to understand how to argue against him or why so many popular antisceptical arguments fail. (1991: xiv)

In the course of further characterizing this group, and describing the analogy between their views and David Hume's pessimism about our ability to refute the sceptic using rational arguments, Williams notes that:

> The most thoroughgoing Humean pessimist among contemporary philosophers may well be Thomas Nagel. However incredible in ordinary circumstances, from the objective standpoint scepticism is the only possible verdict on our supposed knowledge of the world. (*Ibid.*: 15)

Williams bases this overall assessment on the discussion of epistemology in *The View from Nowhere*, which I shall now describe.

Nagel opens his discussion in *The View from Nowhere* by connecting two questions. The first is whether knowledge is attainable at all. The second is whether we can form an objective conception both of ourselves and of the world. He addresses the literally incoherent ambition suggested by the metaphor of "the view from nowhere":

> The objective self is responsible both for the expansion of our understanding and for doubts about it that cannot finally be laid to rest ... The most familiar scene of conflict is the pursuit of objective knowledge, whose aim is naturally described in terms that, taken literally, are unintelligible: we must get outside of ourselves, and view the world from nowhere within it. (*VN*: 67)

The metaphor of a view from nowhere is simply that, a metaphor, but it points towards an unrealizable ideal. The unrealizability of this ideal does not impede its intellectual authority for us. That explains Nagel's central claim in this discussion, namely, that objective knowledge "is inescapably subject to scepticism and cannot refute it but most proceed under its shadow" (*VN*: 71).

In the next chapter I shall discuss Nagel's account of the objective self, described in this passage, but here I want to draw out the role that this ideal plays in generating Nagel's conception of scepticism. He elaborates further:

> Since it is impossible to leave one's own point of view behind entirely without ceasing to exist, the metaphor of getting outside ourselves must have another meaning. We are to rely less and less on certain individual aspects of our point of view, and more and more on something else, less individual, which is also part of us. But if initial appearances are not in themselves reliable guides to reality, why should the products of detached reflection be different? ... The same ideas that make the pursuit of objectivity seem necessary for knowledge make both objectivity and knowledge seem, on reflection, unattainable. (*VN*: 67)

So Nagel's conception of objectivity, his Cartesian model of objectification, *invites* scepticism (*VN*: 68, 73). Furthermore, it does so in a way that reveals that scepticism is both true and irrefutable. We are finite and contingent creatures who find ourselves in a world not of our own making: our human point of view can represent, as the case of secondary qualities shows, a constitutive source of error.[17] By "constitutive" here is meant a source of error that could not be avoided by being more epistemically responsible or careful. The human point of view itself is exposed as a defect or limitation. No wonder, then, that the aspirations built into our ordinary concept of knowledge cannot be realized: we keep trying to escape ourselves but we cannot:

> We cannot accept [the] appearances uncritically, but we must try to understand what our own constitution contributes to them. To do this we must try to develop an idea of the world with ourselves in it, an account of both ourselves and the world that includes an explanation of why it initially appears to us as it does. But this idea, since it is we who develop it, is likewise the product of interaction between us and the world, though the interaction is more complicated and more self-conscious than the original one. If the initial appearances cannot be relied upon because they depend on our constitution in ways that we do not fully understand, this more complex idea should be open to the same doubts, for whatever we use to understand certain interactions between ourselves and the world is not itself the object of that understanding. However often we may try to step outside of ourselves, *something will have to stay behind the lens*, something in us will determine the resulting picture, and this will give grounds for doubt that we are really getting any closer to reality.
>
> (*VN*: 68, emphasis added)

This is a crucial passage for understanding the connections that Nagel forges between his conception of objectivity and how that idea leads directly to the truth of scepticism.

Michael Williams notes that Nagel tries to "take the edge" off his concession that philosophical scepticism is true by suggesting that a "reconciliation" is possible between the objective standpoint that generates scepticism and our subjective standpoint, such that we can still live "in the light of the truth" (1991: 16; *VN*: 231). The aim is a kind of relativized pluralism: scepticism is true from one standpoint and not from another, and what we have to do is try to reconcile the two standpoints to the greatest extent possible. The question is, once again, the relationship between Nagel's Cartesian and Hegelian models of objectification and what one is to say when their results clash. Williams thinks that the conclusion is forced and that the Cartesian model has to dominate:

> Living in the light of the truth requires more than recognizing the impossibility of integrating our everyday outlook with the results of philosophical reflection: it requires acknowledging the final truth of scepticism. If this were not so, there would be no point in calling the philosophical standpoint "objective": how things look from the "objective" standpoint is how they are. (1991: 16)

Perhaps distinguishing clearly between the two models of objectification might avoid this question by preventing this clash of standpoints from arising in the first place. We do not have to address the question of how we can reflectively live with the truth of scepticism if the argument for its inevitability is implausible. Perhaps the connection between Nagel's view of objectivity and the price we pay for that view, namely, acknowledging the truth of scepticism, is not as tight as he claims.

I do not think that we ought to concede that aspiring to develop an absolute conception of the world forces us to concede the inevitability of scepticism. This is one point at which I think Dancy's concern that Nagel sometimes equivocates in his arguments between the two models of objectivity described in Chapter 1 is well placed (Dancy 1988: 8–9). I quoted, in particular, the crucial passage that speaks of the knowing subject as always "behind the lens" (*VN*: 68). But this whole passage seems to move from features of Cartesian objectification to features of Hegelian objectification in a way that undermines the argument.

It is the model of Cartesian objectification that Nagel interprets as presenting to us the problem of the constitutive dependence of the "appearances" on our human point of view. Nagel would be begging the question if he simply asserted that whenever we form a more objective conception, for all we know it might be *just as* tainted a set of appearances as our first-order experiences. So he needs to add that, for all we know, higher-order reflection might be tainted because it may be determined in a way now concealed from us. That would be true if it, too, depended on contingent features of the human epistemic subject. We cannot rule that out because we can never bring this knowing subject into our field of vision. That subject is always "behind the lens".

However, it is the Hegelian model of objectification that presents the separate problem that when we respond to this challenge by invoking higher-order reflection, the knowing subject himself or herself always "stays behind the lens". This claim is no part of the Cartesian conception. Dancy notes that:

> The place where Nagel has conflated Hegelian with absolute objectification is in the words "something will have to stay behind the lens, something in us will determine the resulting picture". The first of these is true on the Hegelian conception, the second more to the absolute conception. Crucially, one cannot argue from the first to the second. The fact that something will have to stay behind the lens does not show that any individual feature or features of that something will determine the resulting picture.
> (1988: 9–10)[18]

There are, therefore, grounds for challenging the tight connection that Nagel forges between his account of objectivity and the truth and irrefutability of scepticism. However, for purposes of exposition I shall set further evaluation of this issue aside and describe how Nagel develops his views.

Nagel proceeds to classify all theories of knowledge as a response to scepticism on the basis of his assumption that scepticism is unavoidable and strictly irrefutable. Such theories fall into three groups: the sceptical, the reductive and the heroic (*VN*: 68). As I have noted, the general pattern of sceptical argument that Nagel describes here is that offered by A. J. Ayer in *The Problem of Knowledge* (1956): sceptical problems are all under-determination problems. There is an evidential gap between our ostensible claims to know and the evidence that we cite in support of those claims. Nagel argues that scepticism alerts us to this gap; reductionism tries to close it by fiat via the simple tactic of reducing our knowledge to our evidence; the heroic epistemologist acknowledges the gap, but simply "leaps across the gap without narrowing it" (*VN*: 69). Given his realism Nagel sees his choices as scepticism, which is a truthful representation of our epistemic predicament, and heroism that is equally authentic in its response to scepticism, even if not entirely satisfactory as a response to it.[19]

Nagel's constructive solution is to accept that scepticism is irrefutable because it is grounded on the same model of Cartesian objectivity that sustains his realism and then works in its "shadow". It sets an unattainable ideal in contrast to which we try to develop the degree of self-transcendence that we can achieve, bearing in mind our constitutive limitations. The mathematicization of nature and the consequent perspectival ascent described in Chapter 1 once again form Nagel's paradigm for a genuine gain in objectivity (*VN*: 74–7). Not all intellectual progress has this character. Not all such progress advances our reflective self-understanding in the special way that involves forming a conception of the world that is maximally independent of our peculiarities. Nagel thinks it is important to this project that it produce an understanding of the mind that itself forms increasingly less perspectival self-conceptions. That ambition will be described at length in Chapter 3.

Self-understanding is so important to Nagel because the source of our capacity to form a more objective view of ourselves must lie, precisely, within. We have a capacity for reason and that is a source of *a priori* knowledge. It is our capacity for theory that allows us to become more objective:

> The position to which I am drawn is a form of rationalism … we have the capacity, not based on experience, to generate hypotheses about what in general the world might possibly be like, and to reject those possibilities that we see could not include ourselves and our experiences. Just as important, we must be able to reject hypotheses which appear initially to be possibilities but are not. The conditions of objectivity that I have been defending lead to the conclusion that the basis of most real knowledge must be a priori and drawn from within ourselves. (*VN*: 83)

Nagel's rationalism is not committed to indubitable foundations for knowledge (*VN*: 85). It is an account of our capacity to theorize as a capacity whose exercise cannot be reduced to the accidental, scattered and idiosyncratic evidential input to the system of knowledge as a whole. Those inputs have to be endorsed, theorized about and integrated into a more objective understanding. The principles that underpin those processes are not themselves the product of experience: "Although the procedures of thought by which we progress are not self-guaranteeing, they make sense only if we have a natural capacity for achieving harmony with the world far beyond the range of our particular experiences and surroundings" (*VN*: 84). Nagel notes that Descartes offered a transcendent guarantee for this "harmony with the world" in the form of a proof that God was no deceiver. We can no longer believe that explanation: but the need it highlights is real (*VN*: 85). Nagel thinks that at this historical point in our understanding the honest response is to say that we need an explanation of this general kind, but that we have "no idea" what aspect of the natural order of which we are a part underpins this explanation!

Can one come to some overall evaluation of Nagel's epistemology in *The View from Nowhere*? The situation seems to be this. Nagel traces both scepticism and our capacity for objectivity to a common source in realism. Scepticism is irrefutable and we must work in its shadow. However, it is not entirely clear why that is so: sceptical problems are under-determination problems. Nagel's rationalism tells us that there is a source in reason for principles that can, presumably, compensate for this under-determination of theory by evidence. We can all agree that the under-determination problem in science is less radical than the kind of under-determination of entire classes of belief that is the focus of the sceptic. However, Nagel's constructive solution looks as though it ought to be the same in the two cases. Reason looks as though it can be the source of self-standing principles of reason that can close those gaps between our evidence and our knowledge. If rational principles can have an *a priori* source in our capacity of reason, why do we not have a powerful weapon against the sceptic? Why is Nagel pessimistic about our ability to deal with scepticism?

It is because its ultimate irrefutability rests on the fact that, for any more objective conception we might form, something must remain "behind the lens". Something must do so because it is the person who forms the conception who is always behind the lens. His or her contingent make-up might be a constitutive source of error.[20] However, as Dancy points out, that is only true for the Hegelian model of objectification (1988: 9–10). In the Cartesian model there is no presumption that this is true and every reason to think that there is not such a knowing subject concealed behind the lens. Perhaps Nagel is concerned that any such Cartesian account of the knowing subject would be a reductive one cast solely in terms made available by the absolute conception itself. However, I have indicated that that claim need not be taken to be any corollary of the truth of the absolute conception itself. Nagel seems only too aware of that fact (*VN*: 85). We are left with what looks like an equivocation in his argument that if you aspire to develop an absolute conception of the world, then you are forced to concede the truth of scepticism.

I conclude that Nagel has all the materials available for a more positive response to scepticism: it may indeed express an important truth about our ordinary concept of knowledge, but it can receive an intellectually satisfactory rejoinder. The truth it expresses is not that philosophical scepticism follows from an aspiration to objectivity built into our ordinary concept of knowledge. That is a misrepresentation of our ordinary concept. All that it sustains is fallibilism and an epistemic humility that is appropriate to people who have to take care not to make mistakes (Craig 1990: 129). That which prevents Nagel using his rationalism in this positive, anti-sceptical way is the intrusion into arguments grounded in the Cartesian model of objectification of an assumption that properly belongs in his other, very different model. There need not always be an implicit subject "behind the lens" whose features may, for all we know, be constitutively distorting our outlook.

Interpreting Nagel in this more positive way, as a rationalist who is in a position to acknowledge the truth in scepticism while not being forced to concede that all we can do is work in its shadow, looks ahead to more recent developments in his work. In *The Last Word* Nagel completes his epistemological project in a notably unsceptical way by reflecting on what it is to be a realist about reason itself. It is to those arguments that I now turn.

Realism about reason

As I have noted, Nagel's comparatively brief discussion of epistemology in *The View from Nowhere* was complemented in an important way by the later publication of *The Last Word*. Nagel broadens the scope of his discussion from philosophy, narrowly conceived, to the treatment of the themes of reason and truth in the wider intellectual culture of the humanities.

It has become apparent throughout this chapter that Nagel finds his contemporaries' philosophical attitudes to interpretation and knowledge either superficial or complacent. The content of the recondite theories of meaning or interpretation used to refute the philosophical sceptic fail to convince when set against the naturalness of sceptical reasoning or obvious truths about the contingency of our standing in a world not made for us. Sceptical reasoning shows up such superficiality and complacency for what it is. Nagel's pessimism about our knowledge is shaped by some positive, and unfashionable, commitments about rationality and knowledge. He is a Cartesian rationalist about justification. The positive account of these ideas in *The View from Nowhere* is comparatively cursory; there is not much to do with these positions other than to characterize them and, more importantly, to put them to productive philosophical use. However, they come into explicit focus in Nagel's most recent comprehensive statement of his metaphysical and epistemological views, *The Last Word*. This book systematically studies reason and justification and what it is to vindicate the use of reason.

This short and elegant monograph conceives of its opponents slightly differently from *The View from Nowhere*: from being superficial and complacent, the various forms of subjectivism that Nagel opposes in *The Last Word* seem to have become more dangerous in the sense of less responsible. They have also seeped out from philosophy and characterize our general culture both in the academy and beyond it. Rather than engage in the details of refuting particular versions of subjectivist, relativist and naturalist accounts of reason and rationality, Nagel offers a set of very general considerations intended to stop all such arguments in their tracks. The standpoint from which Nagel writes is recognizably Cartesian, with the major difference that Descartes's vindication of reason depended essentially on a benevolent deity. Nagel wants to keep a central part of Descartes's view, namely, the ideal of an alignment between the subjectivity of an enquirer and an objective order of reasons. As I have noted, Nagel points out that this alignment is secured in Descartes's system by his belief that God is no deceiver (*VN*: 85; M. Williams 1986). Nagel has to secure the same result without this transcendent reassurance, although Chapter 7 of *The Last Word* does discuss whether Nagel's robust realism about rationality itself offers one route to traditional theistic belief.

There are three distinct sets of views expressed by *The Last Word*. The first is an assertion of Nagel's own robustly realist views about the standards of reason. The second is a corollary of the first: any view challenged by a sceptical alternative can be represented, as can its putative rival, as a "first-order" claim within a particular discourse. There is no meta-level framework in which this dispute can be formulated. The third is an attempt to exploit the first two views in a rebuttal of a wide family of views, made up of subjectivism, relativism and naturalism.

Nagel argues that subjectivism, relativism and naturalism are connected by a shared error that they make. Some forms of thought are so basic that we cannot avoid them in any attempt to think. Their unavoidability means that any attempt to debunk them by reducing them to contingent or subjective origins has to use them, too.

Therefore, each of these three views is vulnerable to pragmatic self-refutation. Given the unavoidability of the basic principles of reason, that which seems to be a "second-order" challenge to a reflective commitment to a rational principle can only be another first-order commitment in a misleading guise. Nagel's three arguments in *The Last Word* meet with varying degrees of success.

The first of Nagel's theses is realism about reason. In a sense, this is the most successful of Nagel's claims since it consists simply in a rigorously worked out statement of what it is to be a realist about reason and rationality. The fundamental principles of rationality do not simply claim universal normative authority over our thinking: they exemplify such authority. No contingent origin could explain them as they transcend such contingencies; there is no sharp line here between any such attempted explanation and a scepticism about universal normative authority (*LW*: 32–3). This is, at least, a radically anti-psychologistic view of reasoning of the kind defended by Frege. There is no getting behind or beyond the most fundamental principles of reason: we cannot think without them.

It is a commonplace in epistemology to contrast a foundationalist perspective on justification with competing coherentist and contextualist models and to note the appeal in the latter to the image of Neurath's ship (Neurath 1959: 201). That image captures the idea that beliefs can only be challenged if others are held fixed, even provisionally. That halts any potential regress in the foundationalist's indefinite and linear model of justification (*VN*: 82). That simple scope distinction between justifying all our beliefs or some of them on the basis of others does not impress Nagel. His commitment to the universality of principles of criticism is pitched at the level of formal principles, not the material content of what is believed. Even the coherentist or contextualist relies on inferential principles and it is those that must be context transcendent in the precise sense of universal. They are "the last word" because we cannot think beyond or behind them.

The distinctive apparatus of subjectivity and objectivity figures in this argument in the following way: suppose one questions the objectivity of a particular way of thinking. At one point in this critical assessment, the questioner's stance of questioning objectivity will break down as he or she will be shown to be relying on that very same form of objectivity that is allegedly being questioned. It is important, once again, to emphasize the broad scope of Nagel's concern with fundamental methods of reasoning, not this or that particular belief.

Less successful is Nagel's second argument, namely, that any sceptical challenge to a first-order view ends up being simply another first-order view. Nagel believes that this is a corollary of his realism about rationality. The idea seems to be that since we cannot escape our most fundamental rational commitments, there is no meta-level standpoint from which we can assess them. Therefore, any putative assessment has to take place on the same level and is, in fact, another of our first-order commitments.

There are two problems here. The first is that this position looks like a form of philosophical dogmatism with all the attendant risks of begging the question. The second is that Nagel seems to be oscillating between the claim that all one can do, reflectively, is to reiterate a first-order commitment and yet use that very same fact to answer a different issue about objectivity. Simon Blackburn puts the point very succinctly:

> [T]here are only first-order claims, and philosophers purporting to enter second-order claims are in fact putting forward their own first-order claims, which are typically less plausible than those with which they compete ... But a good part of Nagel's book flirts with a different, second-order response ... that which talks of our "submitting to the order of reasons rather than creating it" ... A true minimalist would ... say that here too we have only ritualistic metacommitments, denying that there is any space for the vision to occupy. We can see why this is so if we put it in terms of what we can call Ramsey's ladder. This takes us from p to it is true that p, to it is really true that p, to it is really a fact that it is true that p, and if we like to it is really a fact about the independent order of things ordained by objective Platonic normative structures with which we resonate in harmony that it is true that p. For the metatheoretical minimalist, Ramsey's ladder is horizontal. The view from the top is just the same as the view from the bottom, and the view is p. (1998: 654–5)

Nagel's third argument is the most ambitious as it expresses his desire to contribute to the wider culture of the humanities and the influence on a wide range of academic disciplines of the subjectivism, relativism and naturalism to which he is opposed. This is an inherently difficult subject matter as it is hard to gauge the extent to which ideas that are debated in the humanities departments of universities do have any wider effect in the culture of which those universities are a part. It is also difficult to determine the extent to which sceptics, relativists and nihilists in the seminar room actually retain those views when they go home at the end of the day: do such people pass the test of being able to live their scepticism (Burnyeat 1983b)?

Setting that matter aside, there is an ironic tension between the success of Nagel's previous two arguments and his third argument. If Nagel succeeds in showing that some forms of thinking are inescapable, or that all sceptical claims are arguments on the same level as the views that they challenge, that does not seem to me to go deeply enough into the motivations for the reductive, debunking views to which Nagel is opposed. That is because of a crucial issue of scope. This point is highlighted by contrasting Nagel's views with those of Bernard Williams. Williams reviewed *The Last Word* (1998) and wrote about similar subjects himself in his last work, *Truth and Truthfulness* (2002). Williams diagnosed our contemporary "culture wars" as grounded in the generalization of a certain style of thinking central to the humanities. The work of Marx, Nietzsche and Freud has been grouped together into a composite "hermeneutics of suspicion": each thinker, in their radically different ways, subjected central parts of our self-understanding to a caustic examination in which their putative epistemic standing is undercut by the operation of merely causal mechanisms that determine our beliefs. Williams's diagnosis of our current intellectual predicament differs from Nagel's: he traces it to this essentially local method of critique becoming falsely generalized:

> Two currents of ideas have been very prominent in modern thought and culture. On the one hand, there is an intense commitment to truthfulness – or, at any rate, a pervasive suspiciousness, a readiness against being fooled, an eagerness to see through appearances to the real structures and motives that lie behind them … Together with the demand for truthfulness, however, or (to put it less positively) this reflex against deceptiveness, there is an equally pervasive suspicion about truth itself. (2002: 1)

Combine this refusal to be hoodwinked with scepticism about truth, and the unstable result is a free-floating, allegedly presuppositionless scepticism that finds characteristic expression in the subjectivism, relativism and naturalism to which Nagel and Williams are equally opposed. However, Williams differs from Nagel in wanting to defend a local, focused and detailed application of this naturalized scepticism, particularly in the case of some of our inherited ethical ideas (B. Williams 1990). These local forms of naturalized scepticism need not be engines of universal scepticism. They can very often vindicate our ideas; but it is important that, sometimes, they do not. Nagel's alternative line of criticism seems to Williams to "install a long-distance, high powered, all-purpose defence system to fight what is in fact a guerrilla war. The irrationalists or relativists or skeptics are amongst us" (B. Williams 1998: 41).

That is why I describe the key issue as one of scope. Williams concedes that Nagel offers two strong arguments against generalized reductionism. Sceptical arguments have to use the most fundamental forms of thought; they cannot simply mention them. Furthermore, a local critique relies on other beliefs and, indeed, other beliefs of the same kind being challenged. If you believe that a historical narrative of how the United States was colonized is a form of ideological distortion, you need more facts of the same kind, namely, historical facts, as opposed to a general scepticism about historical truth. However, Nagel also wants to target the idea of localness itself: any attempt to reduce a claim to the local circumstances of its production can be refuted using his two main arguments. It will either use a fundamental form of thought that it seeks to reject or it can be reinterpreted as itself the expression of a first-order view. Those two arguments, taken together, are very general in scope and seem to rule out a certain kind of local and focused use of sceptical arguments as impossible. In particular, Nagel seems to assume that all naturalistic explanations must be intrinsically reductive. Even if, as Williams agrees, this strategy works for core claims of logic and science, then it ought not to work in addition for much more local ethical ideas. Some of those ideas may, indeed, be ideas that we might want to abandon (B. Williams 1998).

It is difficult to separate this difference in methodological emphases between Williams and Nagel from their different first-order views in ethics (as Nagel would presumably have predicted). Williams wanted to qualify the scope of objectivity in ethics, invoking history to discredit some of our ethical ideas while vindicating others; *The Last Word* contains a powerful statement of a commitment to viewing ethical principles as universal and timeless. However one can note, as Williams does, that there is an internal tension in the arguments of *The Last Word* to the extent that success in achieving its first two aims must impede its success in achieving the third.

The upshot is that *The Last Word* is a forceful expression of Nagel's realism about rationality itself even if its final aim of remedying our current cultural ills is not as well realized. It both deepens and extends the epistemological discussions of *The View from Nowhere*. In the overall context of Nagel's philosophy it plays an important part in clarifying the commitment to immanent principles of reason appealed to particularly clearly in *The Possibility of Altruism*. However, the breadth of the topics to which it applies means that its central theses have ramifications throughout Nagel's work.

Chapter 3

Placing the mind in the physical world

The two areas in philosophy where Nagel has had the deepest impact are moral philosophy and the philosophy of mind. The latter is an area of philosophy where Nagel clearly believes that his distinctive theses can be most productive. It is our thinking about the mind that is, in his view, most in the grip of falsely objectifying theories. Nagel believes that his approach to the subjective versus objective distinction can offer more insight than rival views into the mind, particularly on the issue of locating the mind in the physical world.

This chapter will discuss the various components of Nagel's philosophy of mind. Nagel believes that a Cartesian objectification of the mind would be a self-stultifying form of false objectification. It would be an attempt to think ideally non-perspectivally about the irreducibly perspectival. He has, therefore, consistently tried to develop an approach to the mental that fits the Hegelian pattern of objectification described in Chapter 1. In this chapter I shall describe the two major forms of such objectification that Nagel developed in sequence from *The View from Nowhere*, which expressed the earlier version, to "The Psychophysical Nexus", which expressed the later version. The earlier version is a comparatively orthodox form of dual aspect theory (*VN*: 28–50). It has, however, been replaced in Nagel's most recent work on the place of the mind in nature by a later, unorthodox, form of dual aspect theory based on the prospects for a radical reconceptualization of that which underlies both the physical and the mental (*VN*: 51–2; PN).

Explained via the interpretative framework I have used in this book, this development is, as applied to our thinking about the place of the mind in nature, a change from the first sub-variety of Hegelian objectification to the second sub-variety. In the first sub-variety, the perspectival is insightfully recontextualized by being explained in terms of the less perspectival. By contrast, in the second sub-variety one can state *that* an explanatory relation holds without being able currently to specify *what* it is. Nagel thinks that we are now in the latter situation as both our concepts of the mental and of the physical are radically unsuited to allowing us to formulate an intellectually satisfying account of the relationship between the mental and the physical aspects of reality.

The key to the change between Nagel's two versions of dual aspect theory was an increase in the demands that he places on a satisfactory explanation of the mental–physical relation. He now requires that an explanation of this relationship should meet a demand of transparency. We should just be able to *see* that an underlying nature necessarily manifests itself in physiological, functional and mental ways analogous to the way in which we can just see that a Euclidean triangle has angles that add up to 180°. That is a strong requirement to place on an explanation or an identity statement in a theoretical context. It flows from Nagel's commitment to a philosophical rationalism of the kind described in the previous chapter and from the implication of that view for the nature of scientific explanation. I shall develop an exposition of Nagel's most recent views in stages, beginning with his general conception of how the problem of relating the mental and the physical takes the form for us that it does.

Realism, points of view, and the limits of the imagination

Nagel believes that our problems in understanding the mind have a distinctive structure. They arise from the combination of two substantive assumptions and from one point about methodology. The two substantive assumptions are, first, an uncompromising realism about the mental and, secondly, the belief that mentality can be grasped only from a point of view. The methodological point is that understanding how to reconcile these two assumptions involves an unavoidable appeal to our capacity to imagine. Unfortunately, our imagination is simply not up to the task. Indeed, it plays an important and often unacknowledged role in generating the problem.

What is it that we seek to understand when we try to understand the mind of another? Any satisfactory theory of the mental has to capture an important explanandum, namely, what it is like to *be* a mental subject. This criterion of adequacy for an explanation is presented in one of Nagel's most famous papers and certainly his most famous contribution to the philosophy of mind, "What is it Like to be a Bat?" (1974b), and it states this criterion as follows: "The fact that an organism has conscious experience *at all* means, basically, that there is something it is like to *be* that organism ... something it is like for that organism" (*MQ*: 166). In the same paper Nagel immediately connects this central fact that he seeks to explain to another, namely, that we are conscious: "Consciousness is what makes the mind–body problem really intractable. Perhaps that is why current discussions of the problem give it little attention or get it obviously wrong" (*MQ*: 165). These two ways of describing this important fact, one that appeals to "what it is like", the other explicitly mentioning consciousness, are then connected to a third: "Every subjective phenomenon is essentially connected with *a single point of view*, and it seems inevitable that an objective, physical theory will abandon that point of view" (*MQ*: 167, emphasis added). This further formulation of what appears to be the same thing requiring explanation appeals to the idea of a point of view. That concept was important in the explanation of Nagel's ideas about the subjective and the objective discussed in Chapters 1 and 2 in terms of the perspectival and the non-perspectival (absolute). It is important in Nagel's philosophy of mind, too. The central fact that we seek to explain is that there is something it is like to be a conscious thinker who has a point of view on the world.[1]

Points of view play an important role in helping Nagel to explain why the relation between the mental and the physical seems problematic to us. This explanation is applied to mental state *types*, as opposed to tokens. It is applied to mental state types instantiated by different species.[2] Before describing this role played by the idea of a point of view I shall first explain this type–token distinction. If a teacher keeps a pupil in detention and asks him to write out two hundred times "I must pay attention in class", each of those sentences is an individual token. It is a particular inscription on paper and a physical thing located in space and time. But it is a token of a sentence type: that one type is exemplified two hundred times by its tokens. Types are abstract objects. Their tokens are in space and time, but the types are not. This distinction will prove important in what follows as it makes an important difference whether it is claimed that types of mental state are identical with types of physical state, or whether it is claimed that any particular token mental state is identical with a token physical state.

In setting up why the mental–physical relation seems problematic to us in the particular way that it does, Nagel makes clear that he is discussing mental types. His aim is to bring out a fundamental puzzlement involved in interpreting another creature as having a mind *at all* (Eilan, forthcoming: ch. 1). We believe that creatures like bats have experiences, but in conceiving of what this must be like we are struck by the alien character of such experiences. Our starting-point is that we are familiar with mentality in our own case. But, we do not think that mentality is restricted to that case. Nagel is very clear that, from the outset, our concept of the mind is a general one not restricted to our first-personal acquaintance with our own minds.[3] This assumption will play an important role in his arguments in ethics that I shall examine in Chapters 4 and 6.[4] Nagel assumes, therefore, that non-human creatures have minds, too, in a way that rocks and trees do not. But what is it that we are conceiving of when we form that latter thought?

On the one hand, we are claiming that there is something there, real, in the experienced life of an animal: what it is like to *be* that creature. On the other hand our idea of reality is bound up with the idea of something being accessible from no point of view in particular (as was argued in Chapters 1 and 2). Yet what we are conceiving of as real in this case is precisely something to which we paradigmatically have access in our own case. We presume that the creature paradigmatically has access to it in *its* own case. There is a tension between our commitment to realism and the constraint that ascriptions of mentality must capture a mental subject's point of view. This tension originates from a combination of the Cartesian paradigm of objectification and the assumption that mentality is thoroughly perspectival.

Inevitably, we now wonder if our intuitive commitments are consistent. We view other species as having minds in the way that we do. However, mentality is captured by what it is to take up a standpoint on it. This is not an outright paradox, but when we take the bat's point of view on the world to be real what is it exactly that we are imagining? Our grasp on what it is for the bat to have a mind gets thinner and thinner as we try to imagine the details. There is a tension between Nagel's uncompromising realism about the mental and the role of the imagination in guiding how we ascribe mental states to other people and other creatures. In turn, that role for the imagination is called for because of the perspectivalness of the mental.

A distinctive claim Nagel makes is that the only way in which we can be taken from our first-personal experience of mentality to its ascription to others is by imaginative projection. However, our powers of imagination fail us in a case like imagining what it is like to be a bat. We cannot imagine what it is like – given the bat's physiology, psychological capacities and embedding in its world – to experience the world from a bat's point of view (*MQ*; Alter 2002). Our imagination is too contingently limited. But the problem arises because we need to project into the perspective or viewpoint of any other mental subject. That constraint, in turn, is grounded in the connection between mentality and points of view.

Nagel believes that we are unable to conceive of how to bridge the mental–physical divide because our imagination has two different typical forms of operation. It can operate sensorily or sympathetically. A footnote in "What is it Like to be a Bat?" explains how these two ways in which the imagination operates will *always* generate a sense that the relation between the mental and the physical is obscure to us (*MQ*: 175–6 n.11). There will always seem to be that which Joseph Levine (2001) has called an "explanatory gap" between the ways in which we take mentality to be exemplified in the world and the way in which we take physical things to be in the world. Even if, in fact, the mental aspects of reality are identical to those physical aspects of reality (such as neurophysiological states, functional descriptions and characteristic behaviour) that appear to be correlated with them, it will always seem to us opaque why that should be so. Nagel explains the difference between these two kinds of imagination as follows:

> We may imagine something by representing it to ourselves either perceptually, sympathetically or symbolically .... To imagine something perceptually, we put ourselves in a conscious state resembling the state we would be in if we perceived it. To imagine something sympathetically, we put ourselves in a conscious state resembling the thing itself. (This method can be used only to imagine mental events and states – our own or another's.) When we try to imagine a mental state occurring without its associated brain state, we first sympathetically imagine the occurrence of the mental state: that is, we put ourselves into a state that resembles it mentally. At the same time, we attempt perceptually to imagine the nonoccurrence of the associated physical state, by putting ourselves into another state unconnected with the first:

> one resembling that which we would be in if we perceived the nonoccurrence of the physical state. Where the imagination of physical features is perceptual and the imagination of mental features is sympathetic, it appears to us that we can imagine any experience occurring without its associated brain state, and vice versa. The relation between them will appear contingent even if it is necessary, because of the independence of the disparate types of imagination. (*MQ*: 175–6 n.11)

For a short footnote this passage has had a remarkable influence on contemporary philosophizing about the mind.[5] I shall say more about Nagel's views on the imagination and the difference between mental and physical concepts in the later section "Kripke and Nagel on mental concepts". At this point I shall simply note that according to this early argument, because of a contingent fact about how our imagination works, it would always *seem* to us that there is an explanatory gap between that which is picked out by a mental concept and that which is picked out by a physical concept *whether there is actually such a gap or not* (PN: 218).[6]

This also explains why Nagel's account of the fundamental datum that any satisfactory account of the mental has to explain is accompanied by his reflections on the mental lives of other species. Given our contingent psychological capacities those reflections highlight the origin of the problem of understanding how the mental and the physical could be so much as related. This is a very special and difficult problem because of the nature of mentality and because of certain limitations in our ways of thinking about it. So far, however, nothing has been said to defend the crucial assumption of the discussion that mentality is, indeed, ineliminably perspectival. Nagel has two arguments for this conclusion that I shall now describe.

The case for the perspectivalness of the mental

Cartesian objectification, Nagel argues, makes no sense as an account of the mind. One's subjective point of view is one's starting-point and also one's endpoint. A mental subject's point of view is "the essence of the internal world, and not merely a point of view on it" (*MQ*: 175). But what exactly is the argument for this conclusion?

There would be a danger of equivocation between the Cartesian and Hegelian models of objectification if the basic argument for this conclusion is that mentality can only receive a Hegelian form of objectification because every perspective must be a perspective for *someone*. There is a tempting fallacy here that is well exposed in Nagel's incisive account of George Berkeley's argument for the conclusion that "nothing can be conceived of as existing apart from a thinking thing". That claim was notoriously ambiguous between two readings that Nagel explains with exemplary clarity (*VN*: 93–4). On the first reading, with its scope disambiguated with brackets, the claim is:

> (Nothing can be conceived of as existing) apart from a thinking thing.

We have a triviality: no conceiving without a thinker. But that is a different claim from:

> Nothing can be conceived of (as existing apart from a thinking thing).

That is false: we think of things as existing without thinkers all the time, such as the volcano that was in the location you now occupy before sentient life evolved. I agree that there is more to be said about Berkeley's views on thinking, concepts and imagination than this, and I shall return to this problem again in connection with some of Nagel's remarks about the objective self (Peacocke 1985). But for present purposes the issue is whether or not one can soundly argue that all perspectival representations must be representations for someone simply because they *are* perspectives.

It seems that one cannot. In the previous chapter this sentence came under scrutiny: "However often we may try to step outside of ourselves, something will have to stay behind the lens, something in us will determine the resulting picture, and this will give grounds for doubt that we are really getting any closer to reality" (*VN*: 68). I argued that this was a truth about Hegelian objectification but that it is not true of its Cartesian counterpart. This quotation suggests an argument for the irreducibly perspective-involving nature of mentality along the following lines: forming any conception, even a more explanatory conception, of a perspectival way of thinking is itself an activity that presupposes an active thinker. That is why our thinking about mentality must be perspectival through and through. Any forming of a conception requires a conceiver.

But I do not think that this is a helpful argument in this context. It seems to derive a substantive conclusion from a truism: no perspectives without a subject for whom it is a perspective. This argument seems hopelessly question-begging. "All perspectives are perspectives for someone" is a triviality that those committed to the view that one can give a Cartesian objectification of the mental do not deny (it is, after all, truistic). What such a person would argue is simply that both the subject and its perspective-involving conceptualizations can be given a reflexive explanation that "places" subject, perspectives and world in an explanatory relationship. When that relationship has been spelled out, then the element of perspective is shown simply to be the way in which that subject is "appeared to" by a perfectly objective world. Person, world, appearances and their mutual relationship are all describable objectively in a way consistent with Cartesian objectification (see e.g. Biro 1991: 124–6).

There had better be more than that to Nagel's argument that mentality is irreducibly perspectival. There is more: there is a constraint on the acquisition and use of mental concepts that has no direct parallel to physical concepts and there is a puzzling feature of subjects of experience that demands explanation. I shall describe these two claims in turn. Together they substantiate the claim that we are dealing with an instance of the radically perspectival, as I have defined that notion. They do so without using the idea of a perspectival fact that, in this case, would have to take the form of an ineffable subjective mental reality to which each of us has first-personal access.

Radical perspectivalness is the idea that a point of view, concepts made available only to that point of view and the representations produced from it (using those concepts) need to be explained together. In the case of mental concepts, the form that this general description takes is that mental concepts are directly *experience dependent*. A concept of a mental state like pain, for example, is acquired by your acquaintance with the sensation itself when you attend to your own mental life in introspection. This direct experience requirement has no analogy in the nature of objective and, in particular, theoretical concepts.

This point serves to bring out a peculiarity of mental concepts well expressed by Christopher Hill and Brian McLaughlin in an account that reflects Nagel's influence:

> The experiences that guide and justify one in applying the concept are always identical with the experiences to which the concept is applied. Sensory states are self-presenting states: we experience them, but we do not have sensory experiences of them. We experience them simply by virtue of being in them. Sensory

> concepts are recognitional concepts: deploying such concepts, we can introspectively recognize when we are in sensory states simply by focusing our attention directly on them.
> (Hill & McLaughlin 1999: 448; see also PN: 218)

To use a now well-established terminology, mental concepts are "recognitional-demonstrative hybrids" that combine two functions (Loar 1997; Levin 2007). In some ways they function like acts of inner pointing, acting like demonstrative expressions such as "this" as you turn your attention towards your own mental life in introspection. In another respect they have a recognitional component such that they also classify a mental occurrence as a "this such". Their hybrid function contrasts markedly with the case of physical concepts, such as "perceptual and theoretical concepts", which work very differently: "An agent's access to the phenomena that he or she perceives is always indirect: it always occurs via an experience of the perceived phenomena that is not identical with the perceived phenomena but rather caused by it" (Hill & McLaughlin 1999: 448). I shall discuss in more detail below why Nagel thinks that this special feature of mental concepts can give rise to a certain kind of illusion that one's acts of inner pointing have no ties to other conceptual capacities. But the special feature itself is a datum that all theories have to accommodate.

An example of this special feature is the case of pain. You do not have an experience *of* pain. You simply are in pain. In this first sense mental discourse is perspectival because of the direct acquaintance requirement. You have to stand in this relation of direct acquaintance to the sensation to be competent with the concept grounded on that sensation. That is because the experience enters into the acquisition and the continued justification of uses of the concept itself.

The second respect in which mental discourse is radically perspectival is that our experiences are *for* a thinker in a particular way. I believe that this is the upshot of the searching examination of Nagel's use of the term "point of view" by John Biro (1991, 1993, 2006) in a series of papers about Nagel's use of this metaphor in his philosophy of mind. Biro is primarily concerned with whether or not the idea of a point of view supports what he calls an argument for "radical subjectivity". This would be an argument for the existence of perspectival mental facts, namely, irreducibly subjective facts known ineffably from each subject's first-personal point of view.[7] But Biro's careful analysis of Nagel's arguments yields more than a merely critical result.

Biro argues that the idea of a point of view is equivocal in two ways. We can think of a point of view as a type, such that more than one subject could take up a point of view. Alternatively, we can think of it as a token, such that it is the point of view owned by a particular individual.[8] Furthermore, we can think of points of view as fixed, such that different individuals can take them up (this is the type notion) or as "portable" – a point of view follows each individual around because it is the idea of being from that particular individual's point of view (the token notion) (Biro 1991: 118–19). Biro argues that there is nothing in the type notion that supports any argument for the radically subjective. For that we need the individual, token notion, but the only way to explain what that is appeals to the idea of *ownership* (*ibid.*: 129–33). Representations produced from a token point of view are simply owned by the occupant of that point of view. However, Biro convincingly argues that the relation of ownership does not add to the stock of entities in the world. If, of all the ties in the store, I purchase one token tie, then I now own it. That does not introduce the ineffable property of being-owned-by-Alan.

The same point applies to my mental life. Mental ownership is a puzzling thing, but it is even more puzzling if, in this case, ownership were explained in terms of a set of ineffable perspectival facts. Ownership is a relation: adding ownership to the world is not to add to the inventory of objects, but places two of them in a new relation. I think that this is correct. However, it is not a criticism of Nagel but a helpful clarification of his views. The relevant sense of ownership is going to be difficult to pin down. I do not literally own my mental states in the same way in which I own my ties. Nagel is aware that this is a unique case; normally when we speak of a relation of acquaintance we are describing the mind's acquaintance with something else. However, Nagel's concern is with the mind's acquaintance with itself, necessarily the most fundamental and unique application for this idea of acquaintance (Zahavi 2006).

The constructive interpretation that I shall place on Biro's conclusion is this: it is not simply that each token mental representation can be interpreted as from a point of view. For that set of token mental representations that make up the representations for a particular individual we can conclude that they are all from the *same* point of view. As well as the element of perspective in each representation there is also the unified perspective *from* which each of them *is* a representation. So far, in discussing the metaphor of perspective, we have focused on how different perspectival representations can all be reconciled as depictions of the same reality. Biro's argument shifts the focus to the unity of the viewer: that person for whom all perspectival representations are represented. Interpreted in this way, the claim is that each person's mental life exhibits the distinctive kind of unity that is characteristic of a mental subject.

This is an important part of Nagel's philosophy of mind. Nagel's treatment of the topic shows the influence of Kant. Interpreters of Kant face the difficult task of reconciling two aspects of his views (Pippin 1987; Thomas 1997). In the positive phase of his views, Kant repeatedly appeals to a unified subject of experience. In the critical phase of his views, Kant formulates a radical and influential critique of the view that the pronoun "I" picks out an immaterial substance or, indeed, any kind of substance at all. One way to reconcile these two sets of views would be to describe Kant's view this way: the unity of consciousness is not underpinned by consciousness of a unity. Conscious experience is, in some way to be determined, already unified "formally" as being made up of representations for a single subject. That fact does not require grounding on an individual substance. Nagel holds this view, too. He is as critical as Kant of the illusions generated by our use of "I". However, Nagel's Kripkean view of mental concepts allows him to argue that, in fact, the subject of the first-person pronoun is the functioning brain. The details of this view will be described below. I note here simply another respect in which Nagel takes the mental to be radically perspectival: either all conscious mental representations, or all mental representations generally, must be capable of being interpreted as representations for a single subject.

Overall, Biro separates an argument for radical subjectivity that Nagel does *not* put forward that is very similar to the argument for perspectival facts rehearsed and criticized in Chapter 1. Biro thinks that the only way to cash out the metaphor of a subject of experience occupying a point of view is in terms of mental ownership, but Nagel agrees with this claim. Finally, and most importantly, it seems to me that Biro highlights one respect in which the analogy between points of view and subjectivity needs to be qualified.

The problem, simply put, is that it is not clear that a unified subject of experience occupies a standpoint on the world analogous to a "point of view". It seems less implausible to say that a subject of experience does not occupy a standpoint, but *is* a standpoint. But even that seems strained. You do not, as a subject of experience, occupy a point of view in the way that, as a speaker, you occupy a spatial location that has a bearing on the evaluation of those of your utterances that use the indexical "here". I can only evaluate your utterance by taking into account the location in virtue of which what you said was true. When I evaluate a mental representation of yours there is no comparable point of view "in virtue of which" you can be interpreted as representing truly. The analogy does not go through. But with these limitations to the "point of view" metaphor noted, I think it is safe to keep using the idea.

In summary, there are two reasons why Nagel argues that mentality is irreducibly perspectival. First, our mental concepts operate under a constraint that does not apply to physical concepts: you do not understand them unless your use of them is grounded in, and continues to be justified by, the very experience of which they are a conceptualization. Secondly, all mental experiences are experiences for a subject. We have to be able to understand any system of mental representations as representations for a self.[9] The way in which both Nagel and Biro explain that latter function is in terms of ownership. Mental representations have to be related back to a subject of experience: the precise way in which Nagel does this has to be explained. However, he certainly tries to discharge his explanatory obligations as the section "The first-person standpoint and its illusions", below, will demonstrate.

If our ways of thinking and speaking about the mental are perspectival in these two respects, then they are also plausibly radically perspectival. There has to be direct acquaintance to ground and justify mental concepts, and there has to be a mental subject for whom all mental representations are such. Subjects of experience, concepts and representations from that subject's point of view are inextricably bound together. We can hope for a Hegelian explanation where these perspectival concepts receive a less perspectival explanation (but not a non-perspectival explanation), and Nagel's project is to develop precisely that form of argument. However, understanding the precise form of that project requires a more detailed account of his treatment of mental concepts. That, in turn, requires a background description of the influence on his work of his former Princeton colleague, Saul Kripke, whose influence on Nagel's philosophy of mind has been marked.

Kripke and Nagel on mental concepts

In this section I shall first describe the influence on Nagel's work of Kripke's views on reference and identity. With this preliminary stage-setting in place I shall then describe how Nagel's treatment of mental concepts has gone through successive developments. This narrative will cast light on an interpretative puzzle, namely, how Nagel seemed in his early work to give an account of the acquisition and use of mental concepts that supported physicalism, only for him not to adopt physicalism but to remain one of physicalism's most persistent critics in the philosophy of mind (Levin 2007). Explaining this point will serve to introduce his positive proposal for thinking objectively about the mental. Nagel's later account of mental concepts further clarifies his complex relationship with physicalism.

Nagel repeatedly describes Kripke as an important influence on his work, and without a brief description of his work Nagel's views are hard to understand. For present purposes, the best introduction to Kripke's ideas is to describe a set of assumptions that he challenged. A dominant and historically important approach to philosophy is empiricism. That view seems to have straightforward implications for the distinctions between analytic and synthetic sentences, between necessary and contingent truths and between *a priori* and *a posteriori* ways of knowing truths. Kripke challenged those implications.

The first distinction is between sentences in which the subject term contains the predicate term and those in which it does not. The sentence "All bachelors are unmarried" is analytic as the subject concept **bachelor** contains the predicate concept **unmarried**.[10] By contrast, the sentence "all bachelors are frustrated" is synthetic because the concept bachelor does not contain the concept **frustrated**.

The second distinction is between ways in which a sentence can be true. Philosophers find it helpful to think about these ways using the heuristic of a possible world, a complete alternative way in which things might have been. Appealing to that idea, one can explain the terms "necessary" and "possible" as like quantifiers in ordinary language such as "all" and "at least one". Introduce negation and one can inter-define necessary, possible and contingent truths as follows: a truth is possible if it is not necessarily false; a truth is necessary if it is not possibly false; a truth is contingent if it is not necessarily false and not necessarily true.[11]

The final distinction is an epistemological one: truths are *a priori* if they can be known in logical independence of any facts about experience (for example, if they can be known by an exercise of reason alone). *A posteriori* truths, by contrast, can be known only by appeal to our capacity for experience. The most highly developed form of the latter is scientific enquiry,where theory and experiment work together to produce objective knowledge grounded on experience.

Classical empiricism assumed that the three distinctions that I have described align in a particular way. Necessary truths may be *a priori*, but they are trivial, analytic truths grounded simply in relations between our concepts. (One way in which that latter idea was explained was in terms of grounding in our linguistic conventions of representation.) All knowledge worth having is *a posteriori*, synthetic and contingent. It is science, above all, that gives us this knowledge that is worth having through its formulation of scientific laws that are the basis of successful explanation and prediction. Kripke focuses in particular on identity statements in science that use natural kind terms, but that is because he sees how such terms function as being analogous to how ordinary proper names function.

What does a name like "William Shakespeare" mean? One line of thought is that a name like this functions by having a set of mentally represented descriptions associated with it along the lines of "the famous playwright who wrote thirty-seven plays, worked in London, died in Stratford and bequeathed his wife Anne Hathaway his second best bed". In this case language works by trawling the world with a net: you cast your net, pull in the individual corresponding to these descriptions (or some weighted subset of them) and that is William Shakespeare. Kripke, by contrast, sees proper names as working more like a harpoon: they refer directly to their bearer, functioning like simple tags.

Kripke does not deny that there are descriptions associated with proper names, which assist with the pragmatic speech act of referring, but they are not that in which the semantic relation of reference consists. From the fact that the descriptive content of two photographs, one of each of two identical twins, may leave you unable to pick out one twin rather than another, you do not have to conclude that each photograph is of both of them. You will appeal, instead, to the causal route that placed each twin in front of the camera and produced a token image that is of that twin and not the other. Kripke suggests something similar for the "meaning" of proper names: there is an initial act of baptism, and then each user of the name intends to preserve, in his or her use, this initial connection between name and bearer.[12]

As an account of the meaning of names Kripke's view had antecedents in philosophy, notably in the work of John Stuart Mill (as Kripke acknowledges) (Mill 1843: bk I, ch. I, §5). However, what was exciting about Kripke's view was his use of modal examples to make his case and his extension of this account of the semantics of proper names to the semantics of natural kinds picked out by scientific law. Much of the support for Kripke's view of names came from compelling arguments about the use of names not in different contexts in the actual world, but in different possible worlds. The point of such examples was to argue that proper names are what Kripke calls "rigid designators". They designate the same object in all possible worlds in which that object exists. That allows us to express Kripke's distinctive thesis: the meaning of a proper name such as "William Shakespeare" is not a set of descriptions that constitute its "meaning". That is because one can, without any inconsistency generated by meaning, conceive of a possible world in which William Shakespeare did not write thirty-seven plays, but someone else did instead.

The culmination of Kripke's arguments is his account of scientifically established identity sentences in a theoretical context, such as "water is H_2O". If natural kind terms such as "water" are correctly thought of as working just like proper names, then a distinctive account follows of such identity sentences. Given that a rigid designator is a term that picks out the same bearer in every possible world in which that bearer exists, then an identity sentence with two rigid designators either side of the identity sign "=" is going to be necessarily true. There will be no possible world in which that sentence is not true. Therefore, a sentence such as "water is H_2O" is necessarily true even though it was discovered *a posteriori*. The standard empiricist alignment of the *a posteriori* with the contingent is mistaken. The surprising result is that empirical science gives us knowledge of real necessity. Scientific laws are metaphysically necessary even though they are known via experience and are *a posteriori*.

Kripke's views had a direct bearing on the then current forms of psychophysical identity theory. Pioneered by U. T. Place (1956), the prevailing form of materialism when Kripke presented his view claimed that we had discovered, *a posteriori*, that mental states were type identical to types of brain state. Given that this identity had been discovered *a posteriori*, Place assumed that it must be a contingent identity. That contingency helped to explain away our intuitions that it does not seem as if a mental state and a brain state could be identical: indeed not, but on the contingent version of the theory those possibilities are irrelevant (as, obviously, is the difference in *meaning* between the expressions "pain" and "C-fibre stimulation"). Kripke's unsettling of this combination of epistemic and truth-related categories poses a serious problem for Place's argument. From the fact that such an identity statement is discovered *a posteriori* it does not follow that it is not necessary. Kripke argues that it is, and that leads to a problem: the identity statement (in this type–type) form has implications for other possible worlds than the actual world. If imagination allows us to conceive of genuine metaphysical possibilities, then we can refute Place's theory without leaving our armchairs simply by imagining a scenario in which we feel pain, but our C-fibres are not stimulated.

That is precisely what Kripke proceeded to argue. His "Cartesian intuition" was that reflection on any proposed type–type mental–physical identity could be undermined by the conceivability of a metaphysically possible world in which, for example, a part of one's brain is activated by the stimulation of one's C-fibres, but one is not in pain, and vice versa (McGinn 1980). If that is true, has Kripke not simply abandoned his own distinctive theory of identity statements? Can we not refute the claim that "water is H_2O" in exactly the same way?

No, we cannot. In the case of theoretical identities we can separate out, within our concept of a kind or substance, how the substance appears from the underlying nature that we take to be the explanatory basis of that appearance. It is part of our practice with that concept, and implicit in our grasp of the concept itself, that it is incomplete. We implicitly defer to a more complete understanding that exhibits the nature of that substance by placing it within a structure of scientific law. We can, for example, form the idea of "fool's gold": the idea of a substance that mimics the superficial appearance of gold but is not gold. Fool's gold is, one might say, the *epistemic counterpart* of gold. For all we know, it seems to be gold; it is gold-like stuff. But it is not gold.

However, Kripke argues that in the case of mental concepts we cannot separate out appearance and essence in this way. Hence there is no possibility of an epistemic counterpart of a mental state. If something seems to you to be gold, it might be gold or it might be fool's gold. Only further chemical analysis will tell you which stuff it is. But if something seems to you to be painful, then it is painful. Any epistemic counterpart of a pain *is* a pain. There is no analogous notion of a "pain-like stuff" because pain-like stuff simply is painful (Kripke 1980). So when your refute Place's type–type identity theory by imagining a possible world in which you imagine being in pain without C-fibre stimulation, we cannot reinterpret your thought experiment as simply being about an epistemic counterpart of pain. Kripke believes that the refutation goes through in the mental case, but not for ordinary scientific identity statements formulated *without* the use of mental terms. Theoretical identity statements about the mental–physical relation are importantly different.

Why is this exposition of Kripke's ideas important for understanding Nagel? First, and most importantly, Nagel accepts Kripke's basic thesis that any identity statements that relate mental and physical vocabulary in a type–type psychophysical law must be necessarily true (if they are true) and known *a posteriori*. Kripke accepts that claim in general, but then denies that it is true for psychophysical laws on the basis of his Cartesian intuitions. Nagel offers successive accounts of the nature of mental concepts that undercut those Cartesian intuitions. Mental concepts have various special features that mean that the kind of explanatory gap between their referents that seems to be generated by our mental and physical concepts seems to exist *whether it does or not*. Accordingly, there are aspects of Nagel's view that allow him to accept a Kripkean view of psychophysical laws as necessary and *a posteriori*. That would be a form of physicalism and some philosophers sympathetic to that view have put Nagel's views at the service of their own physicalist reductions of the mental (Levin 2007).

But that is not the whole story. For reasons I shall explain in the next section, Nagel is not happy with the physicalist appropriation of his account of mental concepts. It is no part of our ordinary understanding of such concepts that they pick out a stuff whose nature could be filled in as the physicalist suggests that they can. We can think about mental concepts in more objective ways, but that does not mean taking them at their face value and then claiming that, in fact, such concepts pick out the very same properties that our physical concepts pick out.

Levine, whose work I have already mentioned, argues that while Kripke's Cartesian intuition does not support the metaphysical conclusion that there is an ontological gap between mental aspects and physical aspects, it does support the epistemic conclusion that we face a perplexing explanatory gap (1983: 127–8). That shifts the focus on to how good explanations work. Levine sees them as working as follows:

> Explanatory reduction is, in a way, a two-stage process. Stage 1 involves the (relatively? quasi?) *a priori* process of working the concept of the property to be reduced "into shape" for reduction

> by identifying the causal role for which we are seeking the underlying mechanisms. Stage 2 involves the empirical work of discovering just what those underlying mechanisms are. (*Ibid.*: 132)

A view of this kind also underlies Nagel's work. Nagel's account of psychophysical laws breaks with Kripke's approach over the appropriate standards for psychophysical identity statements. Nagel believes that the special nature of mental concepts implies that in order to understand how such concepts relate to the physical, we need an explanation in which both the mental and physical are necessarily related in a way that removes even the illusion of an explanatory gap. That is beyond our current physics and hence beyond physicalism: it needs a radical change in our conceptions of both the mental and the physical.

Nagel does not demand of psychophysical identities that they share the transparency to the mind of conceptual necessities. Conceptual necessities are wholly transparent to us: we can just see that a Euclidean triangle has angles that add up to 180°. Nagel does not require this of a psychophysical identity statement.[13] However, he does require such a statement to approach a similar level of rational intelligibility. I shall describe the evolution of this view in more detail after discussing Nagel's account of mental concepts. That account has been through several important evolutionary stages, but Kripke's influence is detectable throughout.

A great deal of this chapter thus far has revolved around how Nagel understands the way in which we conceive of mentality. It is worth pulling together the separate strands of Nagel's discussion of mental concepts. I have already noted some of their key features: they seem to be a hybrid of a demonstrative part and a discursive part. The demonstrative part arises because of the requirement that direct experience enters into what it is to acquire and use this kind of concept. Reflection on your own mental life via introspection gives you direct experience of, say, pain. You attend to the sensation and the concept of the sensation is partly that pain feels like *this*. The discursive part brings that experience under a concept: your experience is of "this pain".

But Nagel thinks that there is an illusion endemic in this scenario. It can seem to you as if this act of inner pointing is self-sufficient. You are simply presented with an inner object that demands conceptualizing as a "this-such". But the transition from "this" to "this-such" already shows that there has to be a minimal structure to all your judgements, if we are to talk of judgement at all. Nagel thinks that all such inner demonstrations are tied to a range of conceptual capacities. Your inner judgements, even when they seem particularly transparent to you as unstructured responses to an inner presence, depend on an implicit contrast with other such states. Nagel takes the point from Wittgenstein.

Wittgenstein argued in his *Philosophical Investigations* that it was a mistake to understand ostensive definitions of words as the basic way in which connections between language and world are established. The simplicity and apparent naturalness of such atomistic word–world pairings conceals how much stage-setting goes into this specialized use of language. The point is even more important for "inner" ostensive definitions when the grasp of a mental concept is dependent on a direct experience and yet does a very good job of concealing the presupposed background abilities and conceptual connections that make this act of inner "pointing" possible. Nagel puts the argument as follows:

> The absence of any conceptual connection when phenomena are grasped by ... disparate concepts may conceal a deeper necessary connection that is not yet conceptual because not accessible to us by means of our present forms of thought. To see this, consider how I might investigate reflectively the relations among phenomenology, behaviour and physiology with respect, say, to the cigar I am now smoking. What I must do first is to regard the experience as a state of myself of whose subjective qualities I am immediately aware, which also has certain publicly observable functional relations to stimuli and discriminatory capacities. Even at this first stage there is already the risk of a natural illusion of conceptual independence with respect to these functional relations, because they are concealed in my introspective identification of the experience. But it is an illusion because *introspective identification is itself one of those mental acts that cannot be completely separated from its functional connections* (e.g. the capacity to distinguish this taste from that of a cigarette).
>
> (Nagel 2002: 216–17, emphasis added)

This point is crucial because it shows what Nagel considers is the correct way to think more objectively about the mental. In addition, it illustrates what is wrong with a related proposal on the part of the physicalist who, exploiting Nagel's remark on the limitation of our imagination, develops a competing account of mental concepts at the service of physicalism. I shall now explain both of these aspects of Nagel's position.

Our mental concepts have special conditions of acquisition and use. However, the way in which such concepts conceal in introspection the range of conceptual capacities that they actually draw on creates a kind of illusion. That is the illusion that they are simple names of simple objects. But they are not; they implicitly place sensations relative to a range of implied contrasts. Nagel argues that this allows us to explain one way in which we can think more objectively about the mental that closely parallels the way in which, when a Cartesian model of objectification is appropriate, we can think of physical objectivity in mathematical and structural terms. We can take each individual exercise of a mental concept and place that which it conceptualizes within a similarly abstract and structural conception. We locate the objects of our phenomenal concepts within a quality space. This contextualization is possible only because our concepts of individual phenomenal states draw on a range of conceptual capacities and classify even a bare "this-such" as a "this as opposed to a that". When we classify a taste as the taste of an H. Upmann cigar, we are implicitly contrasting that taste with that of a Cohiba cigar, a cigar and not a cigarette and so on.

Locating mental concepts in a holistic structure in this way is, for Nagel, the correct way to think more objectively about mental discourse taken as self-sufficient. There is a great deal more to be said about a satisfactory overall conception of the mental–physical relation and I shall describe Nagel's views in detail throughout the rest of this chapter. But a necessary preliminary to a satisfactory overall view is the application of a form of objectification of mental discourse that is appropriate.

It is worth noting this because there is another way of interpreting Nagel that characterizes him as a physicalist. He would, thereby, be committed to type–type psychophysical identities. A number of philosophers have drawn on the footnote to "What is it Like to be a Bat?" to identify the contrast between a perceptual and a sympathetic use of the imagination. On this basis they then argue for an account of psychophysical laws that follows Kripke's account of *a posteriori* identities to the letter. However, they also exploit Nagel's point about the unreliability of the imagination as a tool for discerning metaphysical possibilities to undermine Kripke's Cartesian intuition (Hill & McLaughlin 1999; Levin 2007).

Kripke's intuition was that if one can conceivably imagine a situation in which one is in pain, but one's C-fibres are not stimulated, then that establishes a genuine possibility where the type–type identity of pain with C-fibre stimulation is falsified. We cannot undercut it by redescribing it as a case where we are presented simply with an epistemic counterpart of the mental state. That is because any counterpart to a pain *is* pain. But, these philosophers argue, at this point we can appeal to Nagel's footnote about the disparate uses of the imagination in creating this kind of imagined scenario. We project mental concepts using the sympathetic imagination and physical concepts using the perceptual imagination. These very different conditions of application mean that there will always seem to us to be an explanatory gap between that which is picked out by a mental concept and that which is picked out by a physical concept, even when such a gap does not exist. Why not say, then, that we can treat psychophysical identities exactly as the presentation of one property in two ways, one corresponding to a mental concept and one corresponding to a physical concept? If we can say this, why does Nagel not take advantage of his own insight into the unreliability of our modal intuitions in this case and say it too?

The answer is because this form of misguided objectification totally departs from our ordinary understanding of mental concepts. We are trying to capture what these are concepts of "from the inside" (Eilan 2001: 171). Nagel's commitment to realism about mentality is not foreign to our understanding of mental concepts, but is a commitment implicit in them. There must be some understanding of the reality of mentality in which pains are as much a part of the fabric of the universe as muons and phenotypes. It is no part of our ordinary understanding of such mental concepts that they could turn out to be, brutely, the presentation to us of a property also describable using a physical concept (*ibid.*). This kind of physicalism is simply an instance of theft rather than honest toil: it fails to meet an appropriate standard for intelligible identities. An intelligible identity needs preparatory work on an appropriately objective form of our mental concepts that does not do violence to our ordinary understanding of them (Alter 2002). Nagel's proposal about quality spaces is of this form. Furthermore, Nagel's views on the intelligibility of identity statements have been consistent since his early paper:

> Usually, when we are told that X is Y, we know *how* it is supposed to be true, but that depends on a conceptual or theoretical background and is not conveyed by the "is" alone. We know how both "X" and "Y" refer, and the kinds of things to which they

> refer, and we have a rough idea how the two referential paths might converge on a single thing, be it an object, a person, a process, an event, or whatever. But when the two terms of the identification are very disparate it may not be so clear how it could be true ... a theoretical framework may have to be supplied to help us to understand this. (*MQ*: 176–7)

But the most important difference between Nagel's objective phenomenology and the physicalist account of mental concepts is that the former is an attempt to make sense of the realist commitment implicit within our mental concepts themselves. Nagel's proposal also needs a radical revolution in our conception of the physical. But we are not, now, in a position simply to assert that one and the same property is presented to us as both mental and physical in a way that vindicates currently existing physicalist theories of the mental.

In his attempt to find structure within that which is conceived of by our ordinary mental concepts, Nagel seeks a way of thinking objectively about the mental that meets the Hegelian pattern of objectification. We are not seeking to renounce the perspectival, but to contextualize it in terms of that which is still perspectival, but less so. We need to enrich the stock of concepts that we need to think objectively about mental reality, but we are simply unpacking a realist commitment already implicit in how we think of the mind ordinarily. Methodologically we are overcoming the limitations imposed on us by our imaginations: we can progress towards greater objectivity, overcoming the fact that at present we can only think of another's point of view by imagining being in it. The resulting characterization of subjective experience is less perspectival and, therefore, available to a wider class of judgers. (That is because it would draw on fewer of their distinctive peculiarities as judgers.) This is, so far, the mere outline of a proposal that appears in different versions throughout Nagel's work. The project of devising an objective phenomenology is first suggested in "What is it Like to be a Bat?" (*MQ*: 178–9), is further discussed in *The View from Nowhere* (*VN*: 24–7) and features in "The Psychophysical Nexus" too (PN: 213–20, 233).

Nagel's objective phenomenology

Nagel's suggestion is that we can make some progress on the problem of the relationship between the mental and the physical by appealing to the idea of shared structure. The paradigmatic gain in objectivity represented for him by the emergence of the primary–secondary property distinction is partly motivated by the mathematicization of nature in a way that also involves structure (*VN*: 14). The mental analogue appeals to the idea of a quality space and was introduced in "What is it Like to be a Bat?":

> At present we are completely unequipped to think about the subjective character of experience without relying on the imagination ... This should be regarded as a challenge to form new concepts and devise a new method – an objective phenomenology not dependent on empathy or the imagination. (*MQ*: 178–9)

This is an appropriate form of objectivity as, while perspectival, it is not as perspectival as that which it seeks to explain. In particular, it is accessible to a wider class of thinkers seeking to explain and to understand the mental than is the actual content of our experience. (The content, that is, that actually occupies the locations within such quality spaces.) Nagel outlines a view of this kind as follows:

> Structural features of perception might be more accessible to objective description, even though something would be left out. And concepts alternative to those we learn in the first person may enable us to arrive at a kind of understanding even of our own experience which is denied us by the very case of description and lack of distance that subjective concepts afford ... a phenomenology that is in this sense objective may permit questions about the physical basis of experience to assume a more intelligible form. (*MQ*: 179)

Having introduced this promising idea, Nagel later makes some remarks in *The View from Nowhere* about its limitations that seem to me unwarranted (*VN*: 25). I think it is important to take issue with Nagel's own comments on the limits of this objective phenomenology. If, as I have suggested, following Eilan, the project of devising an objective phenomenology is an attempt to unpack the realist commitments within our ordinary understanding of the mental, then if it fails to discharge that task adequately the transition to it will be unmotivated. But Nagel does seem to imply that objective phenomenology precisely leaves out the fine grain of phenomenal experiences. Even worse, he implies that to capture this phenomenology we might need the idea of a subjective reality! But what is this inherent limitation that he sees in his own way of being objective about mentality, originally intended to respect the phenomenology of our experience? His later reservations are as follows:

> If we try to understand experience from an objective viewpoint that is distinct from that of the subject of the experience, then even if we continue to credit its perspectival nature, we will not be able to grasp its most specific qualities unless we can imagine them subjectively. We will not know exactly how scrambled eggs taste to a cockroach even if we develop a detailed objective phenomenology of the cockroach sense of taste. When it comes to values, goals, and forms of life, the gulf may be even more profound. (*VN*: 25)

It is not clear to me from this passage why objective phenomenology leaves anything out at all. Any structural description of a phenomenon obviously leaves something out or it would not be a structural description. However, it does not seem to follow that this is an inherent limitation on the method of objective phenomenology. What is limited is what we try to do in order to supplement the method, namely, to use our imaginations to put back in what structure leaves out.[14] Uncharacteristically, Nagel seems to undervalue what his own method can achieve. It is pitched at the level of general types, and so does not include "the exact character of each of the experiential and intentional perspectives with which it deals" (*VN*: 26). However, it did not *aim* to do so. Given that aim it is hard to see how it can be accused of incompleteness. As a structural description it must leave out material content, but it does not leave out anything relevant to the role that plays in explaining how we can think more objectively about the mental.

Nagel's anti-objectivist arguments

I have already considered two ways in which applying an inappropriate model of objectivity to the mental would, in Nagel's view, be a failure. The first failure would be to insist on applying a Cartesian model of ideally non-perspectival objectivity to the mental in spite of the fact that mentality exemplifies radical perspectivalness. The second form of false objectification was the physicalist's attempt to hijack Nagel's own ideas about the constitutive failings of the imagination. The physicalist put forward an account of psychophysical laws as *a posteriori* necessities. This was combined with Nagel's own suggested method for defusing recalcitrant modal intuitions that suggest that such type–type identities do not hold. I argued that this latter argument failed to capture the kind of objectivity built into our mental concepts themselves. In this section I would like to expand on these points and to explain the sense in which Nagel's philosophy of mind is anti-objectivist, but not anti-physicalist.

Objectivism was discussed in Chapter 2. It is the over-extended, false version of the perfectly true (when restricted) claims made in an absolute conception of the world. Nagel believes that in the philosophy of mind physicalism reappears in the work of many philosophers in the distorted guise of a false objectivism. His primary objection to objectivism in the philosophy of mind is that it overextends a model of knowledge appropriate to theoretical knowledge to cases of knowledge that involve a direct acquaintance requirement. Theoretical knowledge does not, typically, require direct acquaintance on the part of the knower with the object of knowledge. But some non-theoretical (not un-theoretical) knowledge does have this requirement built into it. It is knowledge that is not available unless the knower is directly acquainted with certain kinds of experience that, in turn, ground the concepts needed to formulate that knowledge. In other words, objectivism cannot capture within its explanatory ambitions any instance of the radically perspectival. But the mental is, for Nagel, a paradigm case of the radically perspectival. Therefore, any attempt to treat the mental independently of the direct experience requirement will be falsely objectifying.

Given the influence of physicalism on contemporary philosophy of the mind, it is worth amplifying this set of arguments. A natural way to do this is to examine Frank Jackson's (1982, 1986) well-known "knowledge argument" against physicalism. That is because all the relevant issues are brought out by this argument very well. A physicalist critic would interpret Nagel's view as follows: he elicits, by suggestive counter-examples, a vague intuition that any physicalist account of the mind "leaves out" subjectivity. It is, therefore, radically incomplete and so false. So Nagel's concerns and those of Jackson in his knowledge argument are basically the same. However, this reconstruction of Nagel's anti-objectivism would get his arguments completely wrong. Closer examination of the fierce debate over Jackson's claims will help to clarify why.

In his much discussed thought experiment Jackson described the case of Mary, a colour scientist, who has been brought up in a black and white room. Intensively educated in the room, Mary knows all that there is to know, theoretically, about the nature of colour and its perception. But she has no direct acquaintance with colour in her perceptual experience until she is released from the room into our technicoloured world. She sees an instance of the colour red for the first time in a way that is not an application of her temporally prior theoretical knowledge of colour. It is an instance of direct acquaintance with the property of red.

Jackson claimed that Mary thereby comes to know a new *fact*. That, he thought, was a problem for physicalism. The reason is that physicalism claims to offer a complete account of all the facts that there are. Yet the thought experiment was set up in such a way that in the room Mary already knew all the physical facts. Released from the room she acquires a new fact. So physicalism is not, as it claims, complete. But Jackson was also careful to note that Nagel would never conclude that a knowledge argument of this kind would refute physicalism (1986: 132).

Jackson's caveat was in order as Nagel's relation to the knowledge argument is complicated. That is because Nagel is careful to separate physicalism from objectivism. As Tim Crane has pointed out in his own insightful analysis of the knowledge argument, properly understood the knowledge argument is *not* a critique of physicalism (Crane 2003). Jackson initially represented his argument as a critique of physicalism, and many of his critics have also assumed that this is correct. (Jackson later changed his mind about the relationship between his argument and physicalism; Jackson 1998). According to Crane, there is an equivocation in the knowledge argument concealed within its apparently innocent claim that physicalism is "complete" (2003: 77–8). It is this crucial completeness claim that forces physicalism into the role of giving an account of all the facts that there are including facts about knowledge.

The standard responses to Jackson's original knowledge argument are as follows. First, Mary acquires a "knowing how", not a "knowing that". This is an ability, not an item of discursive knowledge, in a way that disarms the putative challenge to physicalism (the premise that physicalism completely explains all the facts is left undisputed) (Lewis 1990; Nemirow 1990). Secondly, it has been argued that Mary acquires knowledge of a fact she already knew under a different mode of presentation. This identification of an equivocation in the knowledge argument involves a distinction between fine-grained and coarse-grained facts (Van Gulick 1997). Crane shows very convincingly the implausibility of both of these main lines of criticism of the knowledge argument. Even if Mary does acquire an ability, is it not also plausibly correlative with a piece of knowledge, namely, that red looks like *this* (Crane 2003: 71)? The second criticism appeals to Frege's (1948) distinction between sense and reference. This is a distinction between a fact and our mode of access to that fact. However, as Crane (2003: 74) points out, Frege introduced that distinction precisely to explain how two rational thinkers could take up different reasonable attitudes to one and the same fact. It is intended to capture one aspect of what it is to have a subjective point of view. On any reasonable conception of knowledge as a mental state directed to a propositional object, when Mary learns that one referent is picked out by two different modes of presentation, she does learn a new fact. Indeed, Crane argues that in this local and particular sense of the content of the mental act of knowing, there is no harm in calling the object of knowledge a "subjective fact" (*ibid*.: 78).

Crane concludes that what the knowledge argument shows is that there are some kinds of knowledge that depend on direct experience. That is not an anti-physicalist conclusion: physics is simply not a form of knowledge that is experience dependent in such a way (*ibid*.: 80). But the knowledge argument does justify an anti-objectivist conclusion. It is the objectivist who ought properly to be interpreted as making the claim of completeness that the argument undermines. Physicalism, properly understood, is not committed to the completeness claim.

All of these considerations have a direct bearing on the understanding of Nagel's views. I argued in Chapter 2 that one ought sharply to distinguish the content of physics from the content of what Nagel calls "objectivism".[15] Consider the final set of physical theories at the stable endpoint of enquiry. This completed physics makes, in its own proprietary terms, claims about the structure, function and nature of the physical world. It makes no claims about knowledge, including no claims about how it is known. For those distinctive sorts of claims, we need to turn to objectivism.

Objectivism is a meta-level philosophical position that is not just about the physical world, but also about understanding, concepts, modes of presentation, intensional contexts, intentionality and knowledge. It claims that the final physical theory will be able to entail a further set of truths that substantiates the claim that objectivism can be a complete theory of understanding that applies, *inter alia*, to itself. Clearly, these two views have radically differing scope. Physics is true of the world. Objectivism is true of the world and of our knowledge of the world, physics included. It makes the completeness claim that Crane finds objectionable in the putative anti-physicalist (properly speaking, anti-objectivist) argument. It has already been argued, in Chapter 2, that Nagel clearly distinguishes these two views.

Nagel is a critic of objectivism, not of physicalism. His argument is that our conceptions of both the subjective and the objective both need further radical conceptual and theoretical innovations if we are to understand their mutual relationship in a satisfying way. So physics, as currently understood, seems manifestly not up to the task of giving its relation to the mental a transparent basis. However, that is not the same conclusion as the anti-physicalist conclusion that it is false because it cannot offer a complete account of all the facts that there are. (Even the sense of "fact" in which we refer to the content embedded in a knowledge claim.) As Crane points out, physicalism should not even commit itself to the claim that it has to explain how one can learn all the facts that there are. It is not a thesis about knowledge at all: at least, it ought not to be (2003: 80).

It would, therefore, be a mistake to refer to an undifferentiated "Jackson–Nagel knowledge argument" if such an argument is construed as a critique of physicalism. In Nagel's terminology the knowledge argument could play a useful tactical role in exposing the overambitious claims of objectivism. However, that which he identifies as the main problem for physicalism is simply its explanatory inadequacy in the philosophy of mind. Current physics is evidently not up to the tasks that it faces in explaining the place of mentality in the world. Nagel believes that a theoretically satisfactory account of the place of mentality in the physical world needs progress on all fronts simultaneously. We need to be more objective about the mental via the development of an objective phenomenology. We need an enriched conception of the physical. We also need an overall account of how both mental and physical properties can intelligibly be two aspects of an underlying reality. Developing a set of answers to all three questions has been pursued in Nagel's work in two distinct ways. I shall describe each in turn, beginning with the position in *The View from Nowhere*.

The first-person standpoint and its illusions

I noted above that Nagel's argument that the mental is essentially perspectival is based on two claims. The first draws attention to the special character of mental concepts based on the particular way in which such concepts are acquired and used. The second focuses on what it is to be a thinker with a mind at all; it asks what conditions have to be met to constitute that which philosophers call a "subject of experience". I have formulated this second part of Nagel's view as the claim that all the representations that make up the mental life of a person must be representations *for* that person. It involves a person-level unity to a thinker's mental life that has yet to be explained in the context of Nagel's overall views.

The depth and complexity of Nagel's treatment of these issues in *The View from Nowhere* is such that he can be interpreted as addressing both of these grounds of the perspectivalness of the mental in his wide-ranging discussion. Furthermore, in his discussion of what it is to be a mental subject, he covers a diverse range of sub-topics: the nature of first-person reference, the unity of the mental life of a person, personal identity and finally the singularity of an individual consciousness. (I shall defer discussion of that last topic to the section "The objective self" below.)

The overall aim is a satisfactory explanation of the place of mental features in the physical world. To that end, Nagel begins his account by rejecting substance dualism in which the mental and the physical are aspects of two distinct mental and physical substances. He argues that his rejection of psychophysical reductionism does not create a space in reality to be occupied by a non-physical substance. Interestingly, he views such a position as possibly true. However, it is an implausible hypothesis that fails to capture the "intimacy" of the mental–physical relationship. There is just as much difficulty explaining how mental properties or features could inhere in a non-physical substance as there is in explaining their inherence in a physical one. Given that, we might as well cut our losses by taking them to inhere in something that is, at the very least, intelligibly related to the physical world. Nagel concludes that: "the falsity of physicalism does not require nonphysical substances" (*VN*: 29).

Nagel regards as the best available hypothesis the claim that the mental and the physical must pick out distinct features, or properties, but two classes of property that are strongly "interdependent". *The View from Nowhere* thus defends a dual aspect theory of the mental that aims to make intelligible how mental and physical features are interdependent aspects of a single underlying substance. But Nagel is aware that the results threaten to be paradoxical. That is because this view seems to treat our concepts of mentality as picking out phenomena whose nature is open to further specification. That was, after all, precisely the view he that he wanted to resist when he rejected the kind of type–type physicalism that takes our current mental concepts and our current physics as given, and uses Nagel's own views on the imagination to defend physicalism (Levin 2007).

Mental phenomena seem to have further properties not entailed by the concepts used to pick them out. Furthermore, they seem to have properties incompatible with our folk-psychological conception of those properties. In dealing with these two points Nagel appeals to his Kripkean argument that the first class of problematic properties can be dealt with by arguing that our concept of a thing need not pick out all its essential properties. It may have others yet to be specified. But the second case is clearly more problematic for Nagel's view. His argument strategy is to redescribe as many of those cases as possible as meeting his first description. We pick mental properties out in certain ways, but our descriptions leave it open that the properties are correlated with certain others (physical properties) where we can go on to understand how both inhere in an underlying substrate. The candidate that Nagel assumes as such a substrate is the functioning human brain. Thus, in this earlier version of dual aspect theory, mental and physical properties inhere in the functioning brain as an underlying substrate that grounds the "intimacy" of these two kinds of property.

Nagel's main focus in *The View from Nowhere* is to put this hypothesis to the test by considering a radically undercutting thesis, namely, that the self can exist as a simple substance in a way that detaches its own identity through time from that of *anything* physical with which it may be correlated. This seems to be an argument primarily directed against treating the self as a Cartesian simple substance. In fact, however, the situation is more complex. While Nagel aims to recapitulate some of Kant's critical arguments against that simple Cartesian view, he also wants to resist the claims of the reductionist about the self.

This reductionist view has been defended by Derek Parfit in a series of publications (1984, 1995, 1999). Parfit believes that the word "I" and its cognates in ordinary language play an unfortunate role in the way we ordinarily think about ourselves and the world. They serve merely to generate a range of illusions. The primary illusion is an ethical one. It is the false view that personal identity matters, whereas it does not (Parfit 1995). However, according to Parfit it is survival that matters rather than personal identity *per se*. The view that it is identity that matters, not survival, is based on another illusion that our personal identity consists in a simple, but very deep, fact about us. Furthermore, this fact generates an entirely determinate answer to the question as to whether a future experience is mine or not. Parfit thus combines reductionism about personal identity with a view that is not eliminativist about the *concept* of a person. That in which personal identity consists can always be described without presupposing the concept of personhood (*ibid.*, 1999). Parfit goes on to explain that a person's identity actually consists in a set of interconnected psychological facts (facts that are both continuous and connected) in a way that updates Hume's "bundle theory" of the self (Parfit 1984).

Parfit's argument is a constant reference point throughout Nagel's discussion of the self in *The View from Nowhere*. Nagel is concerned to defend the sense in which a subject of experience is a unified locus of mental life without postulating an underlying mental substance, nor reducing personhood to relations between psychological facts. His relationship to these two other views explains why he extensively discusses the problem of personal identity. This is not a detour from his main subject, namely, how the relationship between mental and the physical is best understood. The connection between the two problems is that our concept of the self seems to be of a "pure" and self-contained mental object whose nature is exhausted by our first-personal perspective on it. That is a more general illusion generated from our mental concepts than the illusion of presupposition-free reference to mental objects; the same illusion applies to self-knowledge, too. From within the standpoint of consciousness, one's identity seems wholly translucent to one: "I am I" seems to remain a truth throughout all the other changes that I might undergo, physically or even at the level of underlying character traits. Not even psychological continuity seems relevant from the standpoint of this translucent self-awareness.

Co-personality is the issue of how the mental life of a single subject is unified; co-consciousness is the issue of how the conscious states of a single subject are unified. These are distinct questions that ought to receive distinct answers. However, the two problems overlap. The way in which we ordinarily think about the self makes the fact that it is a unified locus of consciousness one of its central and most important features. When we think about the self, construed as the reference of the first-person pronoun "I", it seems to have a special unity. Furthermore, this unity reveals itself *to* itself in a way that does not depend on any criteria external to the perspective of consciousness. That simplicity and translucency of the use of "I" looks like a major stumbling block for any identification of the brain as the underlying substrate to both mental and physical properties. Nagel's appeal to the functioning brain looks like a radical but implausible solution to the problem that I identified as one of the twin sources of the radical perspectivalness of the mental, namely, that all mental representations must be representations for a self.

To defend his proposal, particularly from Parfit, Nagel surveys the problem of personal identity. Kant and Locke both emphasized that the unity of our consciousness cannot be explained as consciousness of a unity: not, at any rate, the unity of an underlying substance. In the classic discussions of the problem by Joseph Butler (2000) and Thomas Reid (2002), they establish that personal identity may be accompanied by psychological continuity but it is not reducible to it. We seem to have a simple idea of the self. Furthermore, questions about whether a conscious experience in the future will be mine seem determinate and not open to conventional determination. The least unpalatable option seems to be Geoffrey Madell's view that a primitive property of "mineness" attaches to all of my mental states (Madell 1983). Nagel is not happy with that view, but it seems to him to be the least bad of an unsatisfactory range of options (*VN*: 34). However, the argument cannot rest at that unsatisfactory point.

The way forward, Nagel suggests, is to resist the idea that the first-person perspective exhausts our grasp of the concept of the self, as it certainly seems to. It is not as if, from the first-personal perspective, you look within and pick yourself out from among all the other conscious subjects that you could be. When we use "I" to refer to ourselves we do not seem to be recognizing ourselves from among an array of possible objects of reference. But this should not lead us to conclude, Nagel cautions, that the first-person concept is fully transparent to reflection such that the criteria for applying it can be grasped wholly *a priori*. As he notes, the grasp of the concepts of "I" and "someone" are interdependent and one's criterionless self-ascriptions using "I" have to correspond to third-personal uses of the concept. He adds his general, Kripkean, point that to grasp the possession conditions of a concept is not to grasp all the relevant properties of the thing referred to. This is reinforced by the fact that while our first-personal judgements seem transparent to consciousness, they are corrigible. Nagel argues that we can apply the appearance–reality distinction to our first-personal grasp of our own mental lives: "In the case of sensation, the reality is itself a form of appearance, and the distinction one between real appearance and apparent appearance" (*VN*: 36). Nagel concludes that the objectivity that governs mental concepts is *sui generis*. Progress on the problem of personal identity is available if this general account of mental concepts can be applied to it. Noting that judgements of identity differ from judgements of similarity, Nagel's aim is to find a way in which the question of whether a future conscious experience will be mine has a determinate answer.

He argues that there are two main options: to link the concept of the identity of the self to other objectively determinable psychological concepts, all linked to continuity, or to treat the concept of personal identity as basic and irreducible. Nagel argues for the latter, mainly in the face of Parfit's scepticism about what Parfit calls the "simple view" (1973: 140; *VN*: 37–42). Nagel argues that psychological continuity cannot be the basic idea; one can imagine oneself having led a completely different life. What is needed instead is a simple psychological concept that is explanatorily basic, but minimally objective. The question is how our concept of personal identity meets these demands. Such aspects of ourselves as re-identification via bodily or mental continuity (whether first- or third-personal) are "criteria" in the sense of ways in which we fix the reference of the term: they are evidence for identity, not what it consists in.

Pushing this argument a step further, Nagel suggests that while our first-person concept looks transparent to us, our criteria of application for it pick out a phenomenon that may have further features that are yet to be discovered. They will supply both an account of our "true nature" and the principle of its identity. This is hidden from us by the fact that "the idea of the self seems not to be a partial specification of anything" (*VN*: 39). At this point Nagel's argument comes full circle. The apparent detour into issues about the first person and identity turn out to be directly relevant to the hypothesis of the truth of dual aspect theory:

> The concept of the self does not of course imply the truth of dual aspect theory. The concept implies only that if it refers at all, it must refer to something essentially subjective, often identifiable non-observationally in the first person and observationally in the third, which is the persisting locus of mental states and activities and the vehicle for carrying forward familiar psychological continuities when they occur. So far as the *concept* is concerned,

> this might turn out to be any of a number of things or there might be no such thing. But if dual aspect theory is correct, then it is as a matter of fact the intact brain – customarily found in a living animal of a certain kind but not in principle inseparable from it. I could lose everything but my functioning brain and still be me. (*VN*: 40)

This is, as Nagel emphasizes, an empirical hypothesis about the "true nature" of the self not an analysis of the concept expressed by our use of first-person terms. Why the brain? Because it seems to Nagel to be the minimal part of me that could continue in such a way as to underpin the continuity of my self. It is the locus of the psychological continuity with which the identity of the self is associated: "On the evidence, the intact brain seems to be responsible for the maintenance of memory and other psychological continuities and for the unity of consciousness" (*VN*: 41).

Apparently criterionless reference using "I" gives rise to the illusion that I could possibly be disembodied, or a non-physical soul. But this is to confuse epistemic possibility, what I might reasonably believe to be possible in light of what I know, with the metaphysical possibilities dictated by the intrinsic nature of what, in fact, "I" refers to. What it in fact refers to, Nagel hypothesizes, is the functioning brain. He is fully aware that to a certain extent this candidate is not ideal. In particular, a functioning brain might be split to produce two centres of consciousness that are plausibly selves (Nagel 1971a). Alternatively, it might undergo gradual replacement of its cells such that it is not a fully adequate bearer of the self; not, at least, as we understand that idea from the first-personal perspective.

Nagel concedes that his hypothesis does not deliver everything we might have hoped for. We take it that what we seem, without criteria, to pick out as the basis of our selfhood should be a self that preserves such fundamental features as giving a determinate answer as to whether a future mental state is mine or not. If Nagel's answer compromises that, then is he not coming close to abandoning the idea that our intuitive sense of self picks out something? Why not go further and abandon the intuitive conception or reduce it to the psychological continuity with which it is associated? (Again, the pressure here comes from Parfit's competing, reductionist, treatment of the self.) Nagel responds:

> I don't really have an answer to this, except the question-begging answer that one of the conditions that the self should meet if

> possible is that it be something in which the flow of consciousness and the beliefs, desires, intentions and character traits that I have all take place – something beneath the contents of consciousness, which might even survive a radical break in the continuity of consciousness. (*VN*: 45)

Qua candidate, the functioning brain, Nagel argues, may not be ideal but it "is still better than nothing" (*VN*: 45). Furthermore, the hypothesis that dual aspect theory is true solves not only the problem of personal identity, with tolerable deviation from our intuitive beliefs about the subject matter, but also casts light on the mental–physical relation more generally. The subsequent development of Nagel's view does not change the basic elements of his approach. What it does do is apply the transparency requirement for understanding mental–physical identities more rigorously. I shall now turn to the internal evolution of Nagel's views in his most recent papers on the mental–physical relation.

Mental ontology reconsidered: dual aspect theory and Hegelian objectification

The culmination of Nagel's work on the mental–physical relation is his paper "The Psychophysical Nexus". In this section I shall describe the important changes in Nagel's dual aspect theory and how these changes can be interpreted as a shift from the first pattern of Hegelian objectification to the second.

In the first pattern, exemplified by the account in *The View from Nowhere*, the mental is explained by our taking two appropriate steps. The first step is the development of an objective phenomenology that brings out a commitment implicit in our ordinary mental concepts to placing mentality in the world. It does so while respecting the irreducibly perspectival character of the mental. The second step is finding a candidate in the world for being a locus of consciousness and mentality; the functioning brain. This pattern of objectification, as applied to mentality, fits the general pattern of Hegelian objectification. That is because the perspectival is explained in terms of the less perspectival via the project of developing an objective phenomenology. There is no attempt to strip perspective away as illusory as there would be in a Cartesian model. However, while Nagel emphasizes that any theoretical reduction or identity requires some preliminary stage-setting for both the mental aspects of the world and its physical nature, he does not argue that we need radically to rethink our conception of the physical. That latter claim marks the shift to his later view.

The change in Nagel's more recent work on the mental–physical relationship is that he places greater emphasis on the necessity of finding that relationship intelligible or more transparent. To meet this increased demand he turns to a second pattern of Hegelian objectification in which we can specify that there must be a kind of relation between the mental and the physical that would meet this demand of intelligibility, but we are currently unable to state what it is. We cannot now state the nature of this relationship because it requires a revolutionary reconceptualization of the problem on *both* sides of the mental–physical relationship. McGinn, who holds similar views, thinks that because of our contingent limitations as a species the nature of this intelligible connection may be forever closed to us (1991b). By contrast, Nagel thinks that we can reasonably speculate that a scientific understanding of mentality might become available to us in the near future. Any breakthrough in understanding requires a preliminary act of imagining new possibilities for a successful explanation. That is what Nagel seeks to do in "The Psychophysical Nexus".

In *The View from Nowhere* the kind of dual aspect theory that Nagel favours won by default: all the other views considered did not come close to meeting the required standard for explaining the mental–physical relationship. "The Psychophysical Nexus" is more positive: it describes the only possible view that could provide us with a transparent understanding of that relationship. Nagel argues in this rich and subtle paper that his original diagnosis of why Kripke's Cartesian intuition was misplaced no longer seems satisfactory to him. That early account appealed to the differences between perceptual and sympathetic imagination. Nagel now believes that this diagnosis did not go deep enough. He now believes that Kripke's misleading Cartesian intuitions about counterfactual scenarios are relative to our currently impoverished stock of concepts (PN: 206, 216). More generally, the kind of view defended in *The View from Nowhere* seems to concede that we have very tight correlations between mental phenomena and aspects of the physical brain, but Nagel now believes that we need to relativize all such judgements:

> Conceivability arguments for the contingency of a correlation or the distinctness of differently described phenomena depend for

> their reliability on the adequacy of the concepts being employed. If those concepts do not adequately grasp the nature of the things to which they refer, they may yield deceptive appearances of contingency and nonidentity. (PN: 207)

In Nagel's proposed new theory of the mental–physical relationship an underlying substance necessitates both its mental and its physical aspects in a way that approaches the ideal of transparency so as to remove any explanatory gap: "The dependence of mind on brain is not conceptually transparent, but it is necessary nonetheless" (PN: 207). Nagel develops a "task specification" for this underlying substrate:

> It would have to be a third type of variable, whose relation to the other two was not causal but constitutive. This third term should not leave anything out. It would have to be an X such that X's being a sensation and X's being a brain state both follow from the nature of X itself, independent of its relation to anything else. (PN: 221)

Nagel retains his Kripkean account of mental concepts, but the focus has shifted away from the quality spaces in which phenomenal states are located (objective phenomenology) to another of their features. Our concepts of conscious mental states permit us to speculate that they have an underlying essence whose nature is open to a further description:

> To admit the possibility of a necessary connection here, we would have to recognize that the mental concept as it now operates has nothing to say about the physiological conditions for its own operation, and then open up the concept to amplification by leaving a place for such a condition – a place that can be filled only a posteriori, by a theory of the actual type of event that admits these two types of access, internal and external, from within and from without. (PN: 220)

Nagel acknowledges that this general account of natural kind concepts has to be adjusted to the peculiarity of the problem generated by the special nature of the mental–physical relation. Central to this peculiarity is the role played by space. We find it difficult to conceive of how conscious states could be integrated into our spatial understanding of the physical world (McGinn 1991c, 1995; PN: 216). The new stock of concepts will have to overcome that problem:

> The right point of view would be one that, contrary to present conceptual possibilities, included both subjectivity and spatio-temporal structure from the outset, all its descriptions implying both these things at once, so that it would describe inner states and their functional relations to behaviour and to one another from the phenomenological inside and physiological outside simultaneously – not in parallel. (PN: 220–21)

This is going to demand a revolution in our current concepts because we need radically new theories of states and events and their composition.

The underlying nature that is, itself, neither mental nor physical would constitute its manifestations as mental, behavioural, functional and neurophysiological in a way that is necessary and hence transparent:

> The relation between phenomenology and physiology demands an explanation; no explanation of sufficient transparency can be constructed within the circle of current mental and physical concepts themselves; so an explanation must be sought which introduces new concepts and gives us knowledge of real things we didn't know about before. (PN: 233)

I have quoted extensively from Nagel's paper to give a flavour of the radicalism of his proposals. He keeps from *The View from Nowhere* the emphasis on the functioning brain as the locus of consciousness. His more recent positive conception of dual aspect theory now involves the speculation that in the microstructure of the brain there are relations between neural states that mirror macroscopic relations between mental states and a non-contingent expression in characteristic behaviour (PN: 225–6).

How plausible is Nagel's final position? It can seem very speculative, but then everyone working on the problem of consciousness has to admit that the problem seems recalcitrant and that we need new theoretical options (PN: 232). Reduction is an unusual achievement in the sciences, not the norm, and successful reductions often involve theoretical and conceptual innovations both in the reduced discipline and in the reducing discipline. This point has been made by Noam Chomsky:

> Large-scale reduction is rare in the history of the sciences. Commonly the more "fundamental" science has had to undergo radical revision for unification to proceed. The case of chemistry and

> physics is a recent example; Pauling's account of the chemical bond unified the disciplines, but only after the quantum revolution in physics made these steps possible. (1995: 1–2)

Objective phenomenology constitutes Nagel's programme for thinking innovatively in an objective way about the mental. His demand for a conceptual revolution in how we think of the physical underpinnings of consciousness corresponds to the idea that we need a theoretical and conceptual revolution in the physical sciences if we are to explain consciousness. Nagel's arguments in "The Psychophysical Nexus" can be interpreted as complementing, for the physical, his innovative objective phenomenology of the mental in *The View from Nowhere*.

I have described this view as exemplifying the second pattern of Hegelian objectification: Nagel tells us where to look for a satisfactory explanation just as he concedes that he cannot state it. But, as McGinn has perceptively pointed out, one can solve the philosophical problem of the mental–physical relationship even if one cannot solve the explanatory or properly scientific problem (1991b: 1, 16–18). McGinn claims that he can solve the philosophical problem even though he holds the view that solving the explanatory problem is constitutively beyond us. (Just as advanced calculus is too difficult for monkeys.) His point is that we sought, reflectively, to understand why there was a problem and the form that it took for us, and that those two questions have been solved by his own "cognitive closure" theory.

I think that this is correct and that it is a point equally available to those sympathetic to Nagel's more optimistic view. Nagel believes that we can reasonably expect scientific progress, shaped by an imaginative reconceptualization of the form of explanations available to us, finally to explain how a single underlying stuff transparently manifests both its mental and physical aspects. We can reasonably speculate that there is such an explanation even if we cannot currently state what it is. Handing over a question to imminent developments in scientific enquiry can constitute an answer to the philosophical question that troubled us, namely, how is a transparent explanation of the relation between the mental and the physical so much as possible? Philosophy can answer that question to its own satisfaction if it identifies its own limits and tells us that we need new and better theories of the physical to solve the problem, not new and better theories in philosophy.

The objective self

Another respect in which Nagel's work echoes themes from the phenomenological tradition (Priest 2000: 154 n.11, 157 n.27; Ratcliffe 2002), and from the work of Jean-Paul Sartre in particular (1960), is that Nagel is concerned not only with points of view considered as features of individuals (viewed as instantiations of a general type), but also with the singular nature of an individual consciousness. Nagel is one of very few philosophers of mind to take seriously what one might call the problem of ipseity. This is the question of what fact constitutes one's being the particular mental subject that one is. You are born in a particular time and place and have, over the course of your life, had a variety of different experiences that make up your life history. But you can very easily imagine that you were born in a different time and place, or were born in the same time and place as you actually were but have had a completely different life history. However, in both of these imagined scenarios you are still you. Underlying the particularity of your actual history is this deeper particularity – the singularity – that you are you. This is one, rather buried, strand in contemporary discussions of "the first person". However, Nagel is explicitly concerned with this question, as was Sartre (Priest 2000). It forms Nagel's theory of the objective self.

Nagel is aware that he faces an uphill task in formulating the problem. In particular, he is concerned to resist what he calls a "semantic diagnosis". This kind of dissolution, not solution, to the problem explains it away as, to use a Wittgensteinian phrase, a "shadow of our grammar" (Wittgenstein 2001: §§371–3). The peculiarities of our use of the first-person pronoun "I" makes it seem that there is a problem here when there is not. This pronoun behaves like all other indexicals do: for each such indexical expression there is a dictionary entry or "lexical character". To generate something that can be evaluated as true or false, particular utterances containing indexical expressions need to be interpreted as cases where lexical character, relative to a context of utterance (a time, a place or a person), generate a content, or proposition (Kaplan 1989).

The pronoun "I" figures essentially in a description of Nagel's putative problem. Each of us can formulate it first-personally for himself or herself. From Nagel's point of view, the problem can be formulated in this way: what explains the truth of the sentence "I am TN" on any occasion when he asserts it? This problem splits into two subproblems: given that we can conceive of the world from no point of view in particular (in a centreless way) what fact is the fact that the world is centred on my own point of view? Nagel puts it like this: "The first half of the question is this: how can it be true of a particular person … who is just one of many persons in an objectively centreless world, that he is me?" (*VN*: 55). The second sub-problem is this: how can I be *merely* me? This question arises, Nagel believes, from the peculiarities of the first-person pronoun: "From this point of view it can appear that 'I am TN' … is not an identity but a subject-predicate proposition" (*VN*: 55). Nagel's first question concerns the consistency of our being able to think of the world as centreless and yet as containing me, as the particular person I am. I find this part of Nagel's argument elusive. It is difficult not to think that there is a Berkeleyan ambiguity in the argument (Stalnaker 2003b). I explained above the ambiguity inherent in Berkeley's claim that "nothing can be conceived of as existing without a thinking thing" and Nagel's very clear explanation of the nature of that ambiguity. That sentence was either trivial, on one reading, or false, on another. But is there a similar equivocation in Nagel's arguments concerning the objective self?

We can conceive of the world as centreless: as containing no point of view in particular. It still contains the facts that correspond to that point of view, but we do not think of that view of the world as centred on those facts in particular. Of course, we do this *conceiving* from our own point of view (where else?). But that is irrelevant to the content of what is conceived of: what I have conceived of is the world as centreless. That is simply a description of the world that, *ex hypothesi*, leaves out my point of view, but that was precisely what we were instructed to conceive. But Nagel's concern is that it is now puzzling to conceive of the world as centreless and yet also as containing *me*.

I think the basis of this puzzlement is open to question. Suppose, by analogy, one claimed that there could never be a story in which everyone dies on the grounds that there would be no one left to represent the point of view of the story (Stalnaker 2003b). That is clearly an unconvincing argument: it is a formal feature of an aesthetic representation that it is always "as if" from a point of view (Moran 1994: 92). If you pick up a pen and draw a stick figure, that figure is always "as if" viewed from side on, or the front. But that does not mean that you have drawn a stick figure *being viewed* (from side on or from any particular angle). We can, as Stalnaker notes, conceive of a narrative story in which all its characters die: a viewpoint on the story is not a viewpoint in the story. Nagel's puzzlement seems, however, to rest on forming a conception of the world from no point of view and then asking which facts in it make up one's own point of view. It is a mistake to generate a problem by forming a conception of the world that is informationally restricted in a specific way, then asking oneself where one can locate the key item of information that one was instructed to leave out.

I am not convinced that Nagel has found the best way to express the point that he actually wants to make. Fortunately, he also employs a slightly different argument. If one conceives of "being me" as an objective property in the centreless description of the world, Nagel argues that one can always ask the following open question: why does that particular objective property attach to me? Nagel's point is that there is an irreducibly indexical component in how we think about the world. That is why it is present even when we are instructed to think of a centreless world. (This is similar to the central claim defended by McGinn in *The Subjective View* [1983: ch. 5].) That is the basis of Nagel's resistance to a semantically deflationary view that argues that the truth-conditions of any such indexical expression can be captured by a non-indexical counterpart to that judgement. For the semantically deflationary theorist, *any* indexical utterance only generates a content relative to a context, but that is simply how indexicals work (Kaplan 1989). There is nothing special about the use of "I".

Nagel insists that any non-perspectival treatment of indexicals of this kind leaves out the centrality to our thinking of distinctively first-personal modes of presentation to how we conceive of the world. The semantic diagnosis does not make the problem go away: there is a distinctively philosophical use of "I as subject" that the semantic diagnosis has to permit. That use, Nagel argues, is better expressed by the second of his two questions: "how I can be anything so specific as a particular person at all?" (*VN*: 60). Conceding the existence of the centreless view, the question now is how one can be the particular person that one is in this description without a sense of arbitrariness. This is, it seems to me, a much more promising argument in support of the point that Nagel wants to establish.

Nagel is aware that this second formulation of the problem needs to be consistent with his general, Kripkean, treatment of the limitations of the first-person standpoint. He has already argued that imagination is a poor guide to the conception of metaphysical possibilities, and that our true nature is not available to use through *a priori* reflection. That is equally true of reflections on the use of "I". (That concept seems transparent to us, but Nagel has substantiated

Kant's claim that this really is an illusion.) But what remains true after one has accepted these criticisms of the apparent simplicity of our uses of "I", Nagel argues, is that "something essential about me has nothing to do with my perspective and position in the world" (*VN*: 62). That is the bare "thisness" of the objective self, the "last stage of the detaching subject before it shrinks to an extensionless point" (*VN*: 62 n.3). That which seems particularly important to Nagel is that, in forming the objective centreless conception, his being Thomas Nagel does not matter. The properties of TN come to him directly, those of others indirectly, but it all seems alien from the perspective of the subject of whom those are properties.

Nagel's discussion in *The View from Nowhere* then changes tack. From working out how one might develop a conception of an objective self, he changes to the topic of whether forming such a conception might represent an ethical ideal for us. He argues that each of us ought to cultivate a "rather austere universal objective self" (*VN*: 63). That is a recognizable ideal from the tradition of ancient Stoicism, through Kant, to Nagel's own work, but it seems an odd intrusion into the current argument as presented in *The View from Nowhere*. That is because it does not follow that, appealing to Nagel's own Kripkean principles, if one could conceive of one's own primitive thisness either that one ought, or that one could consistently think of oneself as *only* that bare notion. We all have to have further features in addition to our primitive "thisness". Those features might, indeed, be very important in understanding the intellectual authority of the objective standpoint. Nagel himself seems to concede as much, as Chapter 6 will demonstrate, in his own reflection on the limitations of living one's life guided wholly by the objective view. One's particular character or ethical identity, for example, seems essentially to depend on the particularity of one's complex psychological make-up in a way that transcends one's objective self, one's simply being the particular person that one is. Our capacity to form such an objective conception of the self (if we can) is an ethically important fact about us, but it does not determine the extent to which forming this conception is itself something that we ought to do.[16]

Nagel's two questions come together in the following solution to the two problems he identifies:

> We can account for the content of the philosophical thought "I am TN" if we understand the "I" as referring to me qua subject of the impersonal conception of the world which contains TN. The

> reference is still essentially indexical, and cannot be eliminated in favour of an objective description, but the thought avoids triviality because it depends on the fact that this impersonal conception of the world, though it accords no special position to TN, *is attached to and developed from the perspective of TN.*
>
> (*VN*: 64, emphasis added)

So while the centreless view does not contain me, it was produced by me and that explains why it irreducibly bears my imprint.

I shall conclude with a query, a comment and a proposal. The query is whether the paragraph quoted still depends on the faulty Berkeleyan inference. Does it depend essentially on the idea that the centreless view must nevertheless be from a point of view that, since it cannot be in the world so viewed, *must* be at its limit? (This is the point I have highlighted by adding the emphasis to the quoted passage.) There seem to be a truth expressed by the formation of the conception that cannot be expressed in the conception.[17] However, the only grounds given for that is that the objective view *must* figure somewhere and there is nowhere else for it to be.

The comment is over the notion of primitive thisness. Sometimes called by metaphysicians by its Latin name "haecceity", owing to its importance in the work of Duns Scotus as a uniquely individuative property that is not a qualitative property of an individual, the idea has also been defended in contemporary metaphysics by Robert Adams (1979). But others are suspicious of this notion as an illegitimate crossing of the categories of referring to an individual and predicating features of that individual (Wiggins 1968, 2001). If the whole notion is a mistaken one then, given its important role in explaining the problem of the objective self, one has grounds for questioning that latter idea.

Finally, a proposal: I have argued throughout this chapter that Nagel's conception of the mind attaches as much importance to the perspective *for which* objects and properties are revealed as to the objects and properties themselves. We cannot understand the perspective of subjectivity in other terms, notably the mind's acquaintance with other things, owing to the uniqueness of this case. The aim is not further mystery-mongering about the subject's givenness of itself to itself. The mystery can be dispelled by requiring that any account of subjective features has to interpret them as being representable for a self, conceived of as a single point of view (Thomas 2003b, 2006a). Nagel's connected discussion of the first person and the objective self show precisely how that would work. In the case of personal identity, Nagel endorsed Madell's suggestion that: "Being mine is an irreducible, unanalysable characteristic of all my mental states, and that is has no essential connection with anything in the objective order or any connection among those states over time" (*VN*: 34). Can we dissolve the problem of the "thisness" of being the particular person I am by referring to my ownership of the entire range of subjective features that form my mental life? I can anticipate Nagel's reply to this attempt to rephrase the problem of the objective self: that notion of "mineness" is an objective notion to be thrown into the mix with all the other means of objectively characterizing the self as no one in particular.

But that does not seem quite right: commenting in a very similar way to Nagel on any theory of the self as a bundle of subjective features, Sartre commented laconically that he knew himself in not being that bundle. It is too contingent to capture the idea that one is the singular self that one is. But the idea would be that one is the perspective for whom such features are attributed features. Subjective features are representations for a self. That would cash out the idea that, for any such feature, it possesses an irreducible property of being owned (that property cannot, without regress, be an experiential feature). If we are going to take any notion as primitive, mental ownership seems preferable to mental ipseity. We can explain everything with the former notion that we wanted to explain with the latter. This problem of the objective self seems to me to be one of those instances where Nagel both identifies a problem and claims to find it insoluble, but in doing so supplies the materials for a satisfactory solution in spite of himself.

This chapter has sought to demonstrate that Nagel's views on the mind are very wide ranging. He carefully formulates his views while remaining sensitive to the type–token distinction. There may be ambiguities in some of his presentations. However, he develops a comprehensive account of token states (both mental and physical), subjective points of view (as predicated of individuals), and point of view types (predicated inter-subjectively), and of the ipseity of singular individual consciousness. Indeed, he is unusual among philosophers of mind in addressing all of these questions at varying levels of generality. His work is marked by a great degree of creativity, and some of his speculations can seem to be precisely that. But then Nagel may very well reply that at our current stage of understanding of the mental, particularly of consciousness, even the most hard-nosed philosopher of mind is speculating (whether he or she knows it or not).

Chapter 4

The possibility of altruism

Nagel's first major publication was a revision of his doctoral dissertation, which had been supervised by John Rawls. *The Possibility of Altruism* is a slender volume, but it is Nagel's most powerful work. It remains, in the opinion of many, his best book. The method Nagel pursues in this book is that of transcendental argument. Arguments of this kind take some fact that we know to be the case as given and work "backwards" to identify the *a priori* conditions that make this fact possible.[1] Nagel takes as his basic fact the claim that there is a practical use of reason. We do not simply reason theoretically in order to acquire true beliefs; we also apply our capacity to reason in deciding what to do. What must be the case for this to be true? Nagel, like Kant, thinks it is very fruitful to apply this argument strategy not simply to our knowledge of the world, but also to our deliberation and action. The basic question he sets out to answer is what makes practical reasoning *practical*?

What makes practical reasoning practical?

Nagel's transcendental strategy in *The Possibility of Altruism* uncovers two surprising consequences of the initial assumption that reason can be practical. The first is that any such reasoning can be characterized not simply case by case via the identification of instances of good reasoning. We can offer a more reflective account in terms of the *form* of good reasoning.[2] Just as there are formal principles governing theoretical reasoning, so there are formal principles governing practical reasoning. Furthermore, when we have uncovered this formal structure of practical reasoning, we can see that it depends on something else: a conception of the person. In order to engage in reasoning of this kind, identified by the formal principles that we have uncovered within it (by following our transcendental strategy), we have to be capable of thinking about ourselves in a certain way. Each person must think of himself or herself as a single person extended through time and as merely one person among others who are equally real.

Transcendental arguments, as usually conceived of, are weapons against the philosophical sceptic.[3] Their aim, as characterized by Kant, is to identify some very weak assumption that the sceptic cannot deny and to use the method of transcendental argument to uncover surprisingly strong further assumptions that the sceptic cannot consistently deny either. That is not the only way of understanding this use of transcendental arguments, and perhaps it is not the most helpful. However, it worth noting at the outset that Nagel's use of this argument strategy in *The Possibility of Altruism* is consonant with his earlier, Strawsonian treatment of scepticism as being irrefutable, but as a view against which we can offer reasonable considerations.[4] These considerations take the form of noting that the sceptical position imposes certain revisionary costs on our ordinary conceptual scheme.[5] Throughout *The Possibility of Altruism* Nagel argues against his sceptical opponent in precisely the same way: the sceptic, in this case, is a person who denies that reason can be distinctively practical. Those who deny that we are committed to the principles that Nagel identifies and the self-conceptions attached to them cannot be shown to be wrong. However, it can be shown that such a sceptic has to pay an unacceptable price in holding their views. The nature of this cost, in the case of the practical, is an analogue of solipsism that Nagel calls "dissociation".

The solipsist believes that his or her mind is the only mind that exists. One path to this conclusion begins from the fact, noted in Chapter 3, that our basic acquaintance with the mind is in our own first-personal case. The solipsist then reasons that since her access to the minds of others is via third-personal evidence, not direct acquaintance, it is only rational to believe that her own mind exists. (Given, that is, that the inference that other minds exist has an unverifiable conclusion.) Solipsism is, then, a very general theoretical belief. Nagel tries to describe its practical analogue, namely, dissociation. Dissociation is the situation of not being able to ascribe the same mental states to oneself in the third person as one can in the first person. The reasons that Nagel gives for why a person might find oneself in this predicament are explained below.

It is helpful to begin the exposition of Nagel's main argument in *The Possibility of Altruism* by identifying the rival view that Nagel constantly seeks to undermine throughout the book. This view seems to him to be independently plausible and to threaten the argument of the book by getting the same result for less. This alternative view lacks an accurate characterization, so I shall call it "simple motivational theory".[6] The simple motivational theory states that there seems to be a practical use of reason, but that this appearance is misleading. Both sides to this dispute agree that practicality involves motivation in the sense of involving desire. As Nagel himself very clearly states, "it is a mystery how one could account for the motivational source of ethical action without referring to desires" (*PA*: 4).[7] But the way that simple motivation theory adds practicality to practical reasoning is by stating that some of the elements about which we reason are intrinsically motivational states; there is nothing practical about the *reasoning*.

In any case of reasoning, we can draw a distinction between the elements in the reasoning and the inferential principles that guide our steps between the elements. Whereas Nagel focuses on the implicit formal principles governing inference and the conception of the person associated with them, the simple motivational theory asserts that we can make do with much less. We simply add intrinsically motivational states to the elements about which we reason. These are states such that rationally to be motivated by them one simply has to be *in* them. For the simple motivational theorist there is only one kind of reasoning, but it is reasoning about states of two kinds. These states are beliefs and desires or, on a more sophisticated proposal, states with a belief-like "direction of fit" and states with a desire-like "direction of fit".[8] The intuitive idea behind this metaphor is that beliefs aim to fit the world whereas our desires seek a world that fits them. Accordingly, practical reasoning is practical if it in some way involves intrinsically motivating states, paradigmatically, desires.[9]

It is worth bearing in mind that the argument between Nagel and simple motivational theory is over the role of *structure* in practical reasoning, namely, those formal elements that can be picked out by transcendental argument. Both sides to this argument agree that the practical use of reason essentially involves desire. It looks, then, as if there is no disagreement between Nagel and the simple motivational theorist. But the differences run very deep: Nagel's conception of what desires are locates them in a very different context from that of the simple motivational theorist.

For the simple motivational theorist the rational motivation of action is explained by the distinctive role of a mental state within that process of reasoning: desires are intrinsically motivating. In this competing theory, desires can motivate rational action simply by occurring. This distinctive role is "just given". For Nagel, it is the entire complex itself, namely, the implementation of the formal structures of reasoning, the contents within them (both desires and beliefs) and their mutual rational relationship that constitutes rational motivation. Desires figure in this more complex account, but they do so in two ways: either they are motivated by a reason or they are unmotivated. (In the latter case they initiate a chain of reasoning.) It is this latter case that *seems* to support the diagnosis of the simple motivational theorist that desires can simply occur and nevertheless rationally motivate action. However, the correct explanation is that the "brute" occurrence of a desire presupposes all the complex stage-setting involved in understanding a person as a practically rational agent. Such a person implements in her reasoning the formally characterizable principles of good reasoning that transform the occurrence of a desire into a basic reason for action. Without this more expansive view we cannot explain what we mean by the rational inescapability of some reasons, reasons from which (as Nagel famously put it) one cannot "beg off" (*PA*: 4). In this case the idea of rational inescapability is minimally the thought that some reasons have the feature that they apply to everyone. More ambitiously, the claim that moral reasons are rationally inescapable suggests a deeper explanation of that fact. That deeper explanation is that the wide scope of application to everyone arises because reasons of this kind apply to people independently of the contingencies of how they happen to be motivated (Brink 1997).

Here is a simple example of practical reasoning: reasoning prudentially about your own interests in the case of posting the premium on your insurance policy. There is an electrical fault in your flat that will, in ten months time, cause a fire that will destroy much of your property. You do not know this now. What you do know now is that your home insurance policy, which specifically covers fire damage caused by such faults, is now due for renewal. You are at the post-box, about to post the insurance company a substantial annual premium when you hesitate. You reflect on how much money this cheque is for and you think about other things that you want more immediately.

You were planning to upgrade to a new mobile phone, but when this cheque goes in the post you will not be able to afford that for several months. You are assailed by doubts and ask yourself: do I really want to post this now? What do I most want?

As I have described the example, you will in ten months' time face a very serious financial loss when fire damages your flat. At that point you will be very pleased indeed if, ten months before, you had posted your insurance premium and continued your policy. Precisely what you will want at that time is for someone to give you enough money to cover the replacement value of your damaged property. If, at the time of posting your premium, you could see what will happen to you in the future, you would see that you have a very good reason to post the premium. However, we are temporally restricted creatures who occupy a single point in time and our foreknowledge is limited. What differing accounts of your decision to post the premium will be offered by the simple motivational theorist and by Nagel in *The Possibility of Altruism*?

The simple motivational theorist agrees that this is a practical decision: you are either going to post this envelope or not. And for her, such practical decisions depend on the presence of motivational states, that are simply given, and on their deliberative weight. So the only question is: what do you most want, at the time, to do? On reflection you decide that what you *most* want is the new mobile phone; you tear up the envelope, cheque and all, and do not renew your policy.

As I have set up the example, we can see that you have made a serious error. In ten months' time your nearly new mobile phone is going to be auctioned on the internet as you try to recoup your losses. But what kind of mistake was it? What the simple motivational theorist says seems incontrovertible. How could you be guided, in practical matters, by anything other than what, at the time, you most want to do? On the other hand, we can see the force of the thought that you made a serious practical mistake. The strength of your current desires when you considered posting the cheque did not align with what you had most reason to do.

Nagel's counter-argument against simple motivational theory begins with a concession: there are certainly cases that *seem* to meet the simple motivational theorist's description. It is a hot day and you are reading in a hammock. You suddenly want a cold drink. You were engrossed in your book, but you are suddenly thirsty. You start to think about how best to get a cold drink. Of course desires *can* be like this. They can be the beginning of a piece of practical reasoning;

they can, as Nagel puts it, occur *unmotivated.*[10] The desire is not inexplicable; you were not assailed by it in your hammock as you would be if a branch fell off the tree above you and struck you on the head. We can make perfect sense of a person on a hot day wanting a cold drink. (You did not suddenly want to drink warm green paint, for example [Anscombe 1957: 70].) But while the desire is intelligible, it does not rest on anything else. You begin your practical reasoning from it, and it is the element from which you begin to reason. If we described your process of reasoning by writing it down, it would be the content of the first line. That kind of case encourages the simple motivational theorist in her account of the phenomenon; but that is a mistake. Even in this case, Nagel argues, the simple motivational theorist gets it wrong. The state that begins practical reasoning can be unmotivated, but it must be intelligible. For it to be a good reason is for it to be enmeshed in a rational process that is structured by formal principles: it cannot do all that work by being simply given.[11]

Furthermore, not all reasoning about practice, Nagel argues, can be like this, as the case of the insurance premium shows. In that case you made a mistake and you did so by following the simple motivational theorist's advice and asking yourself simply: what do I most want, now? The case has been set up such that you have most reason to pay your premium. Slightly fancifully, we can put the case like this: in ten months' time, standing in your fire-damaged flat, the strength of your regret will correlate with the strength of your wanting, then, to have acted differently now. How can we channel the strength of that desire back into your present decision?

Nagel thinks we need to do three things: change our psychology of desire, change our view of the relation between reasons and desires, and notice the dependence of this piece of good reasoning on an assumption about how we must think of ourselves. On the first point, we need to remind ourselves that desires are not simple, brute, original existences that simply happen to one (analogous, on this view of them, to simple bodily sensations). They are complex states that exhibit the feature of intentionality, of directedness to an object, and they play a functional role in whole stretches of reasoning. Even one's simple desire for a cold drink on a hot day has an intentional object, specifiable with a "that" clause; what one wants is *a hot drink on a cold day.* Desires have a content, on which they are directed, in the way that beliefs have a content on which they are directed and in a way sensations do not. This is what philosophers mean when they refer to many states of mind as propositional attitudes. Clearly, we are starting to theorize common-sense psychology here (as we did in previous chapters), but all that Nagel needs from this idea for present purposes is the thought that we can separate *what* is thought about from *how* a particular individual thinks about it. We can now say that for a desire to be a reason is for it to be rationalized by its propositional object; for it to be a good reason is for it to present your attainment of that object favourably (McDowell 2001: 79).

However, there are good reasons for believing things, too. Good evidence presents you with good reasons for something you know. But there is nothing in that parallel account about practicality. All that could secure this practicality, Nagel argues, is that acceptance of the content of your reason *is* to acquire a motivation to do what it requires: "the presence of a motivation for acting morally is guaranteed by the truth of ethical propositions themselves" (*PA*: 7). The most helpful way to appreciate this point is as the most fundamental assumption we can make here: this *constitutes* practicality in the use of reason.

But now we can make a further point: some desires are not like your sudden desire for a hot drink on a cold day. Those are unmotivated desires that do not depend on any prior condition. But some desires are motivated: they are motivated by your believing that you have a good reason to do something. We cannot leave desires out of practical reasoning; that would be absurd. But some desires are rationally motivated. Nagel does not mean by this the curiously indirect thought that believing that you have a good reason necessarily gives you a motive. Instead the thought is that in accepting a good reason you necessarily have a motive.[12] That must be the case if some reasoning is to be practical, and the "must" in this claim is vindicated by transcendental argument. This thesis is standardly called "motivational internalism": it is the claim that acceptance of the truth of a practical judgement necessarily generates a corresponding motive.[13]

In summary, the basic disagreement between Nagel and the simple motivational theorist is over what can be meant by the practical use of reason. For the simple motivational theorist this question is settled by pointing, within common-sense folk psychology, to a class of intrinsically motivational states. The argument is not whether these are simple, unstructured, "motives", an internal motivational push or more complex states directed to a proposition (although Nagel clearly has views about that issue, too).[14] The question is whether these simple motivational states can explain what needs explaining. What needs explaining is the constitutive question: what makes practical reasoning practical? For Nagel, it is the complex role that a mental state plays in a process that exhibits the right (formal) structure that constitutes the practical use of reason. In rejecting the simple motivational theorist's overly simple account of motivation, Nagel does not deny that practical reasoning involves desire (motivated or unmotivated). The point is that acceptance of a good reason necessarily generates a motivation; otherwise acceptance of a good reason would be left hanging, waiting an independent motivational state to be present, before it could qualify as a practical exercise of reason.

Nagel's objection to the competing picture of practical reasoning offered by the simple motivational theorist is that it is, at least, explanatorily redundant and, at most, dubiously intelligible. In the context of reasoning about practice, coming to your best overall conclusion about what to do *is* to come to a conclusion that is intrinsically motivating. The alternative picture is that you come to your best overall conclusion, but whether you act or not depends on the presence or absence of an independent, intrinsically motivating state. But suppose this internal psychological mechanism that supplies simple motivations misfires: you come to your best overall practical conclusion, but do not act because this independent state simply does not arise. In this case you are clearly open to rational criticism: you failed to act on a reason that was, *ex hypothesi*, your best reason. "What", your exasperated friend or adviser asks after the fact, "were you waiting for?" Answering "I was waiting for the desire to do it" might, depending on context, be comical or tragic. Either way it seems a caricature of the practical use of reason.

Suppose your motivation-supplying mechanism misfires in another way: every five minutes throughout the day, without prior warning, you suddenly get an overwhelming urge to drink warm green paint. Even if this is an intrinsically motivational state, it gives you no reason to act on it; indeed, the reason it does give you is to try to get rid of it. Because it cannot be made sense of within the overall pattern of your practical concerns, it is not intelligible: the simple motivational theorist is wrong to think it can do its motivational work simply by *occurring*.[15] It can only play that role within a pattern of practical reasoning and a pattern exhibited by the right kind of agent. The first kind of case shows that such a conception of motivation is redundant: we do not need it to explain what needs explaining. The second raises the question of whether we can so much as make sense of this as an explanation of the practicality of reasoning.

Timelessness and a unified self-conception

In the example of the insurance premium it seems that you are making a serious practical error. Why? Because a future reason of yours is not being appropriately reflected in your current desires. When you elected not to post the premium payment that would have been responsible for your future reason to pay for replacement goods being met, you were guided by what you most wanted to do at the time. However, it now seems that the strength of that desire was not a reliable guide to what you had most reason to do. That is because it played the wrong kind of role in your reasoning: your focus should have been on the desire's objective content. That is not to discount the desire; it is to give it appropriate weight in your deliberations. This weight stems from its objective content. What is "objective content"? At this stage of Nagel's work (and this is one of his earliest uses of the contrast between the "objective" and the "subjective"), the terms "objective content" and "subjective content" are applied solely to *all* of one's pre-reflective motivations. They involve the application of a reflective test to those subjective motivations in order to see which of them is, in fact, a good reason.

The intuitive idea is this. You currently have a wide range of motivationally effective states that would if the occasion arose, figure in your reasoning as, at least, *prima facie* reasons.[16] Call these your subjective motivations. There are three characteristics of these motivations: they are yours, they are yours now and they have objects. When they function as reasons they show attainment of that object in a favourable light. In the case of prudence, Nagel's idea is that if a subjective motivation really is a reason for you, we have to see its reason-giving force as, in a sense, *timeless*. Going back to the insurance premium example, the simple motivational theorist exploits the thought that all that could move you are your current desires because they are all that can occur *now*. But reflection on the case shows precisely what is wrong with that: it is your future reason that gives you a reason, now, to post the premium even if it is not what you most want to do. In the balance of conflicting reasons you ought to want to do what you have most reason to do, namely, to pay your premium. Therefore, your only current desires that are relevant are those motivated by your future (timeless) reason. It is the reason that is doing the work, via the current desires that it motivates, in marked contrast to the simple motivational theorist's competing picture.

This can seem highly implausible: how can there be rational "action at a distance"? How can a future reason of yours exert such control over your current action? Nagel's response is that it is not this thesis that is counter-intuitive, but its denial. He gives the example of intending to travel to Italy, knowing that he will require some rudimentary knowledge of Italian, but doing absolutely nothing about it before his arrival (*PA*: 58–9). This does not seem, to us, an example of a practically rational agent. It is a feature of rational agents that they have a capacity to bind their will, in a non-alienating way, by taking rational decisions about their own future. This example highlights the point precisely by describing this completely opposite case where your future reason fails to exert any control over your present actions (Pink 1996; Bratman 1999).[17] We take it, on the contrary, that forming a reasons-supported intention, now, to carry out some action in the future simply *is* what it is to exert rational control over one's future action (Pink 1996).

Nagel also wants to emphasize, in the insurance premium case, how one must think about oneself for this example to be plausible. You must think of yourself as a single person extended through time in order to explain your rational agency. The issue of how we can conceive of a person as diachronically identical through time is itself a hotly contested philosophical problem, as was noted in Chapter 3, so we can exploit Nagel's transcendental strategy to hedge about his claim here. It is part of how we conceive of ourselves, in our ordinary ways of thinking about rational agents, that if we are to take people as rational agents who can bind their will by taking rational decisions, then we must be able to think of ourselves as a unified agent through time.[18]

If this seems counter-intuitive, consider its opposite. If we replace diachronically unified agents with agent stages (for example, by splitting people into temporal stages of themselves), how does *each of the stages* succeed in binding each other through time by forming intentions based on reasons? Suppose that when you deliberate about whether to pay your insurance premium you are not strictly and literally the same person as the one who will, in ten months' time, have good reason to replace all of his or her possessions at the insurance company's expense. You and that future person are related as person stages, with whatever qualifications are required to specify that you and that person stage are so related that this future stage is a future stage of you and not of anyone else. (This proposal replaces strict identity with a looser relation as we saw Parfit suggest in Chapter

3.) How does a reason for that future person stage become a reason for you now?

If we try to model this relation in terms of the relationship between you and other rational agents who exist at the same time as you, we might give answers such as the following: you accept the future person's reason because you trust him or her, or accept his or her testimony.[19] But all such proposals fall to a simple, but devastating, objection: trust and testimony are based on rational grounds, and this move simply launches an infinite regress.[20] If your current reason is based on that of a future person stage of you because you trust her, for example, what explains that fact? You trust her because she is independently well placed to grasp that reason at that future time. But whatever is involved in that future person stage of you accepting a good reason, it is exactly what is involved in your directly accepting that reason now. So the thing to do is literally to "cut out the middle-man" and accept that you have an identity through time that explains the timelessness of some of your reasons!

That is why Nagel assumes that the temporal neutrality of reasons that explains the rationality of prudential judgements over time can only be true if we think of ourselves in a certain way. Associated with the principles that are implicit within reasoning about prudence is a self conception. That will prove very important for the analogy that he wants to develop with reasoning about other people's interests, namely, altruism, for that is his primary concern.

Prudence, altruism and resentment

The point of this discussion, of course, is not transcendentally to deduce the rational foundations of the insurance industry. Nagel hopes that his argument about cases such as posting your premium will seem to you rationally compelling in a case where you reason prudently about your own interests. His further aim, however, is to argue by analogy that the features uncovered in the case of prudential reasoning about your own future interests are reproduced in the case of reasoning about another person's interests. He wants to explain how it is so much as possible to act in another person's interests, that is, to act altruistically. Again, the "how so much as possible" formulation indicates that this question can only be answered by a transcendental argument.

Here, too, Nagel is very much concerned to ward off the rival explanation offered by simple motivational theory. As he points out, virtually every ethical view acknowledges altruism in the undemanding sense he seeks to describe, namely, action done for another that does not reflect any selfish or self-interested motive on one's own part (*PA*: 79). His main rival, once again, is a view that traces this kind of motivation to "indiscriminate general sentiments of sympathy or benevolence" (*PA*: 79). Nagel does not deny that there can be such a source of moral motivation, but to be genuine reasons they must be cashed out in terms of objective principles that also supply motivation when these contingencies of motivation are *not* present. There is a formal structure implicit within any system of practical reasons, such that those genuine reasons operative within it can be directly motivating. In the sense I have already described in the case of prudence, acceptance that you have a good *moral* reason suffices to motivate the virtuous person. A standing repository of independent, intrinsically motivating states is simply redundant.[21]

Nagel is aware of the serious point of disanalogy between prudential and altruistic reasoning: even in the insurance case, where your present desires were a poor guide to your own best future reason, we were dealing with temporal perspectives on *your* life. However disparate the perspectives, they were all perspectives from your standpoint. But altruism of the kind that interests Nagel is about different people. Indeed, as a student of Rawls, the separateness of people and their individual lives is something that Nagel is at pains to emphasize throughout his work (Rawls 1971). (Its importance in the normative ethical theory described in *The View from Nowhere* will be explained in Chapter 6.) So we can have, at best, an argument from analogy between prudential and altruistic reasoning, and there is a point of disanalogy that is so striking as to be unavoidable. When you act for another person's sake, surely this reason must be based on something in *you*. Simple motivational theory supplies the answer that if you act for another person's sake, then that is because you want to do so; the action depends on your current desires and their comparative strength. And, as Nagel notes, this is not to imply that even the most altruistic action is covertly self-interested; he notes Butler's point that when I want a person's happiness for her own sake, what I want is her happiness, not the satisfaction of my desire that she be happy (*PA*: 81 n.1).

Nagel responds to these countervailing intuitions with an argument structurally similar to his argument in the case of prudence: what makes practical reasoning, as such, so much as possible in the case of altruistic motivation? The answer is, once again, formal principles of practical reasoning and an associated self-conception as oneself among other people who are equally real. He repeats the arguments levelled against the simple motivational view of prudence in which what you have most prudential reason to do is determined by the strength of your current desires. This is transformed, in this case, into the view that you have a reason to help another person for her own sake if that is what you most want. Such a view, he argues, mistakes how unmotivated desires work for how motivated desires work. The simple motivational view does not even raise the questions of how desires are possible and it lacks appropriately broad scope.

The clue to the correct view, Nagel suggests, is the experience of resenting something done to you (*PA*: 83, 145; Wallace 2007). When you resent something done to you, you do not merely express the view that you did not want it done, did not like it and that you did not want the other person to act as she did. That, it seems, does not go far enough. Resentment is based on the thought that there was a *reason* for that person not to act unkindly to you. It was a reason plainly available to her such that you could reasonably expect her to have respected that fact. You do not just dislike her action towards you; you resent it in a way that cannot be captured solely through talk about her or your wants. Intuitively, resentment as opposed to dislike has a ground, namely, a reason that is equally available to both parties. It is this reason that captures the idea of being wronged *by* someone.

This, Nagel thinks, is the nerve behind "if I were you" arguments in ethics:

> The argument appeals to a *judgement* that you would make in the hypothetical case, a judgement applying a general principle which is relevant to the present case as well. It is a question not of compassion, but of simply connecting, in order to see what one's attitudes commit one to. (*PA*: 83)

Recognizing these feelings in one's own case depends, once more, on seeing oneself as a person among others equally real and of the possibility of seeing things from the other person's point of view. Your resentment is grounded on the fact that there was a reason not to harm you that was available to the other person. But what does that imply about your own case? That you see your not being harmed as, itself, something of intersubjective importance: it grounds a claim on other people.

But is it true, in this case, that one can detach from the intersubjective importance of the reason not to harm you the fact that you are its object, that your "needs, actions and desires" ground a reason that is not *particularly* yours? Nagel thinks this *is* implicit in the very idea that your treatment is something you resent. Does it not, thereby, have to figure in the deliberations of the other person as a reason for anyone? It is not just that I do not want to be harmed. I resent it because there is a reason for it not to occur. That reason is at least shareable between me and the wrongdoer who harms me. Nagel argues that this only makes sense if the reason is a reason for anyone such that the roles of wrongdoer and victim can be reversed. Your own desires and interests are, therefore, only "worthy of consideration" if they ground reasons that are *anyone's* and not merely yours (*PA*: 84).

Nagel thinks that it does not require any argument to persuade you to take up that view of your own case. It is simply intuitively evident to you. If that is correct, then altruism as Nagel seeks to characterize it follows simply and directly from that intuition. You merely need to direct that very same attitude to the desires and interests of another person's as being as "worthy of consideration" *as* anyone's. But if we are blind to that argument, we can be brought to see its force by reflecting on the presuppositions of resentment and the basis of "If I were you" thinking. Those presuppositions are the parallel, in ethics, of the considerations that made sense of the rationality of prudential judgements whose force does not depend on the strength of what you currently want. That is the core of an argument that Nagel develops at much greater length. I shall now describe it in further detail.

Formulating Nagel's test

I shall begin with some of Nagel's comments about the relation between his view and previous discussions in ethics of the nature of ethical egoism. This is, as it were, a historical aside given that Nagel has already conceded to the simple motivational theorist Joseph Butler's point that if I want your good, what I want is your good for your own sake, not the satisfaction of my desire. This implies that the simple motivational theorist is not an egoist and can allow the content of desires to be non-egoistic: an important concession. But there is a dialectical point to be registered in Nagel's discussion, namely, that ethical egoism contrasts with altruism in a way that can be illuminated by Nagel's previous discussion of prudential reasoning. Egoism contrasts with altruism just as, in the discussion of prudence, dated reasons contrasted with timeless reasons (*PA*: 84). Nagel's discussion tries to preserve, point by point, the analogy between the rationality of prudence and the rationality of altruism.

Furthermore, Nagel's discussion of egoism involves one of the most famous passages in *The Possibility of Altruism* worth quoting for its intrinsic interest as a summary of his basic intuition:

> An egoist who needs help, before concluding that anyone else has reason to assist him, must be able to answer the question "What's it to him?" ... The pain which gives him a reason to remove his gouty toes from under another person's heel does not in itself give the other any reason to remove the heel, since it is not his pain. Anyone who thinks he is an egoist should imagine himself in either role in such a situation. Can he truly affirm that the owner of the heel has no reason to remove it from the gouty toes? Particularly if he owns the toes, it shows a rare detachment not to regard the pain as simply *in itself a bad thing*, which there is *reason for anyone to avert*. It is difficult, in other words, to resist the tendency to *objectify the negative value* which one assigns to pain, or would assign to it if one experienced it, *regarding the identity of its owner as irrelevant*. (*PA*: 85, emphasis added)

Nagel's foundational thought is well exhibited here: objectification of intrinsic value or disvalue is to treat it as good or bad in itself (such that the particularity of its owner is not relevant) and to treat it as generating reasons of wide practical scope that apply to anyone. The egoist claims that a person's interest can only be the object of the altruistic concern of any other person's if it is in the latter's interest to be so concerned. Nagel finds this psychologically very implausible: it commits the egoist to saying very odd things when she is, herself, victimized by another's wrongdoing directed at her.

The starting-point of Nagel's own argument is one's own first-personal case. His derivation of a "requirement of universality of practical principles" begins from there. Just as prudential reasoning depended on the timelessness of reasons, so altruism is based on an analogous formal principle. Nagel calls this formal principle the requirement of objectivity: "that all reasons be construable as expressing objective rather than subjective values" (*PA*: 88). (His central aim is to substantiate this use of the phrase "rather than".) This formal principle is, in turn, the "practical expression" of an underlying conception of the person. That conception is that one is "merely one person among others, and of others as persons in just as full a sense [as oneself]" (*PA*: 88). Nagel draws here on an idea discussed in the previous chapter, namely, that our idea of the mind is an inherently general one. The way in which this idea is applied here is to support the view that thinking in an objective way about oneself is interdependent with thinking of other people as real people with minds and perspectives on the world like one's own. I noted in Chapter 3 that Nagel thinks the conceptual problem of other minds is more fundamental than its epistemological counterpart.[22]

Since Nagel's method is that of transcendental argument, it must begin from an assumed state of affairs whose prior conditions are identified by regressive argument. Nagel's starting point is that people do have "primary reasons for action". If they pursue their own interest, then the possibility of acting for the sake of another person's interest can be demonstrated to them. In order both to enable and to streamline his argument Nagel makes a range of assumptions that structure his discussion.

His first assumption is that all actions can be represented as events. In a way that seems counter-intuitive to common sense, Nagel regiments all talk of actions into a different vocabulary where an action is the event that is identical to someone's promotion of a state of affairs (an outcome). This is taken also to be true for the limiting case where actions are done for their own sake. (This latter case is treated as one in which actions promote their own occurrence.) His second assumption is that all reasons are derived from principles. Thirdly, all principles are universal in form and take as their scope all people. Derivatively, all reasons are universal too: for every token reason there corresponds a predicate, *R*, such that it figures in a universally quantified proposition of the form:

> Every reason is a predicate *R* such that for all persons *p* and events *A*, if *R* is true of *A*, then *p* has prima facie reason to promote *A*. (*PA*: 47)

Where, then, does the crucial distinction between objectivity and subjectivity apply? It applies to the *scope of application* of a reason that is discernible within the scope of the universal quantification. The full definition is as follows:

> Formally, a subjective reason is one whose defining predicate *R* contains a free occurrence of the variable *p*. (The free-agent variable will, of course, be free only *within R*; it will be bound by the universal quantification over persons which governs the

> entire formula.) All universal reasons and principles expressible in terms of the basic formula either contain a free-agent variable or they do not. The former are subjective; the later will be called objective. (*PA*: 90)

This obviously calls for a good deal of explanation.

First, Nagel uses the terminology of "bound variables", taken from logic, to capture an idea that is more easily grasped in ordinary language, namely, anaphoric reference. Anaphoric expressions "pick up" a reference that has been already established by another referring term, such that the two expressions are referentially dependent on each other. Suppose I tell you that "Jack went up the hill and he is tired". In the two phrases "Jack went up the hill" and "he is tired", in a given context of use we can take the "he" in the second clause to refer back to the referent picked out by the use of "Jack" in the first clause. So that which Nagel intends by appealing to bound variables in the expressions of reasons derived from his principles is to clarify whether the reasons apply to anyone, or have an "open" reference that needs to be "picked up". That would involve particularizing reference to an individual agent. But it is important to note that this point is subsidiary to the universality of Nagelian principles: this issue of open or closed reference occurs in reasons expressions corresponding to principles, not in the principles themselves. Furthermore, all reasons expressions begin with a universal quantification over all agents and events. The issue is whether, within the scope of that quantification, an "agent variable" occurs "free" (with an open reference) or "bound" (with a reference that has been determined).

Secondly, there is the issue of substance behind the terminology: subjective reasons are those that give "distinct but related ends of action for different individuals". What distinction is this account trying to capture? The intuitive difference is between a reason such as this:

> Everyone has reason to promote the happiness of parents.

and a reason such as this:

> Every child has reason to promote the happiness of his or her own parents.

Statements of reasons, then, but not the principles corresponding to them, can restrict their scope of application in a certain way. I shall call this idea that of the "practical scope" of a reason. Ordinary language is not really sensitive to this distinction; we tend to speak indiscriminately about reasons being "for" people. Nagel is explicit, however, that classifying principles using his terminology is not merely a matter of grammar, but primarily a matter of interpretation. A single sentence might ambiguously express either an objective or a subjective principle or reason, and only interpretation can determine which reading is the more plausible.

Reasonably enough, Nagel draws on his own theoretical account to allow him to disambiguate that kind of sentence, namely, whether a sentence such as:

> Everyone should improve his mind.

can be read subjectively. If it is read subjectively, then it gives the person picked out by the pronoun "his" a reason to improve his own mind, but does not give anyone else a reason to improve that person's mind. Furthermore, it does not give anyone else a reason to improve their *own* mind. If we interpret the sentence in that way, then in our interpretation we decide that the "free agent variable" in the sentence makes a particularizing reference to the subject of the sentence in such a way that that person's reason is restricted. That interpretation of the reason ascription is such that it "prevents the transmission of derivative influence to any acts of another person" (*PA*: 93). This is very important to the formulation of Nagel's theory of practical objectivity that I shall describe in the next section.

However, Nagel claims that the same token sentence can be read objectively if "it assigns *objective* value to the pursuit of mental self-improvement" (*PA*: 93). Assigning objective value corresponds to assigning the reason wide scope because objective values can transmit their "derivative influence" across agents. This asserted equivalence is very important for the arguments both of *The Possibility of Altruism* and of the later *The View from Nowhere*: objective values and wide practical scope are coextensive. They occur in all and only the same cases, and the wide scope is explained by the objectivity of the value.

I do not think anyone could pretend that the ideas Nagel is trying to fix here are clear. Aware that his discussion has been a very abstract one, Nagel helpfully gives several examples of principles intended to illustrate the rationale for classifying each as objective or subjective. Each covers a case where G. E. Moore is crossing the road and takes evasive action to avoid being run over. What kind of reason is this? We need to examine the principle from which it is derived.

First are Nagel's terminological stipulations, which I have already described: the reason is the reason for an event, where the event promotes a state of affairs in which G. E. Moore stays alive. Secondly, all principles are universal quantifications over persons and events. Here are some candidate principles from which the reason could be derived. In each case they are informally specified and then formally specified in the manner Nagel suggests:

(1a) That the act will prolong G. E. Moore's life.

Rewritten to bring out the interpretation of the sentence as:

(1b) For all persons, and for all events, (if an event will promote Moore's life, then a person has reason to promote that event).

Compare:

(2a) That the act will prolong his life.

Rewritten as:

(2b) For all persons, and for all events, (if an event will promote a person's life, then that person has reason to promote that event, i.e. promote his own life).

Finally:

(3a) That the act will prolong someone's life.

Rewritten as:

(3b) For all persons and for all events, (if [there is at least one *q*] such that the event will promote *q*'s life, then any person has reason to promote that event).

According to Nagel, principles (1) and (3) are objective, but (2) is subjective. Why is this?

Principle (2) is subjective because the word "his" is a free agent-variable. Following the pattern of analysis described above, when one interprets principle (2) as subjective, one interprets the particularizing reference to an individual in this sentence in such a way that the reason ascribed to that person is the following: that the individual concerned has reason solely to promote his *own* life.

By contrast there is, as Nagel immediately comments, "no open reference to the doer" in the objective principles (*PA*: 91). They are reasons to bring something about that are reasons for anyone. That practical scope is the key to these interpretations can be brought out by considering a borderline case.

In this case different valid interpretations can yield either a subjective or an objective interpretation of the principle.

> (4a) That the act is one that will promote the life of its agent.

It could be given exactly the same reading as (2a) and rewritten in the same way:

> For all persons, and for all events, (if an event will promote a person's life, then that person has reason to promote that event, i.e. promote his own life).

But Nagel argues that it can also legitimately be rewritten as:

> For all persons, and for all events, (if *A* is an act which will promote the life of its agent, then *p* has reason to promote *A*).

What is the difference between these two interpretations? The first is directly analogous to the interpretation of sentence (2a), so it is being treated as subjective in the way that sentence (2a) is treated. However, there is an equally permissible objective interpretation of the same sentence. What is the difference here?

It is the difference between a case where an agent has reason only to prolong his own life and a case where anyone has a reason to prolong the life of the agent performing an act. This, of course, covers the agent's own reason but its scope transcends that. It gives to anyone who is an agent of an act of that kind a reason to promote his or her own life. There is a reflexive reference back to the agent in this formulation, but the key issue is once again the scope of the principle: every agent has reason to perform that act that is the prolongation of his or her own life. We need to be careful, then. Reflexive reference back to an agent might be part of an objective principle: the issue is not grammar, but practical scope. How we interpret the latter is the key to these interpretations. So we need a guiding theoretical account to help us devise such interpretations, namely, Nagel's underlying model of objectivity and what it tells us about the significance of the practical scope of a reason.

Sidgwickian objectivity

Nagel's careful terminological choices and stipulations are part of the evolving dialectic of *The Possibility of Altruism*, but I think it is helpful to stand back from the argument as exposited there and identify its central assumption. That is what I shall call a Sidgwickian model of objectivity because of its origin in the work of the Victorian moral philosopher, Henry Sidgwick. Sidgwick argued in his *The Methods of Ethics* (1981) that the kinds of intuitions mobilized in the first two chapters of this book concerning the absolute conception had an ethical analogue. That metaphysical idea, applied to knowledge and belief, depended on the idea of reality as substantial, unitary and independent of us. Only such a conception would be able to discharge its distinctive explanatory role of grounding perspectival representations such that they turn out to be from no point of view in particular in a Cartesian model of objectivity. Can an analogous idea be developed for practical reasons? Sidgwick thought that it could by focusing on the idea of value.

It is helpful to contrast his view with Mill's famous "proof" of the principle of utility (Tollefsen 1999: 62). Mill argued that:

> No reason can be given why the general happiness is desirable, except that each person, so far as he believes it to be attainable, desires his own happiness. This … being a fact, we have … all the proof … that happiness is a good; that each person's happiness is a good to that person, and the general happiness, therefore, is a good to the aggregate of persons. (1969: 234)

Mill's sequence of inferences at the end of this quotation seem to Sidgwick too optimistic. His concern was this: what guarantees that an aggregate of individuals seeking their own good are, in fact, seeking the aggregate good for all persons? If we independently want moral reasons to be universal, authoritative over desire and inescapable, then we want each individual agent to be motivated by token reasons of the same type to ensure coordination between the distinct ends of action of different agents. To enforce that, we need to back up an agent's own desires with the independent good at which he or she aims. That is secured, in Sidgwick's account, by making that independent and objective good valuable "from the point of view of the universe" (1981: xx, 82, 420). It discharges this role just as the absolute conception of the world helps to explain the various perspectival representations on it.

Sidgwick does not overlook the inevitable perspectivalness of how we characterize ethics, but he uses an analogue of the basic argument for the absolute conception to show how all individual reasons have to be understood as perspectives on a single, integrated and totalizing whole in order to preserve some of the key aspects of those reasons.

In this case, however, the relevant ideal of objectivity is that of an evaluative whole: "I obtain the self-evident principle that the good of any one individual is of no more importance, from the point of view ... of the Universe, than the good of any other" (Sidgwick 1981: 382). One part of Sidgwick's view, the consequentialist part, argues that this totalizing vision of an integrated "mathematical whole" of goods is not dependent on any individual agent's point of view in particular. It can, nevertheless, motivate individuals even if that which they fragmentarily grasp as the whole good is not, in fact, their own good. The latter is a mere appearance that can be subjected to an analogue of Cartesian objectification.

Sidgwick's most famous phrase is "the point of view of the universe". He thinks that this is the only appropriately objective standpoint for action (although, foreshadowing Nagel's own hybrid theory in *The View from Nowhere*, Sidgwick acknowledges the competing demands of prudence leading to his famous "dualism of practical reason" (Brink 1992). This account of objectivity lies in the background of Nagel's arguments: it encourages an analogy between evaluations and literal perceptions. Just as one argument for the absolute conception of the world takes it that assuming the existence of that conception explains individual perspectives on it, so those practical reasons of an individual that correspond to timeless and intrinsic values are construed as perspectives on an integrated evaluative whole. As the subsequent argument will demonstrate, this assumption plays an important role in the overall argument of *The Possibility of Altruism*. It does so by providing an underlying metaphysical guarantee for Nagel's motivational internalism.

Applying Nagel's test

The stage is set for the application of the objectivity requirement to an agent's reasons:

> The thesis which I propose to defend is simply that the only acceptable reasons are objective ones; even if one operates successfully with a subjective principle, one must be able to back it up with an objective principle yielding those same reasons as well as (presumably) others. Whenever one acts for a reason, I maintain, it must be *possible* to regard oneself as acting for an objective reason, and promoting an objectively valuable end. (*PA*: 96–7)

The target of this crucial argument is the claim that altruism is not possible because all reasons are fundamentally egoistic. The egoist claims that reasons have, of their nature, restricted practical scope to the person for whom they are a reason. They are grounded in that particular person's subjective values.

Nagel repeatedly insists that the distinctions he is drawing in *The Possibility of Altruism* are purely formal. One and the same object can be viewed, evaluatively, as simply good, or as good for a particular person (where it is not simply good that that person stand in a relation to that good). That is a difference in the "formal" characterization of that value.[23] Alternatively, we can switch to the language of reasons and say that a subjective reason is a reason whose full content needs to be filled in by a particularizing reference to an agent. By contrast, an objective reason is a reason for anyone. These formal remarks, however, are ways of treating values and reasons to which we are already committed and can only be applied to evaluative commitments that we already have. Nagel repeatedly insists that *The Possibility of Altruism* does not offer a theory of value that is *not* formal. The scope of his account is very restricted because his aims are very limited: they are simply to show that altruism, acting on another person's interests, is possible.

As Nagel notes, he has entered so many qualifications to the subjective versus objective contrast that it is hard to see how his argument can involve two contradictory positions: there is no simple dichotomy between egoism and altruism. There are many non-altruistic objective principles and non-egoistic subjective principles. It looks as if what Nagel calls his "formal result" has serious limitations without a general theory of what is valuable.

Nagel concedes all this, but it is at this point that the limited scope of his argument comes to the fore: he is entitled to assume, he thinks, a great deal of common agreement on some shared values. The argument of *The Possibility of Altruism* will not work without this assumption. We all do, in fact, agree that there are some common goods, shared interests and other things valued as ends, and for Nagel's purposes that is enough. Add his formal result and the possibility of altruism will have been demonstrated. In keeping with his general treatment of scepticism, Nagel does not view denying his "formal result" as delivering anything like formal contradiction or incoherence. What he aims to show is that a person who denies Nagel's formal principle pays a high price in terms of how he or she can think about his or her practical commitments. Denying Nagel's thesis commits one to a practical analogue of solipsism, namely, dissociation.

Why does denial of Nagel's principle lead to this cost? Anyone who is already committed to some ethical reasons can legitimately interpret them as subjective reasons on one condition: that any such reason be cashed out as an objective reason. If you remain committed to a reason that fails this test, you have denied the possibility of altruism and are open to a distinctive kind of rational criticism. You are not, strictly speaking, guilty of a belief in solipsism. If you do not accept that all your subjective reasons need backing from an objective counterpart then you are *dissociated*. What does this mean? *It means that you cannot make the same judgement about yourself in the third person that you can in the first person*. That is, certainly, an odd predicament. When you deliberate, first personally, about what you ought to do, you can come to accept a subjective reason. However, finding yourself in that position produces the odd consequence that in thinking about yourself and your own deliberation, you cannot ascribe the very same reason to yourself third personally that you accepted first personally. Why not?

The answer is that Nagel's internalist connection between accepting a reason and, necessarily, being supplied with a motivation explains what he means by a "personal practical judgement" in the first person. However, only if the reason accepted from that perspective is an objective one can we see *that very same practical judgement* is available to anyone. "Anyone", here, can of course be you. But only if the reason is objective can you make the same ascription to yourself in the third person that you can in the first. You are related to yourself, in the relevant respect, just as others are related to you (and vice versa).

Doing the substantive work in the background here is the Sidgwickian notion of objectivity. Common sense might suggest to you that the first-person–third-person asymmetry in how you think about your own mind is a separate distinction from the individual–other people distinction. However, in the light of the Sidgwickian model these distinctions can be aligned. Thinking about yourself objectively is the same as thinking about yourself as if you were another person. (The discipline of objectivity is the same in the two cases.) Your reasons are not distinctively yours; if they pass the test, then they are made up of two factors, namely a value that is intrinsic and timeless and a reason that is a reason for anyone. The latter fact *explains* the truth of internalism. The reason why acceptance in the first person of a good reason necessarily generates a motive is that objective reasons carry motivational import within themselves. They simply *are* reasons for anyone. There seem to be reasons that depart from this characterization, and we should take this appearance at face value: there really are subjective reasons. But Nagel's crucial test shows that unless we can back them up with objective reasons, they will leave us dissociated. The test shows that they really are, if acceptable, only the misleading guise of objective reasons. What the model of Cartesian objectification in *The Possibility of Altruism* implies is that, if they fail Nagel's test, then they are not acceptable reasons at all.

One way to argue for Nagel's conclusion would simply have been to describe the Sidgwickian notion of objectivity and let its rationally compelling features speak for themselves. This simply is what it is to bring an intuitive notion of objectivity to bear on practice. However, Nagel's strategy in *The Possibility of Altruism* is, rather, to develop an independently compelling refutation of simple motivational theory and an attractive model of practical reasoning, to use those arguments to support his thesis of motivational internalism, and then to demonstrate how the latter is only defensible via a Sidgwickian notion of objectivity. The word "only" is important here: the aim of Nagel's transcendental argument strategy is to argue regressively through the conditions that make the idea of reason in practice possible. The concern that most troubles his critics is that this is not so: motivational internalism can be, and ought to be, defended independently of the Sidgwickian model of objectivity. That does not, strictly speaking, mean that the latter is false. Nagel could offer an independent defence of it. But, in the argument strategy of *The Possibility of Altruism*, the aim of its central transcendental argument is to identify the Sidgwickian model as an essential precondition of motivational internalism and thereby to articulate what constitutes the practical use of reason.

The argument evaluated

Nagel's argument is lengthy, complex and subtle. There is, however, in the surprisingly limited critical literature on *The Possibility of Altruism*, a single objection to the argument that seems the most important (Sturgeon 1974: 380; Darwall 1983: 125–9). It is the concern that, at a crucial juncture, Nagel's argument involves an equivocation. The overall dialectical significance of this is that one can accept his critique of simple motivational theory, the motivated–unmotivated desire distinction and indeed his internalism without accepting that the price of doing so is commitment to the Sidgwickian notion of objectivity.

The equivocation is this: it is best captured in terms of the meaning of word "judgement" (Darwall 1983: 127). That word is process–product ambiguous, as the word "construction" is in the sentence "I went downtown to see the construction". Did you go and see the process of construction or the product that has been constructed? "Judgement" is ambiguous in a parallel way: it can refer to a mental act, the exercise of a capacity of judgement, or it can refer to the object judged. In the latter sense, in philosophy, we mean the intentional content of what is grasped, such as a proposition. Consider now the formulation of the thesis of Nagel's motivational internalism. That was expressed as the claim that in judging that one had a good reason to act, one was thereby necessarily motivated to perform that act. But what two things does this principle connect? Does it necessarily connect an act of judgement to motivation, or does it necessarily connect an object of judgement (a proposition) to motivation?

On reflection it seems that the former claim is by far the more plausible. In coming to accept a good reason (judging) a person is thereby necessarily motivated in that act of judgement or acceptance. Motivation does not attach to the *proposition* in some ghostly way. Motivation is a psychological phenomenon, and the event of being motivated is necessarily generated by another psychological event, namely a person's judgement that she has a good reason. Stephen Darwall articulates the problem very clearly:

> If motivational content has to do with actual motivation or attitude, in what sense does the personal practical judgement have motivational content? Is it part of *what one judges*? Or is it part of one's *judging*, namely, the attitude that one normally has when one judges that there is reason for one to do A? Nagel's argument requires it to be part of *what* one judges, part of its content. That is what must change with one's perspective if one cannot hold true the very same things *about* oneself. But what reason do we have to believe that the attitude itself is part of *what one judges* to be true when one accepts the personal practical judgement rather than the attitude one normally has toward an act on *judging* there to be a reason to perform it?
>
> (Darwall 1983: 127–8)

But, with this ambiguity resolved, the distinctive explanation that Nagel offered for the truth of his internalist thesis no longer seems plausible. The claim was that internalism was explained by the Sidgwickian claim about objectivity because objective reasons simply are grounded on timeless and intrinsic values that support reasons of wide practical scope. They have motivational import before the agent grasps them: it is there, waiting to be grasped. But resolving the ambiguity means that we no longer have to accept that putative explanation. We can accept everything that Nagel says about the falsity of simple motivational theory, the motivated versus unmotivated desire distinction and his appealing internalism without the further commitment to Sidgwick's model.

Nagel has two responses to this argument that I shall describe and evaluate in turn. First, he explicitly considers the competing explanation and gives grounds for its rejection:

> Such an account fails to preserve the impersonal view, for the motivational content of the general subjective principle has now become simply "For each person, if I am that person, then I should act as the principle prescribes for him". But that is nothing more than the personal maxim that I should do as the principle says. Since no impersonal attitudes to one's action can derive from such a maxim, nothing has been done towards meeting the congruency condition. (*PA*: 117–18)

For Nagel, appeal to counterfactual acceptance is not enough. But the new question is whether it is his rejoinder that is question-begging in this context. His Sidgwickian account of objectivity is here simply being asserted, even though an equally good explanation of motivational internalism can be expressed in counterfactual terms. (This alternative explanation is cast in terms of what *would* follow were an appropriately configured agent to accept a true ethical proposition.) There is a Sidgwickian basis for Nagel's counter-argument. He expresses a concern already articulated in the tradition of ethical reflection within which he is working. As Christopher Tollefsen (1999: 63) notes, Kant had already expressed a concern that desire based motivation was not only too contingent, but also distributed "subjectively". In a sympathetic reconstruction of this line of argument originated by Kant and developed by Sidgwick and Nagel, Tollefsen comments:

> [Objective reasons] provide a shared motivational backing for moral norms, which could be commonly appealed to by all agents, and which could motivate without reference to the individuality

> of any agent. There is a parallel with reasons for belief: objective reasons for belief are reasons that, inter alia, are the same for different believers. This underlies a conception of science as moving from things as they appear to us, to a characterization of things independent of their subjective appearances. (*Ibid.*: 63–4)

Note the explicit analogy Tollefsen makes between a notion of objectivity derived from our conception of the physical world as a substantial and unitary whole and a conception of a world of shared reasons that can motivate without reference to the particular person that one is. But, as I have already discussed, the opponent of this whole line of thought will argue that the "point of view of the universe" simply supplies the wrong model for objectivity in the case of the practical. We do not have to see our good reasons as all elements of a single, convergent, unified conception, and that is because there is a brute difference between theoretical reasons for belief and practical reasons for action (B. Williams 1985: 67–9). It is simply a philosophical error to treat practical reasons as backed up by a unitary system of values that constitutes, as Sidgwick claimed, a totality analogous to a "mathematical whole" (B. Williams 1997c).

I concede that those sympathetic to Nicholas Sturgeon and Darwall's critique need to say more. Suppose that the acceptance of a good reason does not necessarily generate a motive in a person? Suppose that the entailed motivation simply does not occur? From Nagel's point of view the grip of morality has been weakened by making the internalist connection depend on the contingencies of the psychologies of agents. But one of the starting-points of the argument was the datum from our moral experience that moral reasons are both inescapable and rationally authoritative. That is why the overall aim of *The Possibility of Altruism* was to determine structural truths *a priori* that constrain all possible psychologies (*PA*: 13–14; Korsgaard 1996a; Thomas 2006b: 87–97). Clearly, this is a large topic, but at the very least a plausible rival view will have to supplement the account at least this far: acceptance of a good reason is necessarily motivation generating in *the right kind of agent*, namely, a virtuous person. A virtuous person is characterized precisely as a person with the right stock of concepts and power of discernment to judge the presence of good reasons and with the correct psychology, such that moral reasons are for him or her automatically inescapable (McDowell 1978; Thomas 2006b: ch. 4).

If Nagel's central argument does not succeed, is *The Possibility of Altruism* a failure? Obviously not. The book succeeds in restating, with both elegance and rigour, the distinction between motivated and unmotivated desires descended from Aristotle (Dent 1984: ch. 4). In doing so it offers a convincing account of practical reasoning and a telling critique of simple motivational theory. It connects the temporal neutrality of reasons to a conception of the agent as unified. The nerve of its argument, a Sidgwickian model of objectivity, remains independently compelling even if the precise form in which it makes altruism rationally compelling was not entirely satisfactorily worked out.

Nevertheless, one aspect of the book's importance lay in what came next: the central ideas, reinterpreted and restructured, laid the framework for Nagel's later work in *The View from Nowhere* and his hybrid ethical theory. This shift can be described as an analogue, in practice, for the shift from a Cartesian to a Hegelian model of objectivity in a theoretical context. In *The Possibility of Altruism*, subjective reasons are tolerated, but only if they turn out to be objective reasons: this is analogous to the relation between subjective appearance and reality in a Cartesian model of objectification. In *The View from Nowhere*, subjective reasons are transformed into an autonomous category of agent-relative reasons that are now placed alongside a category of agent-neutral reasons as a genuine category in their own right. This is analogous to the relation between different perspectives in a Hegelian model of objectification. However, Nagel's central controlling idea of Sidgwickian objectivity retains its central place even in this new Hegelian model of ethical objectification: agent neutrality directly expresses it, but it also exerts a controlling pressure on those reasons that ostensibly depart from it, notably in the form of tolerating them, as I shall explain in Chapter 6. A necessary preliminary to that discussion is Nagel's wider consideration of what it is to bring objectivity to bear on the will.

Chapter 5

Practical objectivity, freedom and a realistic autonomy

The preface of *The Possibility of Altruism* showed that Nagel was already beginning to revise and develop his view on the nature of reasons and ethics more generally. Further publications in ethics followed, but the next systematic presentation of his views on practical philosophy as a whole was a very influential discussion in *The View from Nowhere*. It is a wide-ranging account, focused on the idea of bringing the constraint of objectivity to bear on practice. It ranges from issues about freedom and autonomy, the subject of this chapter, to normative ethics, the subject of the next. Ethical impartialism remains the dominant approach to contemporary normative ethics, and in Nagel's work it receives a sophisticated statement and defence. I shall begin, however, with a more abstract consideration of how objectivity applies to practice via Nagel's discussion of the traditional problem of free will as that is how Nagel chooses to preface his own discussion in *The View from Nowhere*. Nagel structures his account very much as a reaction against the work of Peter Strawson, notably Strawson's well-known essay "Freedom and Resentment" (1974b). Some of the themes from Chapter 2, where I discussed Nagel's reaction against the context of Oxford philosophy of the 1960s, will be echoed in this chapter, for the issues of scepticism and responsibility are central to Nagel's analysis of the problem of free will.

The problem of freedom

Nagel initially characterizes his subject matter in the most general terms: it is the bearing of the ideal of objectivity on the practical. The problem of freedom is one aspect of this subject matter. Nagel's aim is to use his subjective–objective distinction in a way that will cast new light on how this problem is to be characterized.

The traditional problem of the freedom of the will contrasts free action with action that is causally determined. In a variation of this formulation, a distinction may be further drawn between two kinds of causation: a *sui generis* "agent causation" and event causality more generally. In the former case, an agent causation theorist argues that agents are substances, not events. Furthermore, an agent can originate a sequence of events (paradigmatically by taking a decision) and is, therefore, a cause of her free actions, but is not herself caused by anything else (Chisholm 1976; Donagan 1987). Nagel argues that this contrast is misconceived. The problem of free will arises, rather, because one can view action both from one's first-personal, subjective standpoint and from an objective or external standpoint: "The essential source of the problem is a view of persons and their actions as part of the order of nature, causally determined or not" (*VN*: 110). For Nagel, the agent causation theorist's formulation of the problem in terms of two kinds of causality misses the real point. Indeed, so does the more traditional conception of the problem as solely about how causality relates to agency. How is Nagel's dichotomy of the objective and the subjective contextualized in this discussion?

The term doing the work is "objective": Nagel gives two non-equivalent formulations of what he means in this context by an objective view. The first is that an objective view sees an agent and her actions merely as a part of nature. The second formulation is that an objective view takes a third-personal, explanatory stance towards actions as opposed to a first-personal or deliberative stance. That these distinctions do not neatly align with each other can be brought out by considering the kind of rational control of oneself that is, to a certain degree, the taking up of a third-personal and explanatory perspective. I mentioned in the previous chapter the idea of alienated action control (Pink 1996). Consider the lack of self-trust involved when you not only set an alarm clock, but also place it out of reach! That seems to be a way in which we can sometimes think about our own agency: this kind of control is in one sense alienating, but we are familiar with this kind of strategy for delivering reliance on our future self even in the absence of self-trust. It does not seem to me as clear, however, that we think of our actions as part of nature in quite the way Nagel intends. What he means is that we can always think about our actions as located in an ever-expanding conception of the world as merely a series of natural events of which our action is simply one.

Nagel argues that the most basic perspective on action for appreciating the problem of freedom is not the perspective from which you view your actions as a part of nature, but the perspective from which they seem to be *merely* parts of the natural order: "That conception ... leads to the feeling that we are not agents at all ... against this judgement the inner view of the agent rebels" (*VN*: 110). Events simply happen; our actions are events, so they simply happen, too. The way in which Nagel appeals to this "natural" description of our actions as a way of interpreting the problem of freedom seems to me problematic in way that I shall explain below.

Nagel distinguishes three distinct problems about freedom: the nature of agency, of autonomy and of responsibility. At the outset of his discussion he notes that he does not take himself to have anything to contribute to the philosophical discussion of agency. Citing the influence of Brian O'Shaughnessy's book *The Will: A Dual Aspect Theory* (1980), Nagel argues that the idea of action is simply basic and irreducible. But, while basic and irreducible, this account of action is a hybrid one in that it is conceptualized as a basic *psychophysical* category. This fact, however, does not in itself contribute to solving the problem of free agency. It is part of O'Shaughnessy's view that while action has an "internal" or mental aspect, taking oneself to be free is no guarantee of the truth of that belief. You can take yourself to be free when you are not.

Nagel's focus in *The View from Nowhere* is, therefore, on the two other ideas of autonomy and responsibility. As mentioned above, his discussion is a reaction to the position taken on the relationship between the problem of free will and the nature of responsibility by Strawson in "Freedom and Resentment" (1974b). In that essay Strawson challenged the usual understanding of how discovering that human action was part of the causal order of nature would threaten our ordinary notion of responsibility. As standardly represented in the traditional formulation of the problem of the relation between free will and moral responsibility, the moral sentiments that structure our reactions to other people are understood to be grounded on a *theory*. Furthermore, it is a theory that could be undermined by being shown to rest on a further, false belief about a presupposition of our freedom, namely, that our actions are uncaused or caused by agents in an irreducible way. The threat that determinism posed to the ordinary notion of responsibility was assumed to take precisely that form: it showed that a presupposition of our continuing to "believe in" responsibility is false. Responsibility depends on freedom, freedom depends on an absence of causation, and determinism shows that presupposition to be false. Again, in the traditional version of this problem, those opposed to this deterministic argument share with their opponents the crucial assumption that the truth or falsity of determinism is crucial to justifying ascriptions of responsibility.

Strawson responded that both sets of arguments misrepresented the nature of those ethical sentiments that he called the "reactive attitudes" (*ibid.*: 6). These attitudes form part of a standpoint of engagement, whereas the traditional discussion focuses on attitudes that involve disengaged, detached attitudes such as moral praise and blame:

> I have mentioned punishing and moral condemnation and approval ... These practices or attitudes permit, where they do not imply, a certain detachment from the actions or agents which are their objects. I want to speak ... of something else: of the non-detached attitudes and reactions of people directly involved in transaction with each other; of the attitudes of reactions of offended parties and beneficiaries; of such things as gratitude, resentment, forgiveness, love, and hurt feelings. (*Ibid.*: 4)

These attitudes are simply part of our human lives lived together; we can imagine them suspended in particular cases, for particular reasons, but it does not follow that this is because they have been locally *falsified*. They do not rest on a theory, so they cannot be shown to be false by a conflicting theory. The reactive attitudes may play an important role in constituting our shared ethical lives, but they do not do so by constituting a network of presupposed beliefs. Our shared ethical lives are implicated in a complex presupposed structure of mutual reactions, but these reactions are ethical sentiments, not beliefs. If they do not rest on a belief, then they cannot be falsified; to assume that they can be merely shows that the problem has been misrepresented in a particular way – it has been over rationalized and presented as an issue about belief whereas it presupposes a basis in sentiment (*ibid.*: 24).

The issue of objectivity is transformed, in Strawson's discussion, into the prospects for a stance of objectification. The reactive attitudes structure a stance that we take towards others that we can intelligibly suspend in particular cases, replacing it with an objectified stance that we take up towards others when we view them as subjects for treatment and control. Developing the most interesting version of the "ordinary language" response to scepticism, Strawson argued that people could be normally judged to be responsible or judged to be competent subjects for moral assessment. However, failures in such competence are precisely failures in particular ways, or a placing of an agent entirely outside the scope of the attitudes (*ibid.*: 2–3, 7, 16–17). There seems to me be a significant convergence here between Strawson's views and those of Austin: our default position is that we take people to be competent, absent some specific excusing condition that explains a particular failure of responsibility in the case of a particular action (Austin 1961b). The shift to the objectified stance occurs when we no longer judge a person to be competent at all. The overall effect of Strawson's account is to protect what matters in our ordinary way of thinking about freedom and responsibility from any general threat arising from the truth of a metaphysical thesis, such as the global truth of determinism (Strawson 1974b: 11). In so far as Strawson's conclusion is reassuring or optimistic, Nagel's discussion seeks to challenge it as complacent just as he judged any reaction to scepticism that was grounded in our actual conceptual scheme as complacent.[1]

Nagel opens his discussion by explicitly contrasting his views with Strawson's. Nagel argues that there is a single way in which "objectivity threatens ordinary assumptions about human freedom", but that this threat motivates two separate problems (*VN*: 111): the problem of autonomy in the case of our own freedom and the problem of responsibility in the case of the freedom of others. However, to appreciate the way in which objectivity threatens these ordinary assumptions one needs to focus on the formulation that actions conceived of objectively are conceived of solely as events in an increasingly comprehensive view of the natural order. Once again, causality is not the issue in this argument:

> An objective view of actions as events in the natural order (determined or not) produces a sense of impotence and futility with respect to what we do ourselves. It also undermines certain basic attitudes toward all agents – those reactive attitudes ... that are conditional on the attribution of responsibility. (*VN*: 111–12)

Noting that Strawson's discussion focuses primarily on the latter, Nagel continues:

> The threat to our conception of our own actions ... is equally important and equally deserving of [being the problem of free

> will]. The same external view that poses a threat to my own autonomy also threatens my sense of the autonomy of others, and this in turn makes them come to seem inappropriate objects of admiration and contempt, resentment and gratitude, blame and praise. (*VN*: 112)

Nagel also notes, at the outset, that the traditional problem of free will is one of the most recalcitrant of philosophical problems and that he does not believe that any of the existing options put forward as a solution or a dissolution of this problem are particularly plausible. The reason for this is that it is "impossible to give a coherent account of the internal view of action which is under threat" (*VN*: 112–13). I will now describe the way in which this account of an objective view of human actions undermines not just our view of autonomy, but also our view of responsibility. I shall then question whether this is the right way to set up the problem.

The problem of autonomy

Nagel argues that the problem of autonomy arises when we try to combine an internal, deliberative and first-personal perspective on actions with a view of those same actions as "simply … part of the course of events in the world that contains us" (*VN*: 113). It seems to each of us that when we deliberate about our actions, we select from a range of possibilities. However, the third-personal perspective offers a very different account of those same actions. This "external" view offers a much wider range of relevant information about the agent and her choices. This wider information is about the circumstances of choice, "conditions and influences lying behind the action" and "the complete nature of the agent" (*VN*: 113). Nagel immediately concedes that it is difficult to see how one could *fully* take up such a stance towards oneself in action. But that does not detract from the dialectical role that the possibility of such a perspective plays in his argument. It demonstrates that the options for free action that seem available to the agent from the first-personal deliberative perspective are, in fact, closed to her when this wider range of information is introduced.

One might at this point question whether this is the right way to frame the issue. Originally, the contrast envisaged was between first-personal and third-personal views of the same action. However, now that the third-personal view has been supplanted by an "external" view that contains, in principle, *complete* information about the token action, the initial contrast seems to have fallen away. That is because the external view contains so much information that it is hard to see how it could possibly be integrated with a first-personal and deliberative perspective on action.

This is the concern I expressed earlier: take the case where Ulysses has himself tied to the mast to resist the song of the sirens. There is a sense in which we can explain that case as the taking up of a third-personal stance towards his own action. We can acknowledge that kind of action control, alongside forming intentions and the execution of them via decision, as compatible with our ordinary notion of agency. However, that corresponds solely to Nagel's first version of the subjective versus objective contrast in this case. In the first version of this contrast that he gives it is equivalent to the first-personal/third-personal distinction. He has now shifted to a different formulation in which the objective refers to an increasingly comprehensive description of the world that threatens to swallow up the deliberating agent and her actions. However, it is difficult to see how that notion can be accommodated into our ordinary notion of our own agency. We know we are finite and limited in our cognitive resources in a way reflected in our self-understanding as agents. Nagel's second version of an objective perspective is only third-personal in *form*. My worry is that what is envisaged here is no longer an agential perspective: it is not a stance anyone could take up on an action as it is too informationally unrestricted. In the latter sense of "objective" as meaning "a part of nature", this latter idea seems to be the vehicle for a sceptical suggestion that for any such conception of action as a part of nature a more complete description is always available.

Nagel emphasizes that the threat from this external and naturalistic description does not arise from its completeness in any absolute or final sense. It just has to be more complete than the perspective of the first person. Nagel is sensitive to the chain fallacy, which I have already discussed, when he exposits this argument (Anscombe 1957: 34). As mentioned earlier, in the chain fallacy one infers from the fact that "all chains have an end" that "there is an end to all chains". The analogous faulty inference is to conclude that if it is true that, for any objective view, we can conceive of a more objective one that this series terminates on a final, maximally objective view. In this final, maximally objective view one could not conceive of a more objective view than *that*. Nagel is quite clear that he is not making that mistake by invoking the possibility of a more objective view.

Nagel also argues that the threat does not arise from the fact that such naturalistic descriptions will incorporate a causal understanding of the world. The threat posed to our agency is independent of whether or not "the relation between action and its antecedent conditions is conceived as deterministic" (*VN*: 114). The challenge to our ordinary conception of free action is rather that: "From an external perspective, then, the agent and everything about him seems to be swallowed up by the circumstances of action; nothing of him is left to intervene in those circumstances ... Everything I do is part of something I don't do, because I am a part of the world" (*VN*: 114). Furthermore, it is enough to generate this challenge simply to conceive of the availability of such an external view. This is so even if only accessible to an observer with far greater cognitive capacities than ours.

Does this equivocation between the first-personal/third-personal and internal/external perspectives matter? It does change how one conceives of the problem. A subtle shift is introduced into Nagel's exposition when the first personal is re-described as a "form of clouded subjective appearance ... based ... on an incomplete view of the circumstances" (*VN*: 114). That thought seems to be no obvious corollary of thinking first-personally or third-personally about what to do. This *necessary* incompleteness in the first-personal point of view seems, if it is a fault, an inescapable one and one generated by the Cartesian model of objectification. That this is the appropriate form of objectification that Nagel has in mind is clear when he adds that "we accept a parallel subordination of subjective appearance to objective reality in other areas" (*VN*: 114). But in this case, he thinks, such a subordination would be repugnant to our common-sense view of free action. The internal, or subjective, view of free action is, as he puts it "too ambitious" to permit such subordination. We believe ourselves to be, in a deep sense, the authors of our own actions.

But it is noteworthy that the characterization he goes on to give of our intuitive notion of free agency is very ambitious. Nagel believes that our ordinary conception of free action commits us to the view that at the time of action, the outcome that is chosen is freely available to the agent in the sense that nothing up to that point determines the outcome save the choice itself. And my reason for choosing that action is "the *whole* reason why it happened, and no further explanation is either necessary or possible" (*VN*: 115).

Given the difficulties of taking Nagel's account of the contrast that sets up the problem (a contrast between first- and third-personal perspectives) as being wholly located within our own sense of agency, this issue of completeness is crucial. Setting up the problem as he does, Nagel's very strong claim is that our ordinary notion of free action takes the reasons why one acts to be a complete explanation of one's action. That is the claim that conflicts with naturalistic descriptions of our actions that are more complete. They are more complete to the extent that some options that seemed genuinely open from the first-personal perspective can now be seen as closed, but perhaps from a cognitive perspective that is not wholly accessible to us. The question that arises is whether or not our intuitive sense of free action does, indeed, make the crucial completeness claim in such a way as to allow the kind of contrast that Nagel has in mind.

Nagel's alternative formulations of the problem exemplify the same approach to diagnosing how, in fact, the problem arises. He argues that the subjective view of free action offers explanations that are both explanatorily complete and restrictive in the concepts to which they can appeal. They must be couched in terms of the intentional language of "justifying reasons and purposes" (*VN*: 115). Nagel gives the example of a person freely choosing a job. We think that there are reasons "for and against" and that whatever the agent does, we can explain how he or she saw that particular action in a favourable light. The problem, as Nagel sees it, is that if the person takes the job then we will justify what that person did by citing one set of reasons. However, if the person does not take the job, then we will cite the opposing reasons! Therefore, reasons explanation can go "either way". But in the sense in which they can go "either way" they cannot provide a *complete* explanation as required by our intuitive view of autonomy:

> Intentional explanation, if there is such a thing, can explain either choice in terms of the appropriate reasons, since either choice would be intelligible if it occurred. But for this very reason it cannot explain why the person accepted the job for the reasons in favour instead of refusing it for the reasons against.
>
> (*VN*: 116)

This is a very important argument for Nagel. It undermines a compatibilist line of argument that reconciles the more complete description available if one takes up a naturalistic stance towards an action (where such a stance uses a vocabulary drawn from the natural and social sciences) with a first-personal stance on the same action by arguing that in free action one acts on one's best reason. Some events in the world, physically describable, are also token identical with mental events (Davidson 1980b). Among those mental events some are people acting on their best reason. The problem, Nagel suggests, is that whichever course of action is chosen, one can describe it as "acting on one's best reason", but that this picks out different sets of reasons in the two contrasting cases.

However, that argument seems contentious. Presumably, it is open to the response that precisely that which Nagel has isolated is the capacity for executive decision itself (Donagan 1987; Pink 1996). The relevant reasoning is complete, but it is only ever an input to something else, namely an executive capacity for the rational control of action. Even in the case of conclusive reasons there is further work to be done (hence the possibility of weak-willed action). However, to adapt a metaphor from Aristotle, a weak-willed person is like a city with a strong legislature, but a weak executive (Stroud 2000). Theorizing weakness of will is the challenge of explaining cases where an agent decides that the best thing overall is for her to perform a certain action, but then fails to do so. Weakness of will is a complex problem, raising a host of new issues that I do not want to broach here. I note the problem only because it forces on us the importance of distinguishing between all-things-considered evaluative judgements about action (intention formation) and the execution of our intentions in action. But, when a person acts on his or her best reason with no weakness of will, it seems counter-intuitive to take reasons explanations themselves to be indifferent in which outcome they determine. They should explain what you judged that you had most reason to do. Deliberation about what you have most reason to do is what intention formation consists in. Action then expresses the intention on which you decided (Tenenbaum 2007b; Thomas forthcoming (a)).

I think Nagel gives misleading expression to a deeper problem: even if one has given one's conclusive reasons for an action, there is no further explanation as to why those *are* one's reasons. In that sense, Nagel implies, such reasons explanations must always be incomplete. It is the dialectical role of the contrasting, more objective description to flag up this point. While he does not demand that the latter description be absolutely complete, it seems we can always extend the range of information available about a context of choice with the aim of showing how what seemed to be a free option for the agent was not an option.

Having originally claimed that the objective view was one that was not typically part of our first-personal perspective and dramatizing this by substantiating the idea via the fiction of an observer with greater epistemic powers than us, Nagel changes tack. He argues that the incompatibility between the two viewpoints arises because we *try* to integrate the more complete "objective" description into our agency perspective. The problem then arises that we can see that this aspiration cannot be realized without self-evident absurdity. Our ideal of autonomy tells us that we can only act on the basis of self-sufficient rational grounds. We make ourselves more free in so far as every condition on action described by the external view can be rationally underwritten in a more all-embracing view of the basis of free action. But as we push this ideal to the limit, so we reach what Kant would call an antinomy, an irreconcilable paradox. We seem to become nothing other than the principle of free choice itself. We are confronted by an ever-expanding set of conditions that would have to be taken as merely "given" as the basis of free action. However, our ideal of autonomy tells us cannot be merely "given" as they always need to be rationally underwritten (Pippin 1991).

It is essential, in generating this antinomy, that the objective view tells us that we are part of the world. Nagel does not overburden his argument with historical references, but others have pointed out how the modern free will problem originated with late medieval debates over divine freedom. This established the problem of explaining how such divine freedom was compatible with an emerging mechanistic worldview (Taylor n.d.). The answer was to conceive of divine freedom as placed outside a mechanistically conceived of world, but able to intervene in it by an exercise of will. The modern problem of free will is generated when each of us, in microcosm, is similarly placed within a complete mechanistically describable world, but able to be an originator of free action in a purely voluntaristic way. Nagel rejects any analogous solution to the problem for human agents. He regards any such postulation of a transcendental self "at the limits of the world" and able to intervene in the world via its free actions as misguided (*VN*: 119). Nor, as I have already noted, is he impressed by the idea of taking this "*deus ex machina*" view of the free agent and simply inserting it into the causal order as a unique type of agent causation. The result of such a manoeuvre would be an incoherent combination of an ability to originate free action appropriate at the limit of the world with a view of the agent as located within that same world.

The question is whether there is a natural stopping point prior to the point where our ideal of autonomy collapses into paradox. Nagel, characteristically, argues that any such stopping point would be merely habitual or conventional. He implicitly regards all such stopping points as philosophically complacent. Hence, for him, the exact parallel between scepticism about the external world (as described in Chapter 2) and the issue of the freedom of the will.

To resist his parallel conclusion, namely, that the objective view undermines our view of autonomy, I think that one has to question how Nagel sets up his discussion. What is introduced as a distinction, within the perspective of agency, between a first-personal and third-personal perspective is gradually supplanted by a non-equivalent distinction. That distinction is between actions viewed as events and actions as located by an ever more complete description as merely events in a more comprehensive description of the world. There is an interesting analogy with Mill's (1843) conclusion that the antecedent condition of a cause was nothing less than the complete prior state of the universe. If our actions are part of the causal order that is an exact parallel for Nagel's claim that we need a completely objective view of action that is, in principle, unlimited. But how can this be integrated into our understanding of the agential view itself? An agent who needs a complete understanding of all the antecedent circumstances of her actions is no longer recognizable as a finite, limited, that it is to say, *human* agent. In that sense a residue of the early modern form of the problem survives into Nagel's account: his cognitively superior being plays the dialectical role in his argument that God played in the early modern argument.

In terms of the interpretative ideas I have used in this book, this is a further issue where there may be a degree of equivocation between Nagel's two models of objectification. He runs two contrasts side by side: between the first-personal and the third-personal and between the first-personal and the more informationally complete. I have suggested that these cannot be equivalent to each other. The former involves two perspectives on our own agency, whereas the latter involves a perspective on our own agency and an external perspective that undermines our agency because of its potentially unrestricted character. The former contrast is naturally at home in a Hegelian model of objectification where we can see a third-personal perspective as an explanatory context in which our first-personal perspective on our actions operates. The second contrast is naturally at home in the rival Cartesian conception. What compels the move from the first to the second? It seems to me that only Nagel's Cartesian debunking of our first-personal perspective on our own agency motivates that transition. It depends essentially on the assumption that that perspective consists in a "clouded subjective appearance" (*VN*: 114).

This Cartesian debunking of our subjective perspective sees this perspective as both limited and challenged by a more comprehensive natural description of our perspective. The latter, more comprehensive, description closes off certain of the options that seem available from that subjective perspective. That is the basis of Nagel's pessimism regarding a satisfactory rationale for our ideal of autonomy. However, our ordinary notion of an agent's perspective sees a finite and cognitively limited agent as responsible precisely in choosing from a range of relevant alternatives. A compatibilist might argue in response to Nagel that our ordinary ascriptions of freedom are defeasible and open to correction by a more inclusive view. However, "more inclusive" does not iterate to generate a "maximally inclusive" objective perspective (as Nagel himself notes). The fact that, for any action of mine, you could raise an overlooked alternative that I would be negligent not to consider does not iterate to generate a more radical conclusion. That more radical conclusion would be that unless I have ruled out *all* alternatives made available by the comprehensive view of my action as merely a part of nature I cannot act responsibly at all.

Our ordinary ascriptions of responsibility do not require every possible prior condition or precondition of action to be rationally underwritten as the ideal of autonomy seems to suggest. Responsibility for action involves eliminating relevant alternatives in the same way that responsibility for belief does, too. Nagel has certainly identified some of the key, paradoxical, features of our ideal of autonomy. Perhaps, however, it is the shadow cast by that historically determined ideal that is at fault rather than our ordinary folk-psychological conception of free action. If Nagel had elected to embed that kind of account within a Hegelian, rather than Cartesian, model of objectification, then his pessimism about how much of our folk-psychological notion of free action can be defended might have proved to be overstated.

The problem of responsibility

Nagel's description of the problem of autonomy sets the stage for his account of the problem of freedom when applied to our view of the agency of others. He places particular emphasis on the conditions of responsibility that govern our moral reactions of praise and blame. Given Nagel's pessimism about the problem of freedom generally, he is as sceptical about our intuitive notion of responsibility as he is about our autonomy. This is unsurprising given that he takes the essential precondition of our reactions of praise and blame to be our empathetic understanding, whose limitations were explored in Chapter 3. We try to see, from another person's point of view, the reasons bearing on the situation that made him or her choose the action that was carried out. Nagel recognizes that we cannot always do this, and in those cases he says we remain external to the person and experience instead "relief or regret" (*VN*: 122).

Once again, Nagel accepts that our common-sense view allows that a person's actions may be subject to various excusing conditions. So, once again, he tries to start his argument where Strawson's consideration of reactive attitudes ended and to undermine Strawson's conclusion from within the latter's own assumptions. The first general class of such excusing conditions governs those cases where empathy fails. Those are the cases where we judge that the person who is the subject of praise or blame is outside the sphere of those judgements. This may happen, Nagel suggests, when the subject is hypnotized, or under a totally alienated action control. An example of the latter would be the canonical mad scientist directly controlling another person's actions by a further form of indirect control. That indirect control might be control over the events in that person's cerebral cortex that constitute the motor control of action. The second general class of excusing conditions covers cases where the situation is not as the subject took them to be. We still attribute responsibility, but in a restricted sense, as when it turns out that a person acted under duress. But it is the first kind of case that interests Nagel as it (predictably) follows the pattern that leads to a philosophical undermining of all our practices of praise and blame.

The undermining thought is that the whole practice can be represented as lacking any rationale if the entire complex of action, subject, judger and reactions to the subject can be seen as part of a wider context. In that context they are all swallowed up by a description in which they appear merely as events. Once again, the crucial step in the argument is from partial disengagement from our ordinary practices to total disengagement: the inference is from local to global failure. Nagel does not believe that the issue is helpfully conceived of as a matter of finding our subject of praise or blame ineligible for those reactions because her behaviour was caused. The issue is that when a person deliberates and then acts that entire sequence – her rehearsal of reasons that she went through before acting, her status as a practical reasoner – is undermined by a view of the world in which her action is simply another event (caused or not).

Nagel emphasizes that our common-sense view finds a natural resting place that is unavailable to philosophical reflection. He also emphasizes, in Humean fashion, that the perspective afforded by philosophical reflection is not one that we can consistently occupy without our natural sentiments taking over. (This is a point that Strawson emphasized in his argument, too.) Observing that the objectified standpoint on responsibility eliminates the idea that anyone chooses at all, Nagel concedes that we are unable consistently to maintain this perspective. We find ourselves inevitably drawn to viewing others as analogous to us, namely, as agents whose deliberations *matter* in determining the course of the world. But, as in the case of philosophical scepticism, the mere availability of the objective thought is enough to destabilize our ordinary view. This is the case even if we find ourselves overwhelmed by an analogue of natural beliefs. As conceived of in the tradition of philosophical reflection of which both Hume and Strawson form a part, such beliefs lack a rational foundation. They occur naturally. However, their natural occurrence has the consequence that they maintain our commitment to our ordinary beliefs even when rational justifications have been exhausted (Bell & McGinn 1990).

Nagel's focus on praise and blame demonstrates that his primary interest is in the ethical implications of any view of agency that sees it as ineluctably immersed in an objective picture of the world. That makes Nagel's overall aim very similar to Strawson's. A question that arises is whether Nagel has underestimated the resources of Strawson's argument. I noted in Chapter 2 one strand of "ordinary language" responses to the sceptic that combined a positive model of justification with an undercutting critique of scepticism (Austin 1961a; Cavell 1999). The recent development of this positive model in the work of Robert Brandom (1994) and Michael Williams (2001: 150–57) involves arguing that training, and inculcation into our epistemic practices, *constitute* a person as the "right kind" of responsible agent. In Chapter 2, the focus was on whether such a person was constituted as a responsible knower. In the current context the focus is on whether such a person is constituted as ethically responsible. If this presupposition is satisfied, then the competent agent possesses a range of default commitments to which he or she is entitled unless specific reasons can be introduced to challenge them.

In both the epistemological and the ethical case, what matters is how one characterizes failures to know or failures to be responsible. They are always failures in particular ways (Austin 1961b).

Competent agents in normal conditions know, or are responsible, if they eliminate relevant alternatives in their knowledge and deliberation about action. When they fail to know or fail to be responsible a range of excusing conditions standardly explain this (Sie 2005). When an action falls outside this standard range, then focus shifts on to the presuppositions of appraising the agent at all, namely, whether he or she is competent. At that point Strawson's emphasis on objectification as involving a potential suspension of the rational attitudes comes into play.

I think Strawson's "Freedom and Resentment" (1974b) can be interpreted as presupposing this general model: he first of all presses the question of how exactly the truth or falsity of determinism could have a bearing on the attitudes that constitute our shared human perspective on each other's actions (and Nagel agrees that is not the issue). But, more importantly, it is implicit in our ordinary practices of praise and blame shaped by the reactive attitudes, that failures to be responsible are failures in particular ways (Austin 1961c,d). A global failure in reactive attitudes, by contrast, where we shift to a stance of objectified control, reflects a failure in the presupposition that the agent is competent (Strawson 1974b: 7–8; Sie 2005).

The sceptic about our ordinary notion of praise and blame takes the preconditions of our ordinary practices and of the way in which they can be suspended locally and tries to develop an argument that suspends them globally. But that confuses arguments at two different levels. The considerations, within our ordinary practices, that lead us to say that a person was not responsible on a particular occasion are distinct from those considerations that lead us to deny that an agent is competent at all.

Here is an example: when a work colleague of yours flies into a rage in a meeting there may be an excusing condition. Perhaps it is her post-traumatic stress disorder resulting from an incident several months previously where she assisted the badly injured victims of a road accident. If, however, this colleague develops the habit of attacking colleagues in the corridor with no discernible excusing condition to hand then she becomes a candidate for Strawsonian objectification. In this latter case our stance towards her becomes simply one of explanation and control. That is the dual Strawsonian strategy for keeping all cases where agential control is undermined either within a range of normal excusing conditions, or placing the agent completely outside the scope of the reactive attitudes (Strawson 1974b: 8–9, 11). Both strategies converge on the aim of denying a sceptical argument like Nagel's its basis in a representative failure such that the idea of agential control is globally undermined by the permanent availability of a more objective point of view.

In pressing the sceptical claim that we can generalize from local failures to be responsible to a general scepticism about praise and blame, the sceptic is, from Strawson's perspective, stepping outside the preconditions of human life. Nagel is, as usual, critical of arguments of that kind. He pays Strawson the compliment of a detailed, point-by-point refutation.

From Nagel's perspective Strawson's view is a paradigmatic attempt to find a natural stopping point for philosophical reflection. For Strawson the stopping point is a precondition for a shared ethical life, namely, the existence of the reactive attitudes. These attitudes cannot be refuted by rational considerations. The reactive attitudes stand entirely outside justification (which does not make them unjustified). Nagel's view, by contrast, is that our ordinary ideas about responsibility contain a "standing invitation to scepticism", as Bernard Williams remarked of our ordinary concept of knowledge (1978: 64). Once we have raised the internal question of whether or not we can detach to some degree from the moral appraisal of others, there is no principled stopping point that prevents us becoming more and more detached. Once we have begun to generalize, our considerations generalize "all the way out". The train of thought that begins by raising local and familiar sceptical doubts in particular cases takes on a representative significance. Once again, one needs to be careful to specify the nature of the local failures in Nagel's account. A condition that would have closed off an option for an agent can be identified in the more complete information offered by the naturalistic, more objective description of actions as swallowed up by the order of mere events. That wider description of the agent, the context and the circumstances of choice eliminates what seemed to be an open option from the first-personal deliberative perspective.

Any Strawsonian response to Nagel has to argue, in the fashion of the ordinary-language response to the sceptic, that such a sceptic cannot find a case with the following two features. First, that it is a failure for a reason drawn from a contextually specifiable range of possible reasons, the normal range of excusing conditions or the placing of an individual outside all such conditions. Secondly, that it is nevertheless a *representative* failure. Analogously, the sceptic about the external world needs to argue that if you fail to recognize this ordinary object in front of you, then with that failure you lose all your knowledge of the external world. That is because this case was typical, or representative: if you cannot recognize the bittern in the bottom of your garden, then what can you know (Austin 1961b)?

The general line of response suggested by Austin, Cavell and, I have suggested, Strawson is that the sceptic cannot, in fact, find such a representative case (Cavell 1999: 217–21). Failures to know, or be responsible, are always stubbornly particular. The only general notion of failure here is the meta-level judgement that an agent or knower is not competent, but that simply removes a presupposition of appraising knowledge claims or actions *at all*. In a parallel way to the sceptic about the external world, the sceptic about our freedom needs to argue that what happened in a particular case where a person did not act freely could happen in *any case*. A failure in this particular example should lead us to lose confidence in our practices of praise and blame as a whole. These arguments very strongly parallel the general dialectic about scepticism that was described in Chapter 2. Nagel once again takes the line that scepticism is, strictly speaking, irrefutable. We can, nevertheless, draw important lessons from it, and that is how his discussion proceeds in the case of his account of freedom of the will.

A realistic autonomy

Nagel's critical arguments are at the service, as always, of his own positive views. Nagel takes his pessimism about our freedom to lead to a position that tries to preserve as much of a Kantian ideal of autonomy as is realistic. But this is not, he emphasizes, a solution to the problem of freedom. That solution is simply not available: there is no reconciliation between the claims of our first-personal deliberative perspective (in which our actions seem open to us) and the more complete naturalistic description (which makes some of those options definitively closed regardless of how they seemed to us first-personally).

Nagel's positive argument does not fully reconcile his pessimistic description of our irreconcilable stances towards our freedom with his reconstruction of an ethical ideal of autonomy. In this case the tension simply has to be lived with. He describes how one might realize a suitably limited ideal of autonomy in the following terms: it involves a "limited harmony between external and internal, in the shadow of an even more external view" (*VN*: 126). Nagel's explanation casts some retrospective light on how he conceives of the wider problem of freedom. We should aim, in the interests of rational detachment and hence freedom, to develop a maximally complete picture of ourselves. In an interesting and suggestive analogy, Nagel suggests that just as we do not want to be externally coerced, neither do we want to be "bound" by our "motives and reasons and values" (*VN*: 127). We need to stand back (metaphorically) and subject those aspects of our mental life to rational survey and then to endorsement or rejection.

However, Nagel accepts that this process must have a limit: we cannot engage in some practical analogue of Descartes's foundationalism about knowledge (which occurred, after all, in a context in which Descartes explicitly set aside the issue of the demands of the practical). We cannot subject all our motives, reasons and values to rational scrutiny all the time. There must be, as Nagel puts it, a "blind spot" in our aspiration to act from as objective a view of ourselves as possible. The reason for this is that part of our subjectivity must always escape this objectifying gaze, namely, that part of ourselves directing the gaze. The most we can hope for is an "essentially incomplete objective view" (*VN*: 127).

Once again I think it is important to note, if not to reconcile, two aspects of Nagel's view that stem from his two models of objectivity. The inevitability of a "blind spot", of there always being a subject "behind the lens" to draw on the metaphor discussed in Chapters 2 and 3, is an inherent part of the Hegelian model of objectivity. In the Cartesian model, by contrast, we seek a finally complete account that includes the person who develops that conception in its scope. It seems that the positive phase of Nagel's argument opts definitively for the former model; but the key assumption that our first-personal perspective on our agency is merely an appearance plays an important role in setting up the problem (and it properly belongs in the Cartesian model).

The aim is to be maximally objective about our actions, where "maximally" acknowledges that if one is to act at all there must be an essentially uncompletable aspect of the claims of reflection:

> Since we can't act in light of *everything* about ourselves, the best we can do is to try and live in a way that wouldn't have to be revised in the light of anything more that could be known about us. This is a practical analogue of the epistemological hope for harmony with the world. (*VN*: 127)

I have already noted that this does not represent any kind of solution to the general problem of freedom. However, it does seem to me to illustrate some of the conflicting pressures in Nagel's formulation of the problem. On the one hand, we can see this positive account of our maximally objective way of leading our lives as capturing a notion of practical and epistemic responsibility on the part of an agent. An agent cannot be blamed if she has used her best endeavours, attempted to be maximally objective and has accepted (defeasibly) that there *is* no more that she could become aware of within her deliberative perspective such that it would undermine her options.

On the other hand, however, when Nagel set up the general problem of freedom it was as if the naturalistic view of an agent situated in a world of mere events could always supply some more complete description in which that agent's sense of free alternatives open to her was undermined. I noted the ambiguity in whether or not that more objective view was always available to the perspective of agency itself.

However, it is clear from Nagel's conclusion that he takes the pressure generated from the more objective view always to be capable of undermining our norms of responsibility. There is always some defeating condition generated by the more objective view that would show that an agent had not been responsible enough. I have described how those more sympathetic to Strawson's and Austin's views on responsibility might respond. According to Strawson, in particular, there is an ideal of autonomy that operates within our epistemic, practical and moral practices. It involves holding an agent responsible such that the agent merely has to eliminate defeaters made available by his or her objective view of herself.[2] Those defeaters have to be relevant alternatives to a claim made by an agent who meets a presupposed standard of competence. That is an important difference of emphasis from Nagel but, for reasons paralleling the discussions of Chapter 2, he has formulated the most powerful objection to that style of view, not least because of his familiarity with how it is supposed to work.

Bringing objectivity to bear on practice

For Nagel the demands placed on rationality in action are no less stringent than the demands placed on the rationality of thought. We know that there is a more comprehensive naturalistic description of our context of choice that may very well reveal hidden defeaters of our claim to be free: that is, for all we know. But we are constrained to operate in the light of an unrealizable ideal. That is what it is to live reflectively in the light of the truth. We seek to be as objective as we can about ourselves and our situation of choice. But this involves meeting the negative condition of not finding any positive reason to detach ourselves from the reasons, plans and practical commitments to which we are committed. Admittedly, this task is uncompletable, but we are, as in the case of theoretical reason, to go as far along the path of completing this task as we reasonably can.

In order not to see what I do as simply another event in the world, I need to re-engage myself in my life and practical commitments with as much good faith as I can attain. I have to act as best I can within the world, and the responsibility I face as a practical agent seems to be, as Nagel describes it, to take care that I have not overlooked those defeating conditions that are most available to me. They are, metaphorically, the "closest" in that they are made available by the standpoint that would be available to me if I were a little more objective. This looks like the "relevant alternatives" approach to knowledge and responsibility that I have described. However, Nagel places this view in a context that transforms it. It is not a solution to the initial problem but rather a practical amelioration of our predicament.

Given that this is a realistic way forward rather than a solution, it does not matter that these demands are strictly speaking unattainable. It is our rationality, once again, that places us in this predicament. But it also affords the only practical remedy. It does so by allowing us to form the idea of an increase in our objectivity. We can speculate about the content of progressively more objective external views of ourselves and our actions.

I have already noted that Nagel is aware that we run the risk of committing the "chain fallacy" here. We are not entitled to the idea of a most objective view. That would be the view of the context of our actions with the following guaranteed feature: there can be no view more objective than the most objective view. If, reassuringly, this thought about a maximally objective view of our actions remains empty, then we can at least reassure ourselves that the more objective perspective on our practical commitments is on the same scale as those more objective views that subsume it. Our practical commitments are not, as a class, transcended by a finally objective view. In that sense, any analogy for practice of a "God's-eye point of view" in the case of theory is simply not available. Our practical commitments constantly face pressure from the demands of objectivity, but this does not take the form of a once and for all contrast with a maximally objective view. That makes the demand of practical objectivity very close to Kant's "practical" interpretation of the demands of his own Ideals of Pure Reason. Kant thought that what Plato had mistakenly taken to be real ideas, based in our capacity to reason, are in fact more like practical directives. We have various ideas that, properly understood, counsel us to be even more objective than we are already. In Nagel's positive proposal a similar idea emerges: the idea of a more objective view functions as a regulative ideal in the context of our practical freedom.

There are further elements of the demands on practice that Nagel recognizes: that we do not have to conceive of being maximally objective as finding "positive grounds for choice that commanded the assent of an objective will no matter how far removed it was from my particular perspective" (*VN*: 130). He looks, instead, for a more limited form of objectivity. He suggests an analogy with the preservation of objectivity in the case of theoretical reason when you restrict yourself to a hedged epistemic claim about the "appearances". This is a form, Nagel suggests, of objective tolerance: the toleration of reasons for action that you do not believe would be rejected were you to subject them to scrutiny from a more objective view. Reasons pass this test if what they claim is limited. We are not always interested in objectivity in mundane practical contexts. Nagel gives the example of choosing from a menu where he does not care to objectify his desires: he is simply guided by their relative strengths. It would be a waste of time and effort to subject these desires to a more reflective scrutiny. These cases of limited objectivity are permissible because the kind of external perspective afforded on the context of choice by objectivity is simply not relevant here. Desires such as these do not need either endorsement or rejection.

This offers us a model for Nagel's idea of a limited degree of practical objectivity. Nagel suggests that maybe it is like this for us "all the way out". There is a more objective perspective on our actions in which our actions all seem like this, even when they seem to us to involve matters of great importance. The question is whether, from that perspective, the verdict delivered is that our evaluative commitments have been renounced by Cartesian justification or whether they have a limited degree of objectivity that can be lived with. Can they be tolerated by the objective standpoint? If they could, then we could identify with them once again having come to a truthful appreciation of how limited their claims were in the first place. But this identification is, as it were, a little chastened. Things cannot be exactly as they were before.

But this is not, in fact, Nagel's final view of the objectivity applicable to our practical commitments. Interestingly, he sees us as levered out of our state of practical innocence by the fact that desires conflict. Nagel uses the familiar metaphor of "weight" in describing how we decide to be governed by simple desires, but sometimes it seems that desires can have equal weight. It is the possibility of conflict that leads us to objectify our first-order desires. That is, itself, a complex process, and Nagel thinks that it is a process that invites the thought that any objective view is open to challenge from a more objective view.

Nagel describes what he calls "first-order" motivations and conceives of them as forming a complex group that can often contain internal conflict. Reason is brought in to adjudicate these conflicting claims by such simple processes as endorsing some motives and rejecting others with the overall aim of finding mutual consistency. When one takes this step of disengagement it also seems to Nagel natural to ascend to the first kind of objective standpoint that he discussed in *The Possibility of Altruism*, namely, that of prudence. The prudential standpoint is an objective standpoint in the sense that it transcends one's present desires. One is thereby committed to the temporal neutrality of reasons across one's whole life. It is an exercise of practical freedom to disengage from current motivations in this way. Prudence is the first stage of objectification in that it takes one to a more objective perspective on present desire. You are disengaged from the desire's motivational strength, which is open to objective assessment, and you are disengaged from the present moment in order to take up a temporally neutral standpoint.

The further crucial feature of this step to greater objectivity is that the perspective one takes up is *itself* a generator of reasons that can create reasons that did not exist prior to occupying that standpoint. This is the constructivist aspect of Nagel's moral rationalism: engaging in a certain kind of privileged rational procedure can not only endorse or reject existing reasons but can also create reasons. This is clearly an important change: ascending to an objective viewpoint is not like climbing a tall building for a clear view of a cityscape. It is not a merely positional, or epistemic, viewpoint on the reasons you already have. Being more objective about your practical reasons supplies you with new reasons that you did not already possess. This fact will prove particularly important for an assessment of Nagel's views in normative ethics in the next chapter.

This constructivism is in evidence in the simple move from conflicting desires existing, as it were, "first-order" to the second level of reflection. At this level of reflection one has ascended to the standpoint of practical rationality. From this standpoint first-order reasons and desires are not simply viewed as brutely given to the deliberating agent. Nor are these reasons and desires left to order themselves into which are more or less important for action simply by possessing different relative strengths. Nagel is clear that a great deal that happens at this level does not require a constructivist treatment. A great deal of practical rationality simply is endorsement, rejection and finding consistency among first-order motivations. But the step to the objective standpoint of prudence introduces desires explicitly flagged as occurring at different times and other competing kinds of interest that also need to be assessed from an objective viewpoint. We have, at this level, added to the stock of our reasons: "The objective stance here is not merely permissive, but active. The prudential motives do not exist prior to the adoption of an objective standpoint, but are produced by it" (*VN*: 133). In keeping with his shift to treating practical objectivity as involving Hegelian objectification (where not everything that in *The Possibility of Altruism* was called a subjective reason is transcended and renounced by Cartesian objectification), Nagel accepts that this first stage in the development of more objective motivation may modify our first-order desires and supplement them with new reasons. They are not completely eliminated if they are "objectively tolerable". But they have a wider range of competitors as candidates to be the reason that constitutes the deliberating agent's final verdict as to that which he or she has most reason to do.

Nagel concludes his discussion of the problem of freedom and autonomy by reflecting on the connection between his view of practical reason and freedom: "I am agreeing with Kant's view that there is an internal connection between ethics and freedom: subjection to morality expresses the hope of autonomy, even though it is a hope that cannot be realized in its original form" (*VN*: 135). Nagel clearly describes an aspiration: to leave no precondition of rational motivation unendorsed and to ascend to a level of full autonomy where not even your character is something that you can deliberate from (Thomas 2005). It must be something that you can choose from a critical and disengaged standpoint outside yourself. The cost of not doing so is that one cannot accept that one is free: one is reduced to being a mere bystander, watching as one's actions unfold like rocks rolling down a hill or a leaf falling from a tree. Nagel concedes that there are some conditions that it is a matter of sanity simply to accept and also makes the insightful observation that in some respects the conditions of ethical choice are a social matter. (Whether we can lead ethically good lives may depend on whether we live in a society that is just. This highlights a theme central to his arguments in *Equality and Partiality* that will be discussed in Chapter 7.)

Nagel's main point, however, is that the very possibility of the kind of practical objectivity that he has described does not solve the problem of freedom with which he began. It merely forms part of the amelioration of our predicament. In particular, we cannot rescue our ordinary ascriptions of praise and blame, for responsibility for choice (as described in the objective conception) "would have to be found in bad actions as well as good ones" (*VN*: 136). Noting that Sidgwick levelled this charge against Kant, Nagel endorses the argument that if freedom is a condition for moral responsibility, then no one can act freely and wrongly. All we are left with is our ordinary practice of taking up the "subjective view" of those whom we aim morally to appraise. But assuming that this is enough to address the deeper problem of the metaphysics of responsibility is an assumption that can only exist alongside a willed forgetting of the possibility of an objective standpoint. Absent that kind of bad faith, the mere availability of such an objective standpoint undermines all such attributions of responsibility, grounded as they are in a limited and partial perspective. This is an appropriate point at which to make the transition, as Nagel himself does, to issues in normative ethics and to discuss Nagel's own innovative version of an impartialist ethical theory.

Chapter 6

Normative ethics: Nagel's hybrid ethical theory

In the overall structure of *The View from Nowhere*, Nagel's continued discussion of how the demands of objectivity apply to practice extends from his consideration of the problem of free will into moral philosophy. The concept of autonomy forms a natural bridge between these two sets of problems. Moral philosophy is conventionally divided into "meta-ethics" and "normative ethics", and Nagel's presentation broadly follows this division. However, in the absence of any clear way of demarcating first-order from second-order questions in ethics, now that the subject is not taken to be restricted to conceptual analysis, this distinction has become largely a matter of customary usage. Nagel's discussion moves freely between meta-ethical and normative issues. My primary focus in this chapter will be on the transformation in Nagel's Sidgwickian ideal of objectivity in practice, discussed in the previous two chapters, when it is placed in the new framework of *The View from Nowhere*.

Moral objectivity: theoretical and practical

Throughout its history, moral philosophy has considered the problem of moral objectivity in two main ways. The first asks whether moral thought can aspire to the kind of objectivity exhibited by theoretical knowledge; the second construes ethics as an exercise not of our capacity for theory, but of our capacity rationally to direct our action. *The Possibility of Altruism* showed clearly that Nagel works in the latter tradition, and that fundamental commitment remains unchanged in *The View from Nowhere*. Therefore, Nagel opens his discussion with a rejection of many criticisms of the aspiration to objectivity that simply do not apply to his work as they are directed at those who take moral objectivity to be a species of theoretical objectivity. The latter is the view, held by moral realists and cognitivists, such as David Brink (1989), Russ Shafer-Landau (2005) and Thomas (2006b), that some of our moral judgements constitute forms of moral knowledge. These judgements aim to describe, and succeed in describing, an independent realm of moral facts.[1] But in the course of rejecting what Nagel regards as misplaced alternatives to his view he also presents his own positive conception of the task of moral theorizing.

That which Nagel calls the "material" for moral theory arises from our human nature as practical agents with motivational states such as reasons and desires. Reason, in its practical use, gives us a standpoint that not simply ranks, endorses and deletes first-order motives, but (as was emphasized in the previous chapter) one that can add to them by a process akin to construction. In *The View from Nowhere* Nagel advances an even stronger thesis: that values can *only* arise in this way. The idea of being an evaluative realist seems to Nagel deeply misguided. For him there can be no characterization of the idea of value that is independent of the idea of a good reason.

This line of thought makes Nagel an anticipator of what has been called a "buck-passing" theory of value much discussed in recent moral philosophy. It is a focus of attention owing to Thomas Scanlon's development of a view of this kind in *What We Owe to Each Other* (Scanlon 1998). The basic idea is that the ascription of values is asymmetrically dependent on the ascription of reasons.[2] We can always interpret reference to the evaluative features of objects as, in fact, picking out those features that ground reasons for action for some judger. This is, clearly, a refinement of Nagel's basic idea as presented in *The View from Nowhere,* but Nagel's discussion anticipates these more recent meta-ethical developments. To use a slogan that has become popular in expositing Scanlon's view, evaluative talk always "passes the buck" to talk of the grounding of reasons. It is important to note that this is not a reductionist view that claims that one can reduce all values to reasons. The point is, rather, that a relation of asymmetric dependence holds between values and reason giving. Moral theories can exploit that dependence. Nagel refers, therefore, to both reasons and values in a way that is consistent with his view that, whenever we talk of values, we can cash out that talk in terms of some agent being given a reason.[3]

To help make plausible the claim that his is the only possible form of moral objectivity, Nagel draws a distinction between "normative realism" and "Platonism". The former is the idea that we find out truths about "what we and other people should do and want" that are independent of "how things appear to us" (*VN*: 139). Objectivity in ethics does not consist, as theoretical objectivity does, in bringing one's thoughts into accord with reality. It is objectivity brought to bear on our existing commitments as practical agents. Just as a criterial distinction within Nagel's general use of the terms "subjectivity" and "objectivity" is the distinction between appearance and reality, so he equally applies that distinction to an agent's motivations.

That can seem implausible: in what sense, for example, can desires be compared to "appearances"? In fact, Nagel here (as so often in his ethics) follows an ancient precedent and treats conative states like desires as representations, just as he did in *The Possibility of Altruism*. This need not be taken as literally treating conative states as akin to perceptual states, although that view has some very able contemporary defenders (Oddie 2005; Tenenbaum 2007a). However, such states do have an intentional content that can be endorsed (so earn the title "real") or rejected (and relegated to "appearances").

Given this set of assumptions about the only possible form of moral objectivity Nagel gives short shrift to two of the leading anti-realists about moral objectivity, namely, John Mackie (1977) and Gilbert Harman (1977):

> The objective badness of pain ... is not some mysterious further property that all pains have, but just the fact that there is a reason for anyone capable of viewing the world objectively to want it to stop ... No other kinds of truths are involved. Indeed no other kinds of truths *could imply the reality of values*.
>
> (*VN*: 144, emphasis added)

On Nagel's conception we do not take up the objective standpoint in ethics to find truths detached from those to which we are already committed (although we may generate new ones as was described in the previous chapter). The objective standpoint allows us to understand our commitments more deeply in a way that can change them by a process of endorsement or rejection. To use a helpful phrase from Christine Korsgaard, a philosopher with similar views who has been influenced by Nagel, the test to which Nagel appeals is that of "reflective endorsement" (Korsgaard 1996a: 49ff.).

Much of this is recognizably a restatement of the framework of *The Possibility of Altruism*. We begin from people's psychologies as given and subject their existing commitments to a process of reflective scrutiny. This new standpoint is not merely some passive filter, but a standpoint that can generate reasons of its own. This latter point will prove very important in demarcating some of the important changes between *The Possibility of Altruism* and *The View from Nowhere*. The main aspect of the ideal of Sidgwickian objectivity carried over from the earlier book is that our view of the world, even as practical agents, ought to be "centreless". The description of our standpoint that carries the greatest intellectual authority does not place oneself, or indeed any particular person, at its centre. From that centreless view we can either ask what we have most reason to do, or what the world contains (*VN*: 140).

Nagel aligns the centred–centreless distinction with two other familiar distinctions from his earlier discussion: the first-person–third-person distinction and the normative–explanatory reasons distinction. This allows him to contrast his approach with that of Hume, cast in the role of a philosopher of morality who develops a wholly third personal and explanatory view of ethical objectivity.[4] Hume was, in fact, a sceptic about the whole idea of normative reasons, but the dialectical role he plays in Nagel's exposition is as a representative of two views: first, that there is no notion of practical objectivity available that could generate new normative reasons; and secondly, that all normative questions can be replaced by explanatory ones.

Hume is cast in the role of a practical reasons sceptic who views his desires from the first-personal point of view and then switches to the centreless view. All this can do, from such a sceptical point of view, is represent such conative states as akin to Hobbesian "pushes" and "pulls" that motivate the agent this way and that like a ship adrift in a storm. (This is an updating of the depiction of simple motivation theory in *The Possibility of Altruism*). The point of describing a Humean view in this way is to substantiate a model of how perspectival ascent might reveal the "appearances" to be illusory, basing this on an analogy with Cartesian objectification applied to theoretical commitments. It is not important if this application of "appearance" and "reality" talk to practical reasons seems strained as nothing in Nagel's substantive view depends on it. The open question, as he notes, is whether or not he can put forward any convincing examples of how a more objective view can supplement our existing reasons.

Nagel's moral rationalism

A preliminary description of the important change in Nagel's views between *The Possibility of Altruism* and *The View from Nowhere* is that the constraint of Sidgwickian objectivity changes from being a strictly requiring constraint to being a permissive constraint. (This reflects a general shift from a Cartesian to a Hegelian model of practical objectification of our pre-reflective commitments.) In the earlier book, all subjective reasons had to be backed up by objective reasons on pain of a dissociation that was the practical analogue of a theoretical commitment to solipsism. However, in *The View from Nowhere* it is accepted that there is a wide range of reasons that are both subjective and yet are "objectively tolerated" alongside those reasons that are directly objectified. Subjective reasons cannot escape *any* relation to the objective standpoint: the latter has to permit them. But they are no longer required to be objective reasons such that if they fail that requirement they are not reasons at all. The direct descendants of *The Possibility of Altruism*'s objective reasons, agent-neutral reasons, continue to receive a direct form of reflective endorsement that can be seen as preserving, in the new model, the process of perspectival ascent in the earlier Cartesian model. However, in Nagel's overall picture, agent-neutral reasons do not exhaust all the reasons that there are.

The starting-point of any such reflective enquiry, as in *The Possibility of Altruism*, is that which is revealed from the first-personal point of view: one's own beliefs and motivations. Just as in the case of theoretical reasoning, so in practical reasoning I take appearances at face value. I take them as a reliable indicator of what is actually the case (viewing the world theoretically) and of which reasons I have (viewing the world practically). But anyone even this minimally engaged, Nagel argues, is presented with the issue of objectivity. Some of our practical decisions carry no objective weight: perhaps deciding between different flavours of ice cream for dessert or arbitrarily selecting one token can of baked beans from a stack of fifty of the same type in a supermarket. But most practical decisions carry at least this much weight: our reasoning about practice is governed by the idea that one can get the answers to practical questions right or wrong. When a friend comes to me for advice about a serious personal problem, as opposed to advice on choosing a dessert (where there is no disputing matters of taste), I had better take seriously the idea that in advising him what to do we are collectively engaged in a task to which there is a right answer. "Just choose" is going to seem like a very inadequate response to his request for help.

Nagel concedes that this preliminary idea of objectivity is very thin: thin enough to be captured within a sophisticated version of the view that in my discussion of *The Possibility of Altruism* I called "simple motivational theory", namely, Parfit's present aim or "instrumental" theory (Parfit 1984). Strictly speaking a theory of rationality, this view claims that I have most reason to act in a way that maximizes the satisfaction of my current desires. But even present aim theory is pointing in the right direction, Nagel argues, as it introduces generality. It does so by taking up a stance towards reasons in general in which one's own reasons appear as a special instance. That, Nagel believes, is the first step towards the objectification of one's practical commitments.[5]

Nagel argues that this criterion of generality has to be normative as well as explanatory. It is not enough that you see why others are moved by their reasons; you have to see their reasons as ones that you could endorse (or not) in the context of your first-personal deliberation. So the content of their reasons has to be generalizable and therefore intersubjectively accessible. But Nagel also takes this to mean – and this does not seem to follow as clearly – that we are guided in this process by principles that supply a bridge such that we can see each person's reasons as both a reason for them and as potentially reasons for anyone. (I shall discuss this point below in connection with the idea of an agent-relativity in reasons.)

Just as Hume was pushed into the historical role of sceptic about practical reasons, so Parfit is recruited into that role as a contemporary representative of the simple motivational theory described in Chapter 4. That does seem to me a little unfair. In so far as Parfit is not committed to Nagel's distinctive account of desires as potentially akin to Hobbesian motives (pushes and pulls) when not endorsed, so his comparative lack of theoretical baggage makes his view an attractive interpretation of the folk-psychological notion of desire. Nonetheless, Nagel argues that Parfit's theory is too thin and needs to be supplemented by a substantive account of practical reason. He offers two main objections to Parfit's theory: that it cannot accommodate the motivated desires so central to the argument of *The Possibility of Altruism* and that it is a reductive view that abandons normativity and is merely an account of explanatory reasons. One might question the fairness of these verdicts, particularly the second. However, the main task is to see what competitor view Nagel puts in its place, building on parts of the argument inherited from *The Possibility of Altruism*, but revising it and supplementing it in several new ways.[6]

Nagel's classifications: particular versus general, agent-relative versus neutral

As the process of reflective endorsement proceeds throughout *The View from Nowhere*, Nagel develops descriptive and clarificatory terminology to help him theorize important distinctions among reasons. The most important, by far, is the successor to *The Possibility of Altruism*'s distinction between subjective and objective reasons, namely, the distinction between agent-relative and agent-neutral reasons.[7] Between the composition of *The Possibility of Altruism* and *The View from Nowhere* Parfit had coined the terms "agent-relative" and "agent-neutral" in *Reasons and Persons* (1984), applying them in particular to the aims that moral theories give to distinct individuals. Nagel adopts this terminology as a way of developing his earlier "subjective" versus "objective" contrast and applies it to reasons, not to aims. He describes the distinction as "extremely important (*VN*: 152). It is so important because it forms the central way in which he applies the test of Sidgwickian objectivity in this later work. In its application in *The View from Nowhere* to all our reasons, this distinction takes the form of the demand that reasons have to be "understood and affirmed from outside the viewpoint of the individual who has them" (*VN*: 153).

The agent-relative–neutral distinction is introduced as "a second respect in which reasons vary [namely in] their relativity to the agent":

> If a reason can be given a general form which does not include an essential reference to the person who has it, it is an *agent-neutral* reason. For example, if it is a reason for anyone to do or want something that it would reduce the amount of wretchedness in the world, then that is a neutral reason. If on the other hand the general form of a reason does include an essential reference to the person who has it, it is an *agent-relative* reason. (*VN*: 152–3)

Nagel gives an example to help explain what he means by that distinction: suppose that two people, Smith and Jones, have opposed interests. They cannot both be satisfied together. Smith has a reason to bring about state of affairs, *A*, in which Smith's interest is satisfied and Jones's is frustrated. Jones has a reason to bring about state of affairs, *B*, in which Jones's interest is satisfied and Smith's is frustrated. Smith's reason to bring about *A* is because it is in his, Smith's, interest. That is an agent-relative reason in Nagel's sense. Jones has an agent-relative reason too: to bring about *B*. But in neither case can we understand the reason without understanding that it is a reason *for* someone in particular. To understand the reason we have to specify whose it is.

How are we to understand the contrasting case of agent-neutrality? Nagel argues that in these two cases of a person with a token agent-relative reason we need to make "essential reference" to the person whose reason it is. The contrast he intends is a case where we can specify a reason in a "general form" that does not include reference to the person who has it. We can still understand the reason, and it is left open that we could specify a person who has it. However, the latter reference is inessential. It is, in that precise sense, presumed to be a reason for anyone. I would interpret this, as I interpreted the analogous claim in *The Possibility of Altruism*, as the claim that the reason has universal practical scope of application. To use the preposition that we usually use in ordinary language, it is a reason "for" anyone.

The idea of practical scope is a neglected one in practical philosophy perhaps because it is easy simply to assume that all reasons are, in the relevant sense, for anyone. The default interpretation is that reasons are all of wide scope. But John Lucas has attempted to draw a distinction between what he calls "first-personal" and "omni-personal" reasons:

> First-personal reasons … are ones which I am guided by, and offer to others in case they find them persuasive too: omni-personal reasons, as we may term those at the other extreme, are ones which, we claim, should be accepted by everyone, and can never be disregarded or put on one side, and can only be overridden by other omni-personal reasons which, in the relevant situation, are even weightier. (Lucas 1993: 65)

As the argument of this chapter develops, I think it is helpful to bear in mind that the agent-relative–agent-neutral distinction, while not reducible to one between kinds of practical scope, may nevertheless helpfully be elucidated in terms of scope. Certainly, some of Nagel's key claims can be formulated in terms of practical scope alone. It seems to me that further distinctions have been obscured by the success of the agent-relative–agent-neutral distinction that itself has proved highly influential. It has been viewed as a genuine insight into how one might classify not only kinds of ethical reason, but whole normative theories. Nagel, as I shall describe below, is prepared to extend the idea of agent-relativity to values, too. That yields a fourfold classification of agent-relative–neutral reasons–values. That template has been very widely drawn on in recent ethics as a classificatory device, notably in the classification of the main normative ethical theories.

An important use of this classification is to clarify the respective commitments of the normative ethical theory of consequentialism and the theory of deontology. Consequentialism is an impartialist ethical theory that, in its simplest form, claims that the right-making feature of a (token or type) action is that it promotes the evaluative outcome that maximizes (or satisfices) the presupposed value.[8] This account presupposes that this value has been used to rank all outcomes from worst to best.[9]

Deontology, by contrast, argues that the basic idea in ethical theorizing is that of a duty, typically a constraint on the kinds of outcomes that an agent may promote (Fried 1978). The basic idea of using the agent-relative–neutral distinction to sharpen this difference is that consequentialism can be expressed wholly in agent-neutral terms. It recognizes agent-neutral values that everyone has reason to promote. Therefore, it also recognizes agent-neutral reasons.[10] But the deontologist recognizes, alongside these reasons and values, a distinctive class of agent-relative reasons. Indeed, it has seemed to some defenders of deontology that such a view is *forced* to restrict itself to this class of reasons on the ground that any kind of evaluative talk is hostage to consequentialist re-interpretation (McNaughton & Rawling 1995). This just begins to describe some of the complexities of the issue, but it will be clear that Nagel's terminology is central to many contemporary accounts of the structure of normative ethical theories.

In this chapter and the next I shall discuss some of the issues built in to Nagel's terminology. I do not think that this terminology should ever be treated as merely classificatory given how many contestable assumptions go into its formulation. But Nagel himself immediately issues an important caveat about his use of the agent-relative–agent-neutral distinction. He does not intend it to cut deeply when applied to the metaphysical status of reasons and values. It is not about objectification in the sense of how distanced from human concerns and interests a value or reason can be while remaining, recognizably, a category for us. Nagel contrasts the intrinsic–extrinsic value distinction with the idea of being a reason for a particular person or being a reason in general. That points back to the previous classificatory scheme of *The Possibility of Altruism* where objective reasons involved intrinsic and timeless values. Those seem to him to be two quite distinct issues that it is important to keep apart. The agent-relative–agent-neutral distinction, applied to values, is not the same as the intrinsic–extrinsic distinction.

Expanding on this point Nagel further argues that when reasons are presented to us, we usually presume that their achievement by an agent will be subjectively satisfying to that agent. Even on a very objective view of human well-being, if a person's desire or interest is satisfied (in the sense of achieving its end), we will feel satisfied (in the different sense of an occurrent mental state of satisfaction). Nagel contrasts that line of thought with another in which some values are "intrinsic" because "they have an intrinsic value which is not merely a function of the satisfaction that people may derive from them" (*VN*: 153). Interestingly, the most plausible case of such values is, he argues, aesthetic value, such as the beauty of a painting. Borrowing an idea from Kant, Nagel argues that the hallmark of aesthetic interest is that "the object of interest is external". Nagel hopes to acknowledge that such a category of value is possible without leading to the further consequence that such values would be valuable even if no one were ever able to respond to them.

This is a deeply interesting discussion that raises a plethora of issues, but I shall restrict myself to the following: first, Nagel is correct that the issue here is not the deep one of the metaphysical status of values, as all the distinctions that he points to could be drawn presupposing an answer to that question. Secondly, it is of independent interest that there is one area in which Nagel is not prepared to be a "buck-passer" about values, namely, the case of aesthetic judgements. Aesthetic evaluative judgements do not seem to depend on judgements about the presence of features that ground reasons in Nagel's account. I surmise that the reason for this is that aesthetic judgements seem detached from practicality. If a moral realist could persuade Nagel that some cases of moral value were similarly contemplative and that there was an analogy between our ethical interests and "disinterestedness", then the distance between their respective views would narrow. Thirdly, Nagel seems to be operating with the assumption that the distinction between values with a closer tie to subjective interest and values without such a tie to subjective interest aligns with the distinction between the non-intrinsic and the intrinsic. That is an independently interesting theory of intrinsic value, but it is a cross-classification that does not, as Nagel notes, align with the agent-relative–agent-neutral distinction.

Reflective endorsement described

With these preliminary issues of terminology in place, Nagel turns to how he conceives of the authority of practical reflection. His aim is to characterize the test of reflective endorsement. This test involves an agent taking up a reflective stance towards her motivations. This is a stance from which new reasons may be generated and one that informs the perspective of engagement and decision. The objective view exercises a controlling influence either by directly endorsing a reason or motive, by generating a new reason, or by tolerating a reason in a sense that will be explained.

I shall now describe what this involves in more detail. It is worth bearing in mind that action and decision can only be justified from a standpoint of engagement. To act, you need to know who you are and to be identified with your reasons and motives in the sense of being engaged with them. However, disciplined engagement is shaped by the results of a thought experiment in which one's commitments are subjected to the constraint of objectivity. There is (obviously) an incompatibility between detachment and action, but action ought always to be informed by the results of detached reflection.

What this constraint of objectivity does, primarily, is significantly enlarge one's view, such that one comes to appreciate one's subjective perspective as a glimpse of a much wider objective reality about the values and reasons that there are. A central argument of the earlier *The Possibility of Altruism* reappears in *The View from Nowhere*. The move to the objective level forces on you a recognition of the fact that other people are equally real, that those of their reasons and values that survive objectification are as important as yours and, in a sense to be explained, that *their reasons are reasons for you*, too. The problem posed by this requirement of objectivity is as follows: "When we take up the objective standpoint the problem is not that values seem to disappear, but that there seem to be too many of them, coming from every life and drowning out those that arise from our own" (*VN*: 147). This is because, at the objective level, agent-neutral reasons (the successor of objective reasons) possess motivational import *without regard for whose reasons they are*. They have universal practical scope.

By contrast, agent-relative reasons cannot directly have motivational scope at the objective level. That is because the informational restriction used to define the objective stance works in such a way that we do not know whose agent-relative reasons are whose (and they are, irreducibly, reasons for particular individuals). But when you return to the standpoint of engagement in order to discern whose objectively tolerated agent-relative reasons are yours, you have massively enriched "your" reasons with an awareness of the agent-neutral claims of others. They are, quite literally, reasons for you. Hence the risk, cited above, of your own reasons being "drowned out" by the collective demands of other people's objectifiable interests. This is, clearly, a very radical thesis about the effects of taking up an objectified stance towards your own subjective view.

Given that one's starting-point is one's pre-existing commitments, one might reasonably call all this pre-reflective data one's "subjective" or "personal" reasons. The test of reflective endorsement calls for detached scrutiny of those reasons. The first thing that reflection involves is detachment from your particular identity. The transition to a more detached and impersonal standpoint involves thinking of the world in abstraction from its being shaped by your own point of view. From this detached standpoint the agent can think of all other moral agents, without thinking of any particular one of these standpoints of agency as in fact "centred" on his or her self. This is the familiar kind of informational restriction used to set up an objective standpoint: you do not know who in particular you are (Sen 1979). There is nothing incoherent in this; you are asked to imagine a situation that in fact contains you, but in way that abstracts from that fact (O'Neill 1989).

Nagel thinks that such reflection arises naturally from our impulse to take up an objective view of our evaluative commitments. We move from the personal, the particular and the agent-relative to a more impersonal and universal standpoint. At this objective level one's subjective or "personal" reasons have to be critically evaluated. Nagel believes that there are three possible results of this evaluation.

First, reflection may show that some of our reasons are instances of the agent-neutral, applying that term both to reasons and to values. Nagel believes that this conclusion is strongest (counter-intuitively) for what may seem to us paradigms of subjectivity, such as our experiences of pleasure and pain. But that is because such states are akin to perceptions of what is agent-neutrally good and bad. Furthermore, these timeless and intrinsic reasons are reasons for anyone. This general pattern of analysis can be extended to people's basic needs.

Secondly, reflection may show that some of our reasons are instances of the agent-relative. They can now, unlike in *The Possibility of Altruism*, be *acknowledged* at the objective level. However, at that level, one cannot know for whom they are reasons because they have limited practical scope and we do not know at that level which agent we are. The role of the objective level is to tolerate this class of reasons.

Thirdly, reflection may show that some of our subjective reasons will simply be left behind. They will be invisible to the objective standpoint. As the objective standpoint can, therefore, neither directly endorse such reasons nor tolerate them, such reasons will fall outside the scope of objective justification. I shall return to this third, very important, case below. However, Nagel thinks that we will try to overcome this problem by finding proxies for this last class of reasons. These proxies will represent these reasons at the objective level. If we cannot find such proxies, then reasons of this class will fail the test of reflective endorsement.

This threefold distinction is not the most important aspect of objectification: it describes only what may happen to an individual's pre-reflective (subjective) reasons. The most important development at the reflective level, as I have noted, is the massive extension of reasons for an individual to cover the agent-neutral reasons of other people. That transforms what we pre-reflectively mean by an individual agent's reasons. Those of another person's commitments that can be objectified are reasons for anyone, too. Therefore, you can know that they apply to you *without* having to know who you are.

This yields the slightly odd corollary that at the objective level such judgements have motivational import for you even though that level is not itself a standpoint of action. How can you act if you do not know which particular agent you in fact are? Once again, however, this is a key idea carried over from *The Possibility of Altruism* to *The View from Nowhere*. Furthermore, this idea was the focus of the Darwall–Sturgeon objection to the argument of the earlier book. They both argued it was implausible to claim that motivational import can attach to the contents of judgements accepted at the reflective level, even though no agent can act from that standpoint. What he or she does is to acquire motivations that inform action when engaged once again with his or her personal point of view.

At the objective standpoint, therefore, there is a large collection, or aggregation (not fusion), of agent-relative and agent-neutral reasons. This level forces two ethical truths on us, namely, that everyone is of equal value and that all intrinsic values are agent-neutral. The overall result, Nagel thinks, will be the kind of normative ethical theory known as a hybrid ethical theory. The engaged agent has to take into account commitments from the first two classes of reason. The objective standpoint will also seek, as far as it can, to find proxies that represent considerations from the third class at the objective level so as to tolerate them if it is possible to do so. But Nagel is equally clear that this ambition can only be partially realized. I shall argue below that this aspect of his view is responsible for a degree of tension between his pluralist leanings, which seek to represent all our pre-theoretical commitments as neutrally as possible, and his commitment to the ultimate controlling authority of the objective point of view, reflected in the structure of his hybrid ethical theory.

Before proceeding I shall explain both of these views in general terms: both a hybrid theory and pluralism are instances of normative ethical theories. The hybrid theorist begins by taking up an impartial standpoint and reviewing our intuitive ethical commitments. He or she concludes that it is always permissible to rank possible outcomes from best to worst and to select that action that promotes the best outcome using some independent metric of value (just as consequentialism does). However, while one is always *permitted* to do so, one is never *required* to do so. One is allowed, in ranking outcomes, to take into account other ethical reasons grounded in the pervasive importance of the personal point of view of individual agents.

An agent's personal point of view grounds two different kinds of ethical reason: deontic options and deontic constraints. Deontic options consist in a discretion to attach a greater weight to one's own projects and commitments in the evaluation of outcomes. Deontic constraints represent constraints on deliberation that flow simply from the description of proposed action types. Acknowledging a description of an act as murder, for example, prohibits deliberation from considering outcomes containing acts that fall under that description. The hybrid theorist very often regards deontic options as defensible, but deontic constraints as indefensible; Nagel takes a different view.

The ethical pluralist, by contrast, argues that our ethical commitments form a very broad and heterogeneous class (Urmson 1974/5;

Gaut 1999; B. Williams 1997b). There is very little to say to regiment them into a general theory of any kind that can be both true and interesting. Some pluralists argue that one can discern some moderately reflective general duties, but they form no more than a list of duties with no discernible order of priority between them (Ross 1930). Nagel's own work, as I shall demonstrate, has affinities with both positions, reflecting his deepest commitment to theory when theory is available, but also his anti-reductionist instincts not to push theorizing too far when it is inappropriate. Ultimately, however, he favours a hybrid ethical theory, but one that offers an independent rationale for deontic constraints.

Reflective endorsement assessed

While some parts of *The View from Nowhere* significantly revise the argument strategy of *The Possibility of Altruism*, the central argument of the latter survives in a new form. The discussion of Nagel's earlier view in Chapter 4 focused on that which he called "motivational content". Nagel's argument was that the truth of motivational internalism is only preserved when a subjective reason is backed up by an objective reason. An agent's judgement that he or she has a good reason is necessarily motivating, because objective reasons have motivational content *before* an agent comes to accept them. This is also central to Nagel's later argument for hybrid theory.

When one takes up the objective standpoint one views the world as "centreless". However, an objectified set of commitments aggregated from everyone's agent-neutral reasons can still supply motivational content. If, at the objective level, you discover that a practical commitment (viewed as "unowned" by any particular person) is an agent-neutral value, then anyone has a reason to bring it about. That "anyone" includes, by default, you as a special case. But you do not have to re-engage or identify yourself as the particular person you are in order for that reason to supply you with the relevant motivation. "Such a judgement", Nagel argues, "has motivational content even *before* it is brought back down to the particular perspective of the individual who has accepted it objectively" (*VN*: 153–4, emphasis added). This is central to Nagel's version of hybrid theory because of the contrast with the way in which agent-relative reasons function. Agent-relative reasons are perfectly good reasons, but only for those to whom the reason stands in the right relation. That cannot be discerned until one has re-engaged with the reason from the standpoint of one's particular identity.

Is this later argument any more successful than the earlier one? In Chapter 4 I discussed two of the leading critics of the earlier view, Sturgeon and Darwall, and found their objection to Nagel's central argument convincing. They argued that the argument suffered from a fallacy of equivocation. Consider the process–product ambiguity of the word "judgement": it can refer to the act of judging or to the content, what is judged. With this ambiguity resolved, one can explain how Nagel's internalist thesis about moral motivation can be true without accepting his distinctive explanation of it, namely, the truth of the Sidgwickian model of objectivity. That derailed the transcendental argument of *The Possibility of Altruism*. However, I noted that Nagel still had the option of appealing to the intrinsic merits of the Sidgwickian view (rather than arguing that it uniquely explains the truth of an independently plausible motivational internalism). That is what happens in *The View from Nowhere*.

The most fundamental commitment of *The View from Nowhere* is the idea that motivational content attaches to the objectifiable interests of everyone. This is not really argued for: it is, for Nagel, simply that which objectivity in practice amounts to. The unpersuaded will repeat a variation of the Sturgeon–Darwall argument: in so far as I accept that someone else's agent-neutral reason grounds a reason for me, then the event that is my acceptance of that good reason is necessarily motivating. However, the reason is not literally *mine*. Other people's reasons matter, but the way in which they matter is not correctly represented in the Sidgwickian model. When each of us attaches weight to other people's interests in our own deliberations we do not literally make their reasons our reasons. At this point of the argument one might, for example, appeal to the point made by Butler that Nagel conceded early in *The Possibility of Altruism*: a reason can be "yours" in the sense that it figures in your motivations without it also possessing an egoistic *content*. If I want the good of another for his or her own sake, what I want is that person's good, not the satisfaction of my desire. A further consideration against Nagel's later account is that we are to see motivation, at the level of personal engagement with reasons, as already supplied by objective reasons grasped at the reflective level. But what point is there to postulating motivational import to reasons at a level where there is no agency? *Ex hypothesi*, the reflective standpoint is not a standpoint from which anyone can act. It is a standpoint of disengagement from action.

In fact, Nagel needs to tread carefully here as there is a close competitor to his own view in the consequentialist camp that drops the assumption that the objective standpoint is not capable of agency. In *Moral Thinking* (1982), Richard Hare argued that the next stage in the thought experiment of ascending to the reflective level would be hypothetically to fuse everyone's reasons at that level into the reasons for a "world agent" (Nagel 1988; B. Williams 1985: 84–92). That device means that we are no longer sensitive, as Nagel is, to the fact that at the reflective level we know that all the agent-neutral reasons are anyone's, but that all the agent-relative reasons are someone's (and we do not know whose). In Hare's model that does not matter: for the collective agent, both sets of reasons are reasons, and we can proceed to derive an orthodox form of consequentialist theory. Nagel therefore needs to insist on two points: first, the separateness of persons and, secondly, that the reflective level is not a standpoint of agency. But if the latter is true, how can it be a standpoint that (for some reasons) involves considerations that can be intrinsically motivating? I must admit it seems to me that Nagel's insistence on this point is counter-intuitive. But, equally, if he does not insist on this point then his view threatens to collapse into Hare's version of consequentialism.

Concerns about the argument of *The Possibility of Altruism* survive, therefore, in a new form that applies to Nagel's later view. What would be the consequences of accepting that Sturgeon's and Darwall's criticism applies as much to the argument of *The View from Nowhere* as to *The Possibility of Altruism*? In one respect it would be an advantage: Nagel would no longer be committed to the thought that the objective point of view is itself a standpoint that supplies motivational content even if it cannot be a standpoint of agency. However, in other respects this would bring about a serious change in Nagel's emphasis. The idea would be that reflection issues to each agent a reminder that other agents also have a wide range of reasons and values that matter to them as much as your reasons and values matter to you and in the same way. However, reflection does not back up this reminder with the further idea that for each of those agent's agent-neutral objectified reasons and values we can find a counterpart reason that is quite *literally* yours too.

My own view is that the reminder that other people have concerns and values that parallel yours is certainly an ethically important thought. We can all agree that egoistic and selfish people exhibit a serious moral fault (Thomas 2005). The objective point of view, then, retains a great deal of intellectual authority over our practice. However, we might want to balance that consideration with another aspect of Nagel's view that I shall describe in the next section, namely, his sympathies with pluralism. These are reflected in his recognition that the objective point of view has its own costs and blind spots. There is a wide range of considerations for which we try to find objective proxies, but cannot. There are also the costs of objectification itself. If one takes these further issues into account, an acknowledgement of the authority of the objective view has to be balanced by an account of its inherent limitations. In his pluralist moments, Nagel takes these limitations very seriously and with characteristic intellectual honesty draws attention to them.

Nagel discusses all of these limitations to the intellectual authority of the objective view, but ultimately, his commitment to the Sidgwickian model and to the authority of the objective point of view leads him to hybrid theory, not to pluralism. If the former retains some authority, but not, as it were, a complete monopoly over authority in practice, might Nagel's overall view be more inclined to take a pluralist, rather than hybrid theoretical, form? Perhaps, but Nagel is too insightful a philosopher not to have anticipated the line of concern that I have expressed. He offers reasons why he comes down decisively in favour of hybrid theory and against pluralism.

In summary, my concern is that that while at the objective level reflection recognizes both classes of reasons (the agent-relative and the agent-neutral), the reflective agent cannot find out whether she can combine particular reasons from these classes until she re-engages with her first-personal point of view. It can only be when she has re-engaged at the subjective level that the issue of combination arises. I have highlighted an odd consequence: the motivational import of objective reasons at the objective level seems to be idling as it can do no work *at that level*. But Nagel is insistent that it possesses motivational content at that level nonetheless.

Expanding on this criticism a little, a pluralist will argue that the aim of reflection is to seek an overall set of hypotheses that best make sense of our overall commitments. We look for the most plausible set of overall principles that explain and justify the practical commitments that we are prepared reflectively to endorse. But if that is our aim then it seems to me that an agent can only come to an "all things considered" practical verdict when all the reasons that *could* apply to her actually *do* apply to her. The only standpoint from which one can know that this is the case is one of engagement. That standpoint will be informed by the results acquired by objectification and can include the generation of new reasons by that standpoint itself. It can also include reasons sensitive to the costs of engaging in objectification. Importantly, however, it can also extend to those reasons that Nagel has problems objectifying. It is the only standpoint at which *all* of those considerations are available. That seems to me to lead, ineluctably, to the pluralist conclusion that no special authority attaches to objective reasons. The results of objectification will be heterogeneous, and we need practical judgement to discern how an individual agent will balance the various reasons, subjective and objective, that survive reflective scrutiny (including the costs of reflection itself). It might be a serious ethical misjudgement, after all, to live one's life by the reasons made available exclusively from one standpoint to the exclusion of the other.

However, as I have noted, Nagel anticipates this problem. He stipulates that reasons at the engaged level must either be endorsed by the objective standpoint or tolerated by it, but they cannot escape standing in some relation to it: it sets "a standard with which the subjective is constrained not to clash" (*VN*: 155). This standard applies not simply to whether or not something is a reason. It applies, crucially, to practical verdicts: judgements, all things considered, as to what one has most reason to do. Such verdicts must always be a judgement that *could* have been reached from the objective standpoint. We may, in fact, reach it by a different route, from the subjective standpoint, but while the route might be different, the verdict must be independently reachable from the objective standpoint. That is Nagel's objectivist "escape clause" and it commits him to hybrid theory, not pluralism.

From pluralism to hybrid theory

As I have argued, there are conflicting pressures within Nagel's overall reflective theory of morality that he does not seek to reconcile. The first is the controlling influence of the ideal of objectivity. The second is his sensitivity to the range of reasons and values that reflection shows us to acknowledge in our ethical practice. If these represent Nagel's pluralist leanings, however, then he is still not a pluralist! His ideal of objectivity ultimately wins out.

However, *The View from Nowhere* does show a marked appreciation of the inherent limitations of the objective point of view. The first such limitation arises because of the problems of valuing reflectiveness itself. Sometimes, Nagel notes, "individual life and personal relations" involve commitments, the objectification of which would distort those very commitments. Nevertheless, Nagel's overriding ideal of authenticity leads him to claim that "we want to be able to understand and accept the way we live from outside" (*VN*: 155). But if we are always motivated to take up the objective standpoint by that ideal, it is unclear that when one re-engages with one's own life the objective view can replace what one finds in that engaged perspective. Similarly, it is unclear that peaceful coexistence between the two perspectives is possible. The danger of distortion when we try to force all our subjective commitments into the mould of the objectively endorsed (or tolerated) is clearly recognized in passages such as these:

> Sometimes … the objective standpoint will allow us to judge how people should be or should live, without permitting us to translate this into a judgement about what they have reasons to do. For in some respects it is better to live and act not for reasons, but because it does not occur to us to do anything else. This is especially true of close personal relations. (*VN*: 155)

Yet even in this case, having acknowledged the danger of distortion or failure even to recognize the values allegedly in need of objective underwriting, Nagel continues:

> Nevertheless, the possibility of objective affirmation is important. We should be *able* to view our lives from outside without extreme dissociation or distaste … the extent to which we should live without considering the objective point of view or even any reasons at all is itself determined largely from that point of view. (*VN*: 155)

That, however, is explicitly circular. But not all circular justifications are vicious circles: some are simply unavoidable. Furthermore, Nagel's claim here is, as a practical policy, inconsistent and the agent has to choose. You cannot locate, in the thoughts of a single agent, both a policy of living one's life in the light of non-objectifiable ethical considerations and a commitment to objectively tolerating that very same policy. Nagel is aware that there is a choice to be made in this case with costs on either side. Objectivity unsurprisingly ratifies objectivity, but choosing to live a life controlled by the objective standpoint loses some of our ethical commitments in the process.

Nagel recognizes that the objective standpoint itself has some inherent limitations: he believes that working oneself into a completely "alien" or incommensurable set of values is a subjective enterprise that simply cannot withstand objectification. The consequence is that the objective view accommodates an awareness of its own limitations. It includes the thought that there are people living by values that fall outside its scope. More controversially, this limitation can also apply if we find lifestyles or ambitions or personal tastes in value systems closer to ours that we simply find unfathomable: Nagel's (not entirely serious) example is finding marathon runners unintelligible. This is not an instance where the objective view tolerates quirky personal ambitions: it simply does not apply to them! For all these reasons, and in keeping with his general pessimism about theory giving us all that we want, Nagel buys his commitment to an objectified hybrid theory at a cost. He fully acknowledges, in a way that expresses his pluralist leanings, that a wide range of important ethical considerations simply cannot be fully acknowledged by the objective point of view. Yet, in spite of these considerations, the objective standpoint retains an intellectual authority in Nagel's overall account that the subjective view, understood broadly, still cannot attain. This is in spite of the fact that some practical commitments are incompatible with an objectified view of them such that the move to an objective standpoint distorts such commitments irrevocably.

Two versions of hybrid theory: Nagel and Scheffler

I shall now explain some of the details of how Nagel works out his particular form of hybrid theory, as it is a distinctive view in several ways. Among the major approaches to normative ethics hybrid theory is the most recent development. It was an innovation by Samuel Scheffler in his book *The Rejection of Consequentialism* (1994). This book was derived from a Princeton University PhD thesis supervised by Nagel. Before the publication of this book the battle lines in normative ethics were fairly clearly drawn, with the various versions of utilitarianism trading intuitions with critics committed to deontologically focused or virtue-focused rival views. Scheffler took as his starting-point the impartial point of view of consequentialism and combined it with an instrumental notion of rationality. However, from that impartial point of view he also built into his theory a recognition, from the outset, of the importance of the personal point of view.

As I described above, a hybrid theory, generally, is defined by the view that one is always permitted, but never required, to bring about the best outcome from an impartial standpoint. One can also exercise one's agent-centred prerogative, permitting a disproportionate evaluation of outcomes from the personal point of view, in a way that supplies a rationale for deontic options. However, Scheffler's form of hybrid theory finds no satisfactory rationale for deontic constraints. Scheffler's achievement was permanently to change the range of alternatives in normative theorizing in a groundbreaking way. Since Nagel's thinking in this area developed in close parallel to his, a comparison of their respective views will help to clarify Nagel's views, too.

There are significant differences between Scheffler's version of hybrid theory and Nagel's version that emerge when one looks at the details of their respective views. Nagel's version of hybrid theory works like this: take all the reasons and values available at both the personal and the reflective levels and place them together, as a collection, not a fusion. When, from a standpoint of engagement, you reflectively consider your own reasons, there are, alongside the demands placed on you by other people (expressed by neutral values and reasons), agent-relative reasons. What you do not find in your engaged standpoint are the *agent-relative reasons of other people*. So the device of the objective standpoint has already worked to sort other people's reasons into those that genuinely impinge on you and those that do not.

The next important step in the formulation of Nagel's hybrid theory is that in the balance of reasons that are inputs to your overall decision you may prioritize, in your own life, a personal ambition (an agent-relative reason or value) over something of agent-neutral value to you. That seems an intuitively plausible thought in common-sense morality. If we concede that, then that assumption makes available an argument from analogy. If that is sometimes permitted in your own case, then it seems as if you can straightforwardly prefer your own agent-relative reasons to the agent-neutral reasons that represent the claims on you of other people. Furthermore, their claims on you are "capped" at those that can be directly objectively represented. You need *never* promote their agent-relative reasons if that involves unreasonable sacrifice on your part. So, *prima facie*, the space in which one can lead one's own life appears protected against the demands of fully impartial morality in just the way that a hybrid theory intends so to protect it. That is, in essence, the form that

Nagel's version of hybrid theory takes, but he does add some important caveats and restrictions. In particular, if one is weighing one's own agent-relative reasons against the agent-neutral reasons reflecting the claims of others, one might have to use a different standard of evaluation from that which is appropriate in one's own life.

Suppose that in order to pay for your plane ticket to a holiday of a lifetime climbing Mount Kilimanjaro you go without food for a month, restricting yourself to tap water and baked beans. If you are willing to do that, then we cannot fault you for it; it is your autonomous choice over a matter that affects you and no one else. However, suppose that during the last week of your self-imposed regime a disastrous earthquake in a foreign country leaves many people homeless and starving. A representative of Oxfam comes to your door collecting money to provide humanitarian aid for those starving people. In that case, it seems, you are open to criticism unless you take money from your holiday savings and give it to charity. It would be a poor joke to tell the charity collector that because you are going to go without food yourself the starving earthquake victims should go without food also. Indeed, your claim can be represented as making it seem as if they ought to do without in order to help you reach your goal. Those needs that Nagel calls "basic impersonal needs" have more weight when they are those of others than do our own in the first personal balancing of reasons. We can exercise our discretion over our own needs, but not over those of others.

Nagel contrasts four possible views of how to react in cases like the one of the earthquake victims: the reaction of the orthodox consequentialist, that of a Schefflerian hybrid theorist, Nagel's own version of "hybrid theory" and finally a combined proposal with features of both his position and Scheffler's position.

First, the orthodox consequentialist argues that the entire project of attempting to accommodate the validity of agent-relative projects and reasons of autonomy more generally is in principle completely misguided (Honderich 1996). Ted Honderich argues from a standard consequentialist perspective that it is an intellectual rationale for selfishness. For this kind of orthodox consequentialism, practical decision-making should restrict itself to those values that can receive a direct representation at the objective level. Nagel demurs from this hardnosed proposal, responding that "objectivity ... [does not] require of us ... the aim of eliminating perspective from the domain of real value to the greatest possible extent" (*VN*: 173). The key thought, for both Nagel's and Scheffler's versions of hybrid theory, is that this decision to renounce all perspectival values is a personal choice that one can choose to make, or not. But it is not demanded by objectivity *per se*.

Secondly, how would a case like that of the earthquake victims be dealt with in Scheffler's own view? Nagel notes of Scheffler's version of the view that its treatment of this issue is "different from mine but not strictly incompatible with it" (*VN*: 174). Scheffler does not distinguish, among an agent's practical commitments, between those that generate and those that do not generate values represented at the objective level. His more orthodox treatment of the consequentialist component of his view allows the determination of an outcome from an objective (impartial) perspective to range over people's preferences generally. He does not differentiate between the different kinds of reason and motivation that Nagel distinguishes. But, as Nagel notes, that does not affect the idea of an agent-centred prerogative itself. That idea can be formulated independently of the scope of the interests over which it ranges: it could work not by changing this scope, but by assigning different weights to those interests that it *does* cover. However, Nagel wants to draw a distinction, within his moral psychology, between objectifiable and non-objectifiable reasons. Therefore, he cannot be as irenic and tolerant of the whole range of that which can be represented as preferences as Scheffler can.

Honesty compels Nagel, however, to register how this divergence causes special problems within his own view. He does so in describing that which is distinctive about his own version of hybrid theory, making it a third distinct approach to dealing with the example of the objectifiable interests of others. Scheffler believes that we can take up two perspectives on one and the same situation, one impartial and the other reflective of the personal point of view. These two perspectives must generate disproportionate evaluations of the same outcome: that is how the scope of an agent's discretion is calculated. But in Nagel's version of hybrid theory, we only have two contrasting representations of the same outcome for a limited range of moral considerations. That causes a problem for Nagel because in *The View from Nowhere* the subjective (agent-relative) and objective (agent-neutral) can coexist side by side, but only in a limited range of cases. Not only is there no guarantee that they are in fact coextensive, we have compelling reasons to suspect that they are not.

Consider one of Nagel's paradigmatic examples, namely, pleasures and pains. We have a representation of those reasons within our own motives that are capable of surviving objectification. They are represented at the objective level directly and are the basis of both agent-neutral values and agent-neutral reasons. However, in the case of agent-relative reasons we cannot *contrast* how they are represented at the objective level with how they are represented at the personal level. That is because they do not have a direct objective counterpart as pleasures and pains do. But if they are, nevertheless, objectively tolerated as considerations for an agent, then they seem to fall outside the method by which one can calculate Scheffler's prerogative. We cannot generate a disproportion by contrasting how they are generated from different perspectives, both construed as perspectives on outcomes. There is no available contrast to hand. Therefore, Nagel cannot calculate the scope of an agent's prerogative in the same way as Scheffler.

Nagel is concerned that if he calculated his version of an agent-centred prerogative in exactly the same way as Scheffler, then the result would seriously distort the correct ethical result. For example, if we simply add the class of subjective reasons to the reasons that fall within the scope of an agent's prerogative (calculated in Scheffler's way), then the agent is not only getting off the hook morally, but actively conspiring to do so. The hybrid theorist's agent-centred prerogative is a limited discretion permitting one to attach greater weight to those interests that are represented from a personal point of view. But if such an agent is *already* departing from the requirement to bring about the best outcome, impartially considered, then it seems a further distortion in her own interests if she now adds into the balance of reasons further agent-relative reasons. The demands of others recede as the agent starts to stack the deck in her own favour. She does so by bolstering those reasons permitted by the prerogative with further reasons that *could not* be included in the scope of its determination.

Nagel suggests a composite proposal: a "variable prerogative" would work reason by reason. This represents a fourth approach to dealing with objectifiable interests. It has to proceed case by case. In each case it would weight an agent's interests as follows: "An individual is permitted to favour himself with respect to an interest to the degree to which the agent-relative reason generated by that interest exceeds the corresponding agent-neutral reason" (*VN*: 175). This abandons the idea that there is some single way of calculating a prerogative that operates over general classes of reason, or one general class, those reasons "made available" by the personal point of view.

This is, however, another fault line running between Nagel's pluralist leanings and his commitment to hybrid theory; his proposal still only works for those reasons that have an objective counterpart, and many important agent-relative considerations do not. Are most of the central and most ethically important practical commitments of an agent objectifiable? One can only hope so if the theory is going to work. Nagel softens the boundary lines between the two kinds of commitment, namely, the objectifiable and the non-objectifiable, but a difference remains given that many reasons having no objective counterpart at all (*VN*: 175). Thus, if we understand the problem as Nagel does, the issue of distortion remains, both from a consequentialist perspective and from a pluralist one.

The hybrid theorist, whether Nagel or Scheffler, predictably pleases no one, being criticized by consequentialists for departures from the objective standpoint and criticized by non-consequentialists for giving that standpoint too much weight. From the latter perspective the primary concern is that of the correct representation of our pre-theoretical commitments. If thinking objectively about our practical commitments fails to represent entire classes of reason, what special authority attaches to that perspective in the deliberations of a particular agent? It is no answer to be told that that is the perspective that exclusively represents the objectified interests of others. That hands over, too quickly, a crucial class of moral reasons to the objectified perspective. Predictably, like Scheffler's theory, Nagel's hybrid view attracts criticism from those like Honderich who take it to attach too much weight to the personal point of view and those who take it to attach too little weight to the personal point of view and its characteristic values (Thomas 2005).

Interestingly, Nagel's consideration of hybrid theory foreshadows his discussion of political philosophy. With his characteristic breadth of vision, he sees that the question of the extent to which you have to represent the interests of others in your own practical deliberations quickly becomes a political question. It is one that may receive a different answer in a just or an unjust society. Nagel's very interesting discussion of this issue in *The View from Nowhere* (*VN*: 206–7) reached its culmination in *Equality and Partiality* (1991), the arguments of which will be the subject of the next chapter. I shall, over the next two sections, deepen the description of Nagel's hybrid theory in two ways. First, I shall describe his own version of, to borrow Scheffler's title "the rejection of consequentialism". Secondly, having set out the various ways in which Nagel departs from a consequentialist framework, I shall focus on one in particular that is of considerable theoretical interest, namely, his account of deontic constraints.

Nagel's rejection of consequentialism

There are two reasons to discuss Nagel's "rejection of consequentialism" in the course of developing his own view. The first is that, *qua* hybrid theory, his view is defined as much by the restrictions it places on how one ought to interpret the demands of objectivity as by its account of an agent's discretion. The second is that Nagel's taxonomy of the various classes of reason that he believed a consequentialist could only model incorrectly has been deservedly influential. It is worthy of consideration in its own right and leads directly to Nagel's distinctive treatment of the idea of a deontic constraint. Unlike Scheffler, Nagel believes that deontic constraints *can* be given a plausible rationale.

The main problem that Nagel identifies in consequentialism is that it is concerned solely with outcomes. It is not sensitive to how those outcomes are brought about; it is, as Bernard Williams once put it, "simply a matter of which causal levers are within reach" of the agent, not which agent throws the levers (1973: 176). If one *is* sensitive to how outcomes are brought about, it matters very much that outcomes are brought about by the acts and omissions of people. Nagel claims that those acts and omissions are typically reflected in three broad classes of subjective reason. These are the classes of reasons of *autonomy*, reasons of *obligation* and reasons of *deontology*. I shall briefly characterize each class and their mutual relations before describing two of them in more detail (for reasons I shall explain).

The first class of reasons consists in reasons of autonomy. Reasons of autonomy arise because a person has a life of their own to lead. Parts of that life are the particular "desires, projects, commitments, and personal ties" to which that agent is committed (*VN*: 165).

The second class of reasons consists in reasons of obligation. Nagel sees such reasons as stemming from "special obligations we have toward those to whom we are closely related". They function as an agent-relative curtailment on the monopolistic tendencies of agent-neutral and consequentialist reasons. Nagel calls these "reasons of obligation", although he emphasizes that this is not to be understood on the model of explicitly undertaken voluntary obligations like promises or contracts. As Michael Walzer (1990) has emphasized, many of our obligations are simply part of identities that we did not choose; what matters is not that we did not opt in to being sisters, sons or life-partners, but that in each case we have the freedom to break such ties. Some obligations, as the late-nineteenth-century ethicist F. H. Bradley (1999) put it, come with "our station and its duties" without voluntary commitment on our part. Nevertheless, it matters to us that we can free ourselves from such obligations.

The third class of reasons consists in the class of deontological reasons. These reasons arise because the interests of others impinge on your life. The result is that you are enjoined not merely to bring it about that other people do not suffer, but that you are to ensure that this does not occur through your own actions. To illustrate this distinction, suppose you are a schoolteacher in a room of rowdy children. You want to tell them not to shout, so as to bring about an outcome where no one shouts. Do you do so by shouting? It might be the most effective way to bring it about that there is no shouting in the room. But to bring that about, you would have to do the very thing that you are trying to prevent, namely, shout.

This simple case shows that one can bring about an outcome in two ways, and that deontology, as opposed to consequentialism, is sensitive to how outcomes are brought about and may be particularly sensitive to how you, in particular, bring something about through your agency.

Nagel sees autonomous and deontological reasons as related in this way: "Autonomous reasons would limit what we are obliged to do in the service of impersonal values. Deontological reasons would limit what we are *permitted* to do in the service of either impersonal or autonomous ones" (*VN*: 165). What unites all three classes of reason, from Nagel's perspective, is that each falls outside the scope of a consequentialist's single pattern of objectification. For the consequentialist, all reasons must be grounded on agent-neutral values such that they can figure in states of affairs (outcomes) that can be promoted. Nagel can certainly see the appeal of this rival view. He notes, in particular, of reasons of obligation that: "I have less confidence here than with regard to the other two categories that in ordinary thought they resist agent-neutral justification" (*VN*: 165). I shall discuss in the next section Nagel's treatment of deontic constraints. It will emerge that he shares a general understanding of their nature that seems vulnerable to the charge that the whole idea is paradoxical in a way that the consequentialist (and Scheffler) allege.[11] Nevertheless, qualifications aside, Nagel stands by his considered verdict that there are three classes of reason that the consequentialist has difficulty accommodating. That makes, in his view, a decisive case for a hybrid theory and for the rejection of consequentialism.

I will not devote any space to an extended analysis of reasons of obligation as they are not a distinctive part of Nagel's view. There is a sizeable literature arguing that an objective view can accommodate such reasons without distortion and Nagel, as I have noted, tends to agree. For that reason he does not discuss this class of reasons in any detail so I will not do so either. However, it is a priority for a hybrid theory to make space for deontic options: these are, in Nagel's terminology "reasons of autonomy". I shall consider them at length below. It is not, strictly speaking, necessary for a hybrid theorist to find a rationale for deontic constraints. I have already noted that Scheffler thinks they are irrational. However, this simply marks an important point of difference between him and Nagel. Nagel offers a succession of rationales for deontic reasons that I discuss below. Before turning to that important topic I shall explain Nagel's treatment of reasons of autonomy.

I have already noted Nagel's view that subjective states with a direct bearing on well-being, pleasure and pain, prove under analysis to be instances of agent-neutral values that function as the grounds of agent-neutral reasons. Continuing his favourite example from *The Possibility of Altruism*, Nagel argues that even a pain is timelessly and intrinsically bad such that any person has a reason to terminate it. This is, for Nagel, a representative example of the putatively subjective turning out to be directly endorsable at the objective level. However, in the case of other reasons that the objective view *tolerates* such reasons do not turn out, on reflection, to be grounded on the agent-neutral. The entire class of reasons of autonomy fit this profile.

An example is a personal project, an idea that straddles the line between morality, conceived narrowly as the domain of what we owe to each other, and personal ideals (Strawson 1974c). Nagel uses the example of wanting to climb Mount Kilimanjaro. He thinks that this personal ambition makes a very limited claim on other people. If it is your ambition, then it may give you a very strong reason to climb Mount Kilimanjaro. However, it is not a plausible example of something that anyone else has a reason to bring about. Its restricted practical scope implies, for Nagel, that it cannot be analysed as an agent-neutral reason grounded on an agent-neutral value.[12]

This kind of case suggests an extension of some of the ideas appealed to so far; might one not say that this reason counts more for you than for others because the outcome, your climbing Mount Kilimanjaro, is more *valuable* to you than to anyone else? In the case of the badness of a pain, Nagel thinks one can develop an interpretation at the two levels of the subjective and the objective that are in harmony: only apparently subjective, the badness of pain is reflectively revealed to be an agent-neutral reason grounded in an agent-neutral badness (disvalue). But personal ambitions seem different: they seem to indicate an ineliminable role for the idea of an agent-relative value. Nagel credits Scanlon with the insight that "the impersonal value of things that matter to an individual need not correspond to their personal value to him" (*VN*: 167). That opens the way to an explanation of the subjective reasons of autonomy based in, to take the current example, a personal ambition. The value of that outcome can be an agent-relative one.

This is a significant expansion of the range of explanations Nagel can offer, so he needs to make an adjustment to his moral psychology to accommodate it. Rather than simply stipulate that there are agent-relative values, he seeks to explain them. He does so by appealing to the relation between desires, interests and values.

He contrasts two ways in which desire may be related to value. Both can be, misleadingly, described as a value being "conditional" on a desire. In the first way of relating these ideas a person's having *X* when he desires *X* instantiates an agent-neutral value. The satisfaction of that desire is, therefore, something that anyone has reason to promote: hence the agent-neutrality of the reason. However, in the second way in which desire and value can be related, a person's achieving the object of her *X* when she desires *X* is a case where "susceptibility to the value is conditional on having the desire" (*VN*: 167). This is an example of an agent-relative *value* and hence the satisfaction of that desire is only a reason for the person who has it.

Nagel argues that this second kind of case cannot be treated like the case of pleasure and pain. His "simple hedonism" treats such mental states as involving a built-in liking or aversion. This reflects the phenomenological fact that we do not choose to like pleasures or choose to dislike pains. In these cases there is a pro or con attitude directed to a propositional content, but it carries a default setting that we cannot change at will. That is what explains the comparatively direct objectification of these states. But any more psychologically complex practical project or commitment may involve desire in a more complicated way.

This more complex case involves a kind of bootstrapping, where the presence of an ambition is conditional on the presence of a desire generated by that very same ambition. We can distinguish wanting to climb Mount Kilimanjaro from the value of so doing; to that extent desire and relative value are independent. However, the former makes the agent "susceptible" to the value in a way that explains why this value gives a reason to this person, but not to anyone. Practical scope is restricted by the necessity of the enabling desire: if you lack that desire, you will not be "susceptible" to that value. The scope restriction is thereby explained in a principled way. This is one of Nagel's most interesting, and neglected, complements to his distinction between the agent-relative and the agent-neutral.

This marks an important constraint on the ambitions of objectification. As Nagel sees the situation, in many cases we simply respond to value that is independent of our subjectivity. But in many other cases, equally important to our ethical lives, our subjective perspective (with its particular interests and concerns) is that which leads us to pursue certain values. It is, indeed, what makes them values *for us*. (You might say it explains not the values, but our valuing of those values.) Our response to these values, or rather to the conditions that make them possible, is optional. You do not have to take an interest in mountain climbing, valuable though it is to many people. You may instead take an interest in collecting rare books, or in becoming a skilled pianist. You know that each of these activities is taken to be valuable by someone, but unless you share the interest that that person takes in those values, you choose not to engage with them.

This, for Nagel, marks out the distinctive features of the category of agent-relative values and explains why they are related to the objective view in the way that they are. All that the objective perspective can "see" (metaphorically) is not the values themselves, but the reasons that they ground. This explains a principled restriction in Nagel's buck-passing: evaluative judgements always pass the buck to judgements about those features that ground reasons for an agent when viewed from the objective point of view. This is not true – as has just been demonstrated – for judgements made from the subjective point of view. Here the underlying values are invisible to the objective point of view.

The objective perspective leaves behind the particular and interest-relative subjective concern with values that grounds both agent-relative values and agent-relative reasons. That is why agent-relative value, as a category, is not directly representable in it. From the objective perspective, the grounded *reasons* themselves can be seen as both valid and not in need of an underlying guarantee from either agent-neutral reasons or agent-neutral values. But the agent-relative *values*, whose existence is conditional on the occupation of the subjective standpoint, are no longer accessible from that standpoint when one has ascended to the objective level. That is a principled "blind spot" in the objective point of view.

This leads to Nagel's interesting idea of representation by proxy: the objective point of view cannot directly represent agent-relative values. It is a precondition of ascent to that level that one reject those very conditions that make agent-relative values the values that they are for particular agents. But Nagel believes that they can be represented, at the objective level, by proxies. The proxies are the very agent-relative reasons that such values ground. This is true even if those reasons are subject to the restriction that at that level you do not know which of those reasons are yours. What this point emphasizes is the extreme importance to Nagel of the assumption of the separateness of persons. While it matters to Nagel that one does not know, at the objective level, whose agent-relative reasons are whose, that does not matter at all to Hare's world agent. For Hare all individual psychologies are fused into one, so it does not matter if one cannot identify whose agent-relative reasons are whose at that level.

Inconsistently, having identified the category of agent-relative reasons and values in a positive way, Nagel cautions that this is a potential source of ethical error. If reasons of autonomy can roll back the demands of the objective point of view, then an agent might choose to interest herself in a diverse range of values in order to acquire a wide range of agent-relative reasons and values. That is, for Nagel, ethically suspect: another instance of the individual stacking the deck in her own favour by taking on a large number of subjective reasons. He expresses his concern in terms of the intellectual authority of the individual:

> The crucial question is how far the authority of each individual runs in determining the objective value of the satisfaction of his own desires and preferences. From the objective standpoint we see a world which contains multiple individual perspectives. Some of the appearances of value from within those perspectives can just be taken over by the objective self. But I believe that others must remain essentially perspectival – appearances of

> value only *to the subject*, and valid only from within his life. Their value is not impersonally detachable, because it is too bound up with the idiosyncratic attitudes and aims of the subject, and can't be subsumed under a more universal value of comparable importance, like that of pleasure and pain. (*VN*: 168)

The desire–interest pairings involved in agent-relative values are not simply "desires and preferences". While they are described as "appearances to the subject", I interpret this phrase as a neutral, merely diagnostic idea. It not meant to invoke the idea of Cartesian objectification. One might reflect, against Nagel's sentiments in this passage, that if they are appearances they are truthful ones. Climbing Mount Kilimanjaro, to those who want to do so, really is valuable to them in a way it is not to others. Being incapable of representation at the objective level, for principled reasons that Nagel explains, does not make agent-relative values *unreal*. That fact is compatible, of course, with another one, namely, that people can make ethical mistakes. They can make mistakes about agent-relative values, as they can about anything else. But I take it that this passage does not mean to suggest that this whole class of values is vulnerable to this kind of debunking analysis.[13]

Nagel thinks that the discrepancies in the evaluations available to one from an engaged (personal) or detached (objective) perspective show up in how one experiences the respective values in a way that makes the integration of these two evaluative perspectives problematic. Objectively, one's own reasons of autonomy seem to lose the importance that they have from the subjective point of view. Nagel argues that there is an interesting contrast between how a person can view himself from the objective perspective as faced both with "reasons that simply come at him ... independently of his choices" and reasons that he has created for himself by taking up an optional interest in certain values. It remains, stubbornly, in the latter case a "value for him" even though "he" in this case is the subject himself.

Agent-relative value can find no direct recognition from the objective view: it is in its blind spot. It is represented, by proxy, via the reasons that it grounds. But might there be a meta-level surrogate for agent-relative values, namely, the value to each person of getting what he or she wants? If that surrogate tracks agent-relative values, then that is another way in which such values can be tracked by the objective point of view. But the distinctive features of Nagel's moral psychology block this proposal. I noted above that one might hope to take his treatment of pleasure and pain as representative of a wider class of the values of well-being. At least, you might hope this if you are an orthodox consequentialist and are looking to represent as many values as possible from the objective perspective for a reason I shall shortly explain. However, in Nagel's moral psychology pleasure and pain differ radically from "mere" desires and preferences and from desire–value pairings. There is no distinctive value, in Nagel's moral psychology, to desire satisfaction as such.

Furthermore, Nagel thinks that reasons of autonomy work in way that makes it difficult to see how the satisfaction of a person's desires can "create" value in a state of affairs far removed from the desire itself. His example of a state of affairs maximally removed from a person's "inner condition" is an individual's desire for posthumous fame. That desire, Nagel suggests, cannot make that state of affairs valuable for anyone other than the agent. But, conversely, if we can find cases where a subjective sense of well-being is stronger, there may well be a meta-level value to a person's getting what he or she wants that could be objectifiable.

This last point seems very scholastic, but actually it has a direct bearing on the ambitions of consequentialism. Sophisticated versions of consequentialism have developed more and more "objective" conceptions of a person's good that move that idea increasingly further away from a grounding in a person's occurrent mental states, to rational preferences, fully informed preferences, interests or a selection from a list of the objective goods of a life. Nagel offers a further thought here that extends the reach of consequentialism beyond its direct application to agent-neutral values and reasons. Reasons of autonomy, agent-relative though they are, may, in a significant range of cases, be tracked by the meta-value that it is objectively good that a person gets what he or she wants, where that want is itself subject to various conditions.

In any individual's moral experience the problem of reconciling the two viewpoints of the personal and the objective remains. Nagel thinks that some degree of individual dissociation is inevitable (*VN*: 170, 172). Objectively, agent-neutral values supply a motivation for a particular person as the limiting case of their supplying a motivation to anyone. The account at the objective level of agent-relative values is more complex. Their existence is tracked by the acknowledgement of agent-relative reasons. In some additional cases they are further tracked by the surrogate value of it being objectively good that people have their reflective desires satisfied (if those desires form part of a desire–value pairing). However, it remains true that no agent-relative reasons can supply a motivation at the objective level.

Therefore, when you come to apply these thoughts to your own case, from the engaged perspective, you can see that you have certain reasons of autonomy that give you reasons and motives. From the objective perspective, you can see that in a sense it is reasonable for you to have those reasons, but only as the sort of person that you are. They are bound up with the contingencies of your identity and interests. But, as was discussed in the final section of Chapter 3, "The objective self", Nagel thinks that we ought ethically to cultivate a more austere, more objective conception of ourselves. Thinking of yourself in that way, as an objective self, you lack any motive to act on these reasons of autonomy (unless they are in fact yours, which you cannot know at the detached level). And the values that ground them are invisible to the objective view. It does seem, therefore, that one's reasons of autonomy run the risk of seeming fragile and contingent when one tries to reconcile the two perspectives.

Nagel is aware that there is an air of paradox hanging over the claim that mental states such as pleasure and pain have a more secure foothold in the objective perspective than a reason of autonomy. Such reasons can, after all, form an important part of the structure of ambitions and personal projects that make up a life. He seems, as he puts it, to have left out "many fundamental aspects of other people's welfare which cannot easily be given a hedonistic interpretation – their freedom, their self-respect, their access to opportunities and resources that enable them to lead fulfilling lives" (*VN*: 171).

Sensitive to this charge, he responds that in fact we can identify "very general goods" (*ibid.*) that are more like pleasure and pain in sustaining neutral values and hence can be recognized at the objective level. They do not need to be represented by proxy or understood derivatively via a person's individual ambitions or projects. They transcend the contents of consciousness, narrowly conceived, but still "determine the character of life from inside". Adding in the new constraint of universality on agent-neutral reasons, Nagel argues that "liberty, general opportunities and the basic resources of life" (*ibid.*) will also prove to be agent-neutral reasons and values.

The status of deontology

I have already noted that Scheffler could find no rationale for deontic constraints in his version of hybrid theory. That is largely because of his background commitment to an instrumental model of rationality

(Foot 1985; Scheffler 1994: 192–7). The latter model serves to generate a putative "paradox of deontology", an idea that I shall now explain. Suppose that, whatever ethical goal you set yourself, your achievement of that goal is constrained in certain ways. There are some things you simply cannot do in order to bring about a goal. Therefore, your aim-directed activity is subject to that which Robert Nozick called "side-constraints". Consider, to illustrate what he meant by that, my previous example of whether, to stop a roomful of noisy children shouting, you shout "No shouting!" If you do so, then you violate a norm to prevent future further violations of that norm. Analogously, one can imagine a goal-directed or teleological moral outlook that permitted the violation of a constraint provided that doing so minimized the number of such violations overall. From the instrumental, maximizing and outcome-focused perspective of the consequentialist, the deontic constraints of common-sense morality are allegedly paradoxical. That is because, as intuitively conceived of, they do *not* permit violations of themselves in order to minimize further, future, violations. You cannot commit a murder to prevent further murders, for example.

It is hard to find much middle ground in this debate. It is indeed true that from the limited resources that the consequentialist brings to describing the issue, it does seem that there is insufficient material to find deontic constraints anything other than paradoxical. But that is hardly a fair representation of the opposing view. The deontologist, for example, may hold a view in which the perspective of practical reason itself allows one to place rational constraints on the space of proposed actions, not outcomes. From that perspective there is nothing paradoxical about deontic constraints at all (McMahon 1991; P. Hurley 1997). Nagel has his own interesting contribution to make to this discussion, made particularly apposite by the degree of overlap between his view and consequentialism.

To illustrate what he means by a deontic constraint and to point towards that which he regards as their rationale, Nagel uses what is by now a very well-known example. You are involved in a car crash in which your passengers are seriously injured; you find a nearby house where you aim to borrow their car to go and get help for your injured friends. But in the house you find a clearly frightened little girl who tells you that, on hearing your approach, her grandmother took the phone and car keys and locked herself in the bathroom. You go to the door and try to convince her of your good intentions, but she will not open the door and give you the phone or the keys. It occurs to you that if you twist the child's arm, you will convince her to do so. But doing so, Nagel argues, clearly violates a deontic constraint: you simply cannot do something like that. The description of the proposed course of action ought to rule it out from your deliberations.

Given Nagel's theoretical framework, this is a puzzling class of reasons for him. Perhaps that is why he begins his discussion with the observation that this is an "obscure topic" that "complicates an already complicated picture" (*VN*: 175). As a preliminary attempt at characterizing these reasons, Nagel describes them using distinctions that he has already developed. In his interpretative framework, deontic reasons are non-optional, agent-relative, reasons that serve to "restrict what we may do in the service of either relative or neutral goals" (*VN*: 175). They are a new class of agent-relative reasons but, unlike other agent-relative reasons, they represent the way that the interests of others impinge on an agent. They therefore put some strain on Nagel's classificatory scheme and his distinction between the agent-relative and the agent-neutral. They represent the interests of others and yet discharge this role without representation at the objective level. They are "personal demands governing one's relation with others" (*VN*: 176). He draws attention to their token-reflexive feature that they constrain *your* act of bringing about an outcome, not simply its occurrence:

> If there really are such constraints, the following ... [seems] to be true ... You shouldn't break a promise or tell a lie for the sake of some benefit, even though you would not be required to forgo a comparable benefit in order to prevent someone else from breaking a promise or telling a lie. (*VN*: 177)

Simply as a fact of moral phenomenology Nagel finds the existence of reasons like this undeniable. And while, as a system, they certainly function in ways with definite consequences and can be seen to regulate social interaction in a way that might lead one to try to give them an agent-neutral rationale, Nagel argues that this explanation would be too extrinsic to how such reasons actually function.

A more accurate representation of these reasons is, however, problematic within Nagel's framework of assumptions. It is supposed to be the objective view that represents what we owe to each other. In the case of deontic options, a person's special projects can, as Nagel has explained, give rise to individualized engagements with values that give rise to agent-relative values and reasons. However, deontic constraints seem to cross these two classifications: they are relative, but represent the interest of others. "How", asks Nagel, "can there be a reason not to twist someone's arm which is not equally a reason to prevent his arm being twisted by someone else?" (*VN*: 178; see also Darwall 1986).

The child who does not want her arm twisted has an interest in not being harmed; that is, Nagel argues, a neutrally represented interest. So the relativity of an agent-relative deontic constraint cannot be based on the interest that it protects. Nor does it arise from an individualized concern with value of the kind that underpins Nagel's distinctive explanation of agent-relative reasons. Reasons of autonomy, for example, are optional in Nagel's classificatory scheme in the sense of being conditional on interest or desire. However, deontic constraints are non-optional and universal. They do not exhibit any implicit dependence on a prior condition in the way that I have to take an interest in piano-playing to value playing a sonata well.

Nagel certainly understands the consequentialist case against constraints: if your theory is solely outcome focused then how can a person's interest generate a reason against people doing something to infringe that interest *directly* that does not equally prevent that same damage being done to that interest *indirectly*? Yet he sets against this argument the consideration that deontic constraints seem to be the kind of reflectively stable consideration that we want to endorse as a normative truth.

To find a grounding rationale, he appeals to the traditional doctrine of double effect. This is a distinction between intentionally bringing about an outcome and causing an outcome that is foreseen but not intended:

> The principle says that to violate deontological constraints one must maltreat someone else intentionally. The maltreatment must be something that one does or chooses, either as an end or as a means, rather than something one's actions merely cause or fail to prevent but that one doesn't aim at. (*VN*: 179)

This is not the same distinction as another important distinction for deontologists, that between doing and allowing (Brook 1991; Quinn 1994c,d). Nagel argues that his doctrine grounds a more specific rationale for deontic constraints: one ought not to *victimize* another person. Nagel's rationale is distinctive in that it focuses not on the status of the person, but on the relation between agent and victim. It is the relationship of victimization that seems to him the morally objectionable feature of the situation that provides the rationale for these constraints.

The difficulty in recognizing this rationale within the framework of Nagel's prior assumptions is, once again, diagnosed as arising from the clash of the engaged and the objective viewpoints:

> It is as if each action produced a unique normative perspective on the world, determined by intention. When I twist the child's arm intentionally I incorporate that evil into what I do: it is my deliberate creation and the reasons stemming from it are magnified and lit up from my point of view. They overshadow reasons stemming from greater evils that are more 'faint' from this perspective, because they do not fall within the intensifying beam of my intentions even though they are consequences of what I do.
> (*VN*: 180)

This is a recognition of the basic ethical significance of agency, but it is not clear that this explanation precisely matches up with the prior formulation of taking special care not to violate constraints *oneself* (see Brook 1991).

There are two respects in which this earlier discussion of deontic constraints by Nagel in *The View from Nowhere* is noteworthy. (His account was later significantly revised, as I shall describe below.) The first is that Nagel is not the only philosopher to question the consequentialist's myopic focus on the bringing about of outcomes and how this distorts our understanding of deontic constraints. However, he is distinctive in nevertheless "backing up" deontic constraints with a value-based rationale in which they arise from an individual's perspective on agent-relative value. Nagel is prepared to add, alongside the neutral values and reasons of the objective perspective and the relative values and reasons of autonomous reasons, a new class of agent-relative deontic reasons. He already introduced corresponding relative values for the relative reasons that make up the class of reasons of autonomy, but he agrees with Scheffler that conceding that much does not automatically legitimize deontic constraints. Just because they share the formal feature of being agent-relative does not mean that the justification of one carries over to the other. As I noted above, some deontologists are nervous about any value-based rationale for deontology. The grounds for their wariness is that any such account is vulnerable to representation in that which Nozick called "gimmicky" versions of consequentialism in which one simply builds into one's account of outcomes sensitivity to who brought them about (Sen 1983). If that is a general vulnerability, it will apply with special force to Nagel's rationale given that he accepts the authority of the objective point of view.

The second feature of this earlier account of Nagel's is that it seems to mis-describe that which it is trying to explain. (Nagel came to this view himself.) If the fundamental ground of such constraints is the relationship of victimization, are we not looking, ethically, in the wrong place? What about the person victimized? The reason, once again, why Nagel does not cite facts about that person and his or her moral status is that he is concerned to explain the special relation in which two people are placed when a deontic constraint is violated. He notes, very insightfully, that it is with the event, the *violation*, that we are concerned. It is the intentional aiming at an evil, even for the sake of a greater overall good, that is the morally relevant feature. Evil is, of its nature, something at which one ought not to aim. Nagel argues as follows: "Intention appears to magnify the importance of evil aims by comparison with evil side effects in a way that it does not magnify the importance of good aims by comparison with good side effects" (*VN*: 181). When you intentionally set yourself to do evil, it seems to you that you are normatively guided by the very thing that ought to repel you. This, Nagel claims, "produces an acute sense of moral dislocation" (*VN*: 182).

Viewed objectively, acting in this way may bring about the greater impersonal good, but that is not how it seems to you, the agent, from your engaged perspective. But, interestingly, that is not how it seems to your victim either. He or she may, from their objective view, agree that the harm to them ought to happen for a greater impersonal sum of value over disvalue. But it is their engaged perspective that tells them what they may legitimately object to in how they are treated by others. On a fully consequentialist view, if I have to kill one to save five others, then that person has no grounds to object (whereas the five do if I do not kill the one). That, as Nagel points out, seems an absurdly strong demand on the one person selected by me as my victim. He or she lacks any "special standing to appeal to me", even though I have chosen him or her from the six to be my victim where that choice is legitimized by the best outcome objectively considered. But Nagel argues that it is the relation in which we stand that is crucial in explaining why the agent-relative reasons have the moral significance that they do in this case: "This relation has the same character of normative magnification when seen from the personal perspective of the victim that it has when seen from the personal perspective of the agent" (*VN*: 184). Nagel concludes that deontic reasons have to be "admitted" at a "basic level" (*VN*: 185) as reflecting the perspectives of both agents and victims.

Nagel's publications in ethics subsequent to *The View from Nowhere* have reflected an important change in his position concerning the correct rationale for deontic constraints (Nagel 1994a, 1995c). Influenced by the work of Frances Myrna Kamm and Warren Quinn, Nagel now views the rationale for deontic constraints to be rooted not in the intentions and perspective of the victimizer, but in the inviolable status of the person being victimized. This revised account is presented in "Personal Rights and Public Space" (Nagel 1995c). Nagel focuses more narrowly on one form of deontic restriction, namely, rights. He argues that the rationale for the agent-relative restriction that one ought not, through one's own agency, to violate the rights of another is grounded on the recognition of an independent value, namely, the value of inviolability. This is a *status* enjoyed by anyone in a normative system that recognizes it (recognizes it, not creates it). This general account offers an answer to the alleged paradox of deontology:

> It is true that a right may sometimes forbid us to do something that would minimize its violation ... But the alternative possibility differs from this one not only in the number of innocents killed. If there is no such right and it is permissible to kill the one to save the two, that implies a profound difference in the status of everyone – not only of the one who is killed.
>
> (Nagel 1995c: 90)

Rights are, following Kamm's characterization of them, "generally disseminated intrinsic goods" (*ibid.*: 93). They are a fundamental normative idea whose thematization simply adds another level of complexity to Nagel's hybrid view.

Where do we go from here?

The normative ethical theory of *The View from Nowhere* illustrates very clearly the two aspects of Nagel as a philosopher. His fidelity to our ordinary experience leads him to recognize as wide a class of ethical considerations as he can. His commitment to the practical ideal of objectivity leads him to as much system-building as the subject matter can tolerate. The result is a tolerant and sophisticated version of a hybrid ethical theory but, as has been demonstrated, any view of this kind has its internal tensions. Nagel concludes by speculating that this may be because of our historical limitations (in a manner paralleling his ontology of the mental and his hopes for imminent theoretical developments as a way out of our problems). Perhaps hybrid theory is the best view we can come up with now, but imminent historical developments may push us more and more to an objective view.

Nagel offers two interconnected arguments, one from fallibilism and one that appeals to history. His fallibilist argument is that our current views may, for all we know, be in error. Perhaps we are at an early stage in the development of our collective moral ideas such that progress would involve our collectively drawing closer to a more objective view. Objectivity here remains a notion internal to human life. We are dealing with people, with their distinctive peculiarities, and with how to regulate their conduct by a practical use of reason. The entire subject matter is anthropocentric, but that does not mean that there cannot be gains in objectivity relative to that human point of view.[14] These attempted gains, Nagel believes, have to acknowledge that the aim of eliminating all subjective perspectives is not attainable. In particular, Nagel's ambivalence towards the demands of objectivity is evident in his fear that ethics, as we currently understand it, may be disguising selfishness under the heading of reasons of autonomy. The moral progress that Nagel seeks is analogous, in his view, to the progress of science. People will come more and more to modify the scope of the personal in ethics, replacing its demands with those of the impartial perspective. The result will be a moral gain.

I have undoubtedly betrayed my own pluralist sympathies in my representation of Nagel's hybrid theory. Nevertheless, I do think that this historical and fallibilist speculation does scant justice to the range and complexity of Nagel's own view. He emerges as a reluctant hybrid theorist in spite of himself. It seems to me that he is, uncharacteristically, running together two issues, namely, how demanding morality is and what the nature is of the theory that truly represents it. These two questions ought to receive separate answers (Thomas forthcoming (b)). Perhaps, given the current state of the world, a hybrid ethical theory would be very ethically demanding. That seems, in fact, to be a very plausible assumption. But why, in order to capture this sense of demandingness, do we need to abandon hybrid theory and become more objectivist? A correct reflective ethical theory aims to represent what reasons there are, not to determine their comparative weight. Consequentialists typically argue that they are uniquely placed both to recognize the uncomfortable truth that morality is, given the contingent circumstances of our world, very demanding, and to theorize that truth. But that is an unhappy conflation of two quite distinct ideas.

It seems to me that the analogy Nagel points to between scientific and moral progress is not a very strong one. Certainly there are some relatively foundational truths that are part of the modern moral outlook that we cannot now imagine ourselves without, such as equality of moral status reflected in more substantive moral truths such as the vileness of slavery. But that idea is not the proprietary possession of the objective point of view. A more plausible appeal to history, it seems to me, arises from the vitally important connection that Nagel himself emphasizes between his hybrid view and politics. It is in liberal politics that a solution may be found to the reconciliation of the demands of individuals, who believe that they have their own lives to lead, and the demands of others. Perhaps it is in a fully just society that a reconciliation can be reached. Nagel has deeply interesting things to say about that prospect and these are the subject of the next chapter.

Overall, the two aspects of Nagel's philosophy, his uncompromising ideal of living in the light of the truth (including the reflective truth about one's ethical experience) and his systematic theoretical ambitions are never more clearly in conflict than in his normative ethics. The appeal of the ideal of Sidgwickian objectivity remains, even though its role in *The View from Nowhere* differs radically from its role in *The Possibility of Altruism*. One interpretation of Nagel's final considered opinions is that they are unstable, fatally divided between his pluralist instinct to accommodate the full range of ethical considerations and his competing instinct to attach central importance to our power to objectify our pre-reflective commitments. Perhaps another interpretation would be fairer: that this conflicted position is itself expressive of a truth of higher order or, at any rate, is as close to the truth as conflicted beings such as ourselves can hope to attain.

Chapter 7

Justice, equality and partiality

Nagel has made selective interventions in political philosophy throughout his career. Primarily, these have taken the form of individual, highly regarded papers that have had a transformative effect on such issues as positive discrimination, equality, the value of privacy and, most recently, global justice. In the later stages of his career he has turned his attention more consistently to political philosophy. His first book-length contribution to political theory originated as the Locke lectures at the University of Oxford; in a revised form they were published as *Equality and Partiality*. Since the publication of *Equality and Partiality* Nagel has continued to explore themes in the area between moral and political philosophy, and issues of political morality, and has also co-authored a second book on tax policy. However, *Equality and Partiality* expresses his views on political philosophy most comprehensively and also shows how he takes issues in political philosophy to be shaped by the overall conception of philosophy (particularly moral philosophy) that has been traced throughout this book. This closing chapter is devoted mainly to an analysis of its central argument.[1]

In *Equality and Partiality* Nagel succeeded once more in saying strikingly original things about an area of philosophy so thoroughly explored that it seemed all options had been exhaustively discussed. Interestingly, it is the most general feature of his approach, the fact that Nagel clearly takes political philosophy to be continuous with moral philosophy, that is the basis of his originality. The relationship between moral and political philosophy has been debated since systematic political theorizing in the West began with Aristotle. Aristotle explicitly discusses the relationship between ethics and politics and was a political scientist as much as a political philosopher. Nagel's distinctive contribution to this discussion inaugurated by Aristotle is a novel theoretical paradox focused precisely on how moral philosophy and political philosophy relate to one another.

Equality and Partiality argues that our best normative ethical view and our best normative political view cannot be integrated. We have conclusive reasons to support them both, but they inevitably come into conflict. The originality of his view lies in the claim that we do, indeed, face something like a paradox when we reflect on this issue. It is not original to be told, as libertarians have sometimes claimed, that from the perspective of our "natural" moral status, an egalitarian liberalism imposed at the level of the state can be rejected as unduly burdensome on the individual. Nor is it original to be told that a prior commitment to such egalitarianism, at the level of the basic structure of society, may lead to a radical reconstruction of how people may be ethically permitted to behave at an individual level. The troubling part of Nagel's view is how he represents us as theoretically committed *both* to a position that he calls "ethical pluralism" (actually, hybrid theory as was established in the previous chapter) and to liberal egalitarianism in a way that seems superficially plausible. However, the combination leads to a deep-seated incoherence within our own moral and political outlook. I shall focus in this chapter on this central aspect of his view.

While Nagel's position is undoubtedly original, his approach as a whole forms part of a tradition of theorizing about equality with its basis in the work of Rawls. Rawls was a philosopher with whom Nagel had a constructive philosophical engagement until Rawls's death in 2002.[2] When Nagel describes the normative political theory that we have most reason to accept he is referring to Rawls's political liberalism. While I cannot give a fully adequate description of Rawls's well-known views here, a schematic outline of its main features is necessary for what follows.

Rawls's most general concern was with the nature of a legitimate political theory in a modern Western society. This broad theme was discussed comparatively late in his career in *Political Liberalism* (1993). Rawls came to believe that what is distinctive of such a society is that the state, which has a monopoly over the use of force within that political community, has to legislate legitimately to all its citizens even though they hold widely differing views about the good life. How can legislation for all be justified in the face of such reasonable pluralism about what is good? Rawls's solution to this problem was to require that any reasonable view of the good life should be able to affirm, from within itself, the principles of political liberalism. Each can do so as this conception is not the proprietary possession of any: it slots into all those views provided that they are reasonable. Rawls's metaphor for this pluralistic source of support was that his liberal principles form a "modular", strictly political conception. This solution to the problem of the deep-seated moral pluralism in politically modern societies draws on traditions of toleration that are equally part of our modern political experience.

This most general view acts as the framework for Rawls's particular theory about justice, first expressed in *A Theory of Justice* (1971). The central idea of that book is that a model of justice that can give insight into and regiment our existing convictions (and bring out some surprising consequences from them) sees just social choice in conditions of full knowledge as modelled by first-personal prudential choice in conditions of ignorance. The aim of this construction of a concept of justice is insight into that to which we are already committed: so the target notion is our inchoate convictions about liberty and equality that we try to model using various artificial simplifications.[3] Adapting the social contract tradition to his own ends, Rawls asks us to imagine a group of choosers in what he calls an "original position". Each reader conducts the thought experiment of being a co-deliberator with these parties where everyone in this choice situation has to devise a set of principles to govern the distribution of the benefits and burdens arising from their social cooperation. The key feature of this choice situation is that the decision is taken behind a veil of ignorance: identical to the informational restriction that Nagel uses in his modelling of impartiality, this device functions so that the choosers in the original position do not know who they are or which social role they will play in the outcome to be determined. The parties are mutually disinterested and asked to reason prudentially.[4] Rawls believed that in this precisely specified choice situation the parties will choose his two principles of justice, which cover the basic liberties and equality of opportunity as well as his famous difference principle.[5] Rawls states his principles as follows:

> First Principle: Each person has the same indefeasible claim to a fully adequate scheme of equal basic liberties, which scheme is compatible with the same scheme of liberties for all;
>
> Second Principle: Social and economic inequalities are to satisfy two conditions:

- They are to be attached to offices and positions open to all under conditions of fair equality of opportunity;
- They are to be to the greatest benefit of the least-advantaged members of society (the difference principle).

(2001: 42–3)

The subordinated second part of the second principle, is (oddly) the most famous and most widely discussed part of Rawls's view.[6] This well-known "difference principle" permits inequalities in a given distribution only in so far as such inequalities benefit the representative worst-off person under that distribution. The justification for the whole scheme is that no one is any worse off than they need to be in a scheme justifiable to each party.

Rawls was a normative pluralist; his two principles of justice are not intended to cover all aspects of the lives of citizens in a liberal society such as their lives in families or in associational life. One reason for this is that Rawls's society in *A Theory of Justice* is not a voluntary association given that you enter it with birth and leave it with death with no immigration or emigration. However, private associations are voluntary associations, so that if you disagree with the principles governing their internal working you can simply leave and choose another.[7] The primary focus of Rawls's theory was what he called the "basic structure" of society. This presupposed framework of political and socioeconomic institutions has a deep and pervasive impact on the life chances of those born within it.

The moral nerve of Rawls's egalitarianism seeks to reduce (but not to eliminate) the inequalities that arise from what he called the "natural lottery" in the distribution of marketable talents. In his final completed scheme, while it is individuals who are talented and who can legitimately be incentivized when they market their labour, we can think of our pool of talents as a whole as a collective trust for the benefit of all. A further important point for understanding the use to which Nagel puts Rawls's ideas in his own work is that Rawls offers a distinctive treatment of the idea that fair treatment consists in getting what you deserve. Rawls does not believe that there is a justificatory notion of desert available *prior* to setting up the institutions of the basic structure within which people can have reasonable expectations. Within that structure of expectations, you can seek that which you deserve, but outside that structure the idea does no justificatory work. Desert is, for Rawls, a derived and not a basic justificatory idea.

Rawls believed that the specific form of application of his principles in the context of any actual society would require interpretation and political argument, even for the first principle (the liberty principle) and first part of the second principle (the equality of opportunity principle) that are to be secured in the constitution. Nevertheless, it seems plausible to claim that the requirements of his egalitarianism, if applied to the societies with which we are familiar in the contemporary world, would prove to be very demanding. They would involve very significant changes in our political and socioeconomic arrangements.

Equality and Partiality is the latest of those analyses that have sought to determine how feasible Rawls's proposals are if, as Rousseau advised in the opening words of *The Social Contract*, we have to "take people as they are" (1997). To identify the kind of issue that concerns Nagel, consider an account of a "genealogy" of justice that competes with Rawls's view. Hume argued that justice, which he took to be concerned narrowly with the distribution of property holdings, was an artificial virtue because people are naturally benevolent in the sense of ethically partial. However, their partiality was, of its nature, restricted to those to whom they stood in some special relationships. (Reasons of this kind correspond to Nagel's reasons of obligation.) Given that Rawls assumes that in some sense families are naturally just, and given the further plausible assumption that families are a basis of partial attachment, to what extent are the requirements of his view compatible with a society in which familial and partial affection has such a deep effect on the life prospects of individuals? Rawls, after all, seeks to reduce the impact of the natural lottery, not to eliminate it. It is no part of his view to eliminate families by raising children outside the family structure or to eliminate disparities in talents through genetic engineering (were it possible to do so). Given these sources of inequality that are exogenously given, how does Rawls's view succeed in mitigating their effects? I shall now describe the framework of assumptions that Nagel brings to his discussion, many of them by now familiar from Chapters 4 and 6. His special assumptions, as will be clear, go a long way to generating the specific problem with which *Equality and Partiality* is concerned.

Framing the issue

Equality and Partiality's pessimistic conclusion is that we lack a coherent and viable political ideal. The reason for this lies in a division of standpoints within the individual and in the macro-effect of combining different individual standpoints into a collective standpoint, compounded by the effect of time. As I have already described in the previous chapter, according to Nagel's hybrid ethical theory we are genuinely divided between the claims of the personal and the impersonal. If we accept this ethical theory, then a person can blamelessly attach value to his or her personal values and interests. He or she can do so provided that such values and interests are suitably constrained by another of his or her commitments, the impartiality of the objective view. That view represents the agent-neutral values of others as grounding agent-neutral reasons for you, notably those reasons grounded on the "liberty, general opportunities and the basic resources of life" of others alongside the agent-neutral reasons of your own. In spite of the weight of these demands, the ethical legitimacy of the personal point of view might, for example, allow you to spend time developing your own talents and interests or to work harder than you have to in order to provide good things for those close to you, such as your family (extending the idea of the personal, quite naturally, to a decision with broadly political implications).

To focus one's thoughts about the political implications of the kind of issue that I have already discussed in the context of normative ethics, consider this case. Suppose that while putting in extra effort at work to take your family on a more expensive holiday than usual, you discover that the single parent family who live next door cannot afford to replace their washing machine. They are struggling to make ends meet on a low income and every few days you see your neighbour, with three very young children in tow, walking a considerable distance to the local launderette. You might reflect that this state of affairs is a shame, but it is not your fault: provided, that is, that you believe that you live in a just society. You pay your taxes and know that a guaranteed level of free or subsidized welfare is available to support that family. Suppose you do live in a welfare state society.[8] Can you nevertheless continue to work hard for yourself and your family with a clear conscience, knowing that others are not doing so well? After all, you are contributing to a "safety net" of social provision.

Nagel thinks that your conscience ought not to be clear and that this view would be complacent. Morality demands that we pursue the goal of equality more thoroughly. This commitment ought to be built into the fundamental structure of society, and with this demanding and substantive egalitarianism constitutionally secured, we would then be free to pursue our own lives in the light of the kind of pluralist ethical outlook that we take to be the normative ethical truth. Many conscientious citizens of contemporary welfare state societies might identify with this set of aspirations. But Nagel's conclusion in *Equality and Partiality* is that this is precisely the situation that we cannot be in. He believes that even if we do full justice to the demands of equality, we will need a lot more than minimal provision for others in order to lead our own ethical lives with a clear conscience.

Even worse, if we go beyond this minimum and we do meet the demands of impartial equality, we encounter a serious difficulty when we try to pursue our own lives. We find that the operation of the personal, while ethically legitimate at an individual level, has effects at the level of a whole society, and through time that frustrates our very desire for impartial equality. The best way of balancing our commitments turns out to be self-frustrating or self-stultifying. Nagel builds up to this conclusion in stages, beginning with a basis in moral philosophy familiar from Chapters 4 and 6. As this basis has already been extensively discussed above, I shall try to keep the exposition to its essentials in what follows.

Nagel's political anthropology

Rawls's *A Theory of Justice* did not offer any theory of the person.[9] Nagel's first major departure from Rawls's approach is to place a description of the internally complex and conflict-ridden nature of persons at the centre of his liberalism. People are, in Nagel's view, fundamentally ethically divided between the demands of the personal and the impersonal where the latter comes to represent, within the individual, the claims of the social. (This is, in the specific context of political philosophy, the guise assumed by Nagel's dichotomy of the subjective and the objective.) The argument developed from this starting-point proceeds through different stages of reflection that are by now familiar. However, they have a different endpoint, reflecting the fact that the argument has been extended into political theory.

The starting-point is our subjective, pre-reflective, personal condition. We then think of the world in abstraction from our own point of view: the objective conception is "centreless". Following the line of analysis set out in *The View from Nowhere*, at the personal level we do not discriminate between our reasons and motivations as a whole at the subjective level. However, at the reflective level, we can see that some of our commitments prove to be agent-neutral reasons grounded on agent-neutral values. The consequence of this is that those commitments have motivational import for us. Importantly, this is equally true of the corresponding agent-neutral reasons or values of others. There is, in addition, a range of agent-relative reasons tolerated by the objective point of view, but they cannot supply motivation as we do not know whose reasons they are. Finally, some of our personal commitments cannot be represented at all at this level and they have to be abandoned.

Nagel suggests that there is already, implicitly, a transition to political concerns at this level as we seek a social choice function that proceeds in the light of the two truths discerned at the objective level. The first is that everyone is of equal value and the second is that all intrinsic values are agent-neutral. At this point, Nagel argues, we ought to adopt a substantial egalitarianism. Taking the collection of individual reasons and values as a whole, from that impersonal and objective perspective one attempts to find a metric for the alternative ways of answering to these demands that impact differently on different individuals in the light of their own values. This is the problem of collective social choice. But at this level, Nagel thinks we can already perceive that the correct answer will be substantially, not merely formally, egalitarian.

The next stage of reflection arises because we now face a problem in balancing these apparently conflicting demands. Nagel argues that we solve the problem by adopting a political solution in the form of higher-order impartiality. This reconciles the conflicting demands of the personal and the impersonal via a contractualist model of political legitimacy that gives everyone agent-relative ends, but the same end. In a remedy to the defects of standard contractarianism that is beset by problems of free riding because it gives a collective reason for action that does not distribute over each member of the collectivity, contractualism seeks to model a structure in which those who adopt the theory are symmetrically placed *vis-à-vis* each other. Thus, everyone has an agent-relative end specified by the theory, but symmetry is ensured by all those relative ends being the same end when viewed across the entire "constituency" of individuals to whom the theory applies. That is how contractualism works to supply an independently plausible theory of political legitimacy. We believe that each individual affected by a set of political arrangements is entitled to a rational justification for those arrangements that is the *same* justification given to each of them.

Contractualism is usually presented as a theory of rightness, but it is more plausible as a principle of legitimacy. It inverts the contractarian focus on convergent agreement and introduces, instead, what Parfit has called a "complaint model" governing the selection of normative principles. Candidate sets of principles are put forward and we ask which set can be reasonably rejected. In the light of this contractualist model we select the theory that is acceptable by its lights: the theory that has the feature of giving everyone the same agent-relative aim and that no involved party can reasonably reject. That leads, in Nagel's argument, to a further level of reflection, where we structure our social world to reduce the conflict between the personal and the impersonal in the light of the demands of the higher-order impartiality that we have now adopted. At this point we have moved beyond normative ethics and are engaging in political theorizing and construction.

At this point the transition has been made from moral philosophy to political philosophy proper. This higher-order concept of impartiality functions as a political and not as an ethical principle. Nagel cautions that this higher-order solution to the tension between the personal and the impersonal can only reduce the impact of this clash. It will not eliminate it entirely as that is simply psychologically unrealistic. But he notes that the clash between the personal and the impersonal, which higher-order impartiality adjudicates, is not inevitable in all respects: it only occurs when they overlap. But when they do overlap and come into conflict, the higher-order reconciliation effected at this political level of reflection will have been implemented in the institutional design of society so as to lessen the conflict:

> The ideal, then, is a set of institutions within which persons can lead a collective life that meets the impartial requirements of the impersonal standpoint while at the same time having to conduct themselves only in ways that it is reasonable to require of individuals with strong personal motives. But to state this ideal is to see how hard it will be to realize. Its two conditions pull in contrary directions. (*EP*: 18)

At this political stage, an outline of a constructive solution to the original problem seems available. The putative clash between the demands of the personal and of the impartial points of view can be alleviated by institutional design. But this proposal is derailed by a new and special problem. The idea of responsibility plays a different role in a political context than it does in a moral one. That is why

Nagel believes that there can be no direct analogue in political theory for our best normative ethical theory, namely, hybrid theory.

I noted above the paradox that a Rawlsian society is not a voluntary association in spite of the justification for its distributive principles taking the form of a social contract theory. We think of contracting parties as "contracting in" to some voluntary scheme, but there is no "take it or leave it" in the case of a society governed by Rawls's two principles. There is no contracting in or out. Nagel addresses this paradox head on: institutional design has a great impact on people's lives and ought, therefore, to be voluntarily underwritten. Yet, it cannot be entirely so underwritten. To make matters worse, this lack of voluntariness must be combined with a particularly heavy burden of responsibility. Nagel believes that in the case of political responsibility there is no distinction between positive and negative responsibility (*EP*: 99). In the case of state action, there is no difference between action and inaction. The state, as our collective agent, is as responsible for that which it fails to prevent as that which it brings about. Nagel argues that for this reason it would be unacceptable, at the political level, to implement a political theory that is analogous to a hybrid ethical theory. In order to solve this problem we have to apply the fully impartialist theory discerned at the objective level to the basic structure of society. It would be too stringent a demand within ethics, but politics introduces stringent demands because of the special nature of political responsibility. That is the crucial new dimension added in the transition from ethical to political theory.

Nagel invokes an important new idea at this stage of his argument: we have to aim to implement a "moral division of labour" (*EP*: 53ff.). By doing so we incorporate this demanding impartial egalitarianism into the basic structure of our society and hope that this leaves enough social and political space for us to lead ethical lives guided by our best normative ethical theory. However, while that is our ideal aspiration, Nagel thinks that we can see already that it cannot succeed. Impartialist egalitarianism is frustrated by macro-effects arising from the micro-level of individual behaviour. This is true even when such individuals lead their lives in accordance with a hybrid ethical theory assuming that the latter is, in fact, the correct normative ethical theory. The two parts of the view, the interaction of the correct ethical theory in the lives of individuals and the correct political theory imposed by the special demands of political responsibility, come into inevitable conflict. The former works to undermine the latter.

This is a practical conflict where we simply cannot implement two practical policies simultaneously. Nagel believes that we have compelling reasons, explored at length in Chapter 6, to lead our lives according to hybrid ethical theory. There are further reasons, stemming from the special nature of the political and its account of responsibility, to seek a more demanding and unrestricted form of impartialist egalitarianism. But the demands of these two perspectives on one and the same social reality are irreconcilable. That is Nagel's pessimistic conclusion.

His argument does not stop there, however, as he also considers how the argument could be taken forward in the light of his diagnosis. One response is to say that the inequalities that Nagel has focused on have their sources in class and talent, expressed through the influence of families in the former case, and that these are simply irremovable because we have to "take people as they are". The inequalities they give rise to are, therefore, outside the scope of justification. If we have reasons to restrict them, those reasons are, as it were, external to their nature.

A radically opposed view says that once the natural impacts on the social to generate inequality, it is open to justification by the standard we apply to our basic social institutions. Nagel is more sympathetic to this second argument. Nagel shares Rawls's view that we are not responsible for our talents so that inequalities arising from them (except for the "most immediate") are "morally questionable" (*EP*: 121). But that repeats the problematic point the argument has reached without solving the problem at all or suggesting how it might be solved:

> Individual motives remain, and they work against equality in two ways: by inhibiting support for institutions which attempt to reduce inequality, and by putting pressure even on institutions that give priority to the interests of the worse off to tolerate substantial inequalities as the price of efficiency. At the same time these motives seem to play an essential role in the successful operation of a modern competitive economy. (*EP*: 121)

Nagel cannot envisage a transformation of motives that would make this problem go away. Not everyone can be motivated to work hard solely by the intrinsic rewards of their job nor, for that matter, by generalized benevolence. The market is the most efficient transmitter of information about preferences. To meet those preferences people need economic motivations, such as the desire for economic success, which in turn can be directly competitive. It is plausible further to argue that even if such motivations are not directly competitive in particular cases where gains to an individual are at no cost to others, that is not true of the system as a whole. So the desire for economic success is always indirectly competitive.

There are ways in which people can be motivated to restrict their economic motivations: markets are regulated to a greater or lesser extent. Everyone can see the point of controlling what economists call "negative externalities": a good example of this would be environmental pollution. Similar justifications apply to the regulation of competition. By analogy, can we encourage a division of motives where people are motivated to pursue profit with that pursuit being constrained by the demands of impartiality? Nagel suspects not. He argues that the furthest one can go is to support a decent social minimum that would not put in question, as Rawls and his strong egalitarianism does, a "general suspicion of inequalities owing to class or talent" (*EP*: 123). Acquisitiveness is hedged by redistributive taxation with the underlying motivation being the alleviation of sufferings that are not a person's fault, without undue overall cost. All in all, this looks like a philosophical route to the conclusion that an extension of existing welfare state provision is the most realistic way forward. Nagel's point, however, is that if this is our way forward, we have to accept that it has no rationale at the level of theory that is not internally incoherent. That conclusion should certainly trouble anyone who wants to think reflectively about the justice of the society in which he or she lives.

Nagel can see only two ways of closing the gap between this "best-case scenario", which already represents for him a serious compromise with the truth of a demanding impartialist egalitarianism, and the goals set by the more demanding egalitarianism that the objective view demands of us. The first route involves compromising over people's current motivations and pushing for a higher level of minimally decent social provision in addition to fair equality of opportunity. Above the basic minimum, inequalities are not themselves suspect and are in any case lessened by taxation. People above the minimum can blamelessly seek competitive advantage. For those below the line, Nagel assumes that "a guaranteed base will not prevent most people from working, since most people want more than they have" (*EP*: 125). But he regards this option as very much a second best to directly implementing impartialist egalitarianism.

If we could get that far, Nagel envisages a further stage that acts more fundamentally on people's motivations: incentives and innovation would not be in the form of unequal pay. This would be sustained by a general disposition not to be "conspicuously" better off than others. People would want to do well for themselves and their families, but would be reluctant to do well if, comparatively, others in their society were doing badly. Nagel adds that he views a psychological development of this kind as "highly unlikely" (*EP*: 126). Furthermore, it is problematic in its own terms in a way he identifies: it introduces a "gap in incentives to economic efficiency". Those with the highest competitive advantages are motivated to do well, but not as well as possible if that leaves others trailing in their wake. That reluctance on their part will have a negative impact on economic efficiency overall. This view is morally better, but less efficient. He concludes that the more egalitarian scenario is difficult to envisage and that the only psychologically realistic possibility is a more humane form of social democracy.

Given how far this situation falls from his strong egalitarian ideals, he adds that "an acceptable combination of individual and political morality remains to be invented" (*EP*: 129). At this point reflection is complete and the original argument proves to be self-stultifying: the best political solution that we can manage at the highest level of reflection does not pass the test of feasibility. The operations of the personal frustrate the operations of impartial egalitarianism as applied to the basic structure of society. Nagel concludes, unsettlingly, that we have no feasible political ideal of equality.

This is a complex and sophisticated argument. While it "transcendentally deduces" a set of welfare state arrangements as the most feasible trade off between efficiency and equality, it should nevertheless leave one very uncomfortable, as it does so without reconciling a theoretical incoherence in our justification for this state of affairs. I could not, in the scope of this chapter, aim to address every part of this complex overall view. Nagel's intriguing argument requires some further contextualization in order to bring out some of its special assumptions. I shall discuss these before I assess Nagel's central claims.

Nagel's argument contextualized

The first issue that arises naturally is the relation between Nagel's argument and Rawls's own view. The first point to note, as I did at the outset, is that Rawls denied that his theory of justice rested on any particular conception of the person. Nagel's interpretation of the problems facing impartialist egalitarianism, however, are very much shaped by his prior commitment to placing an account of the internally divided nature of people at the basis of his liberal egalitarianism.

There are several very important dimensions across which Rawls's project and Nagel's have very different scope. Methodologically, Rawls is an impartialist and constructivist, but only about justice. Indeed, he seems tempted by the argument that a process of construction needs material in something that is not constructed, namely, independently existing value, which was arguably the same view Kant took of the matter (Rawls 1971; Langton 2007). Rawls does not venture an opinion as to the ultimately correct ethical theory from the point of view of the theory of justice: this theory works with the idea that that question may have an underdetermined answer, as does political liberalism as a whole (Larmore 1990). Furthermore, Rawls does hold the view that Nagel attributes to him about the special demands of justice but it seems to me that he does so only for those parts of his theory of justice that are to be secured in the constitution, not every part of his theory of justice and certainly not the whole of political liberalism. Nagel is clear on this, but it is an elusive point (Thomas 2006b: 317–20).

Rawls does have distinctive views about the interface between the subject matter of the theory of justice, namely, the basic structure, and the lives of individuals. I have already noted his normative pluralism: justice does not apply everywhere. But it does seem to me that it applies pervasively to people's economic lives. Furthermore, each of us has a natural duty to be just and to support just institutions. However, to reiterate the first point, there is no theory of the person in Rawls, so nothing like Nagel's account of our divided selves. By contrast Nagel, like Plato, has his own analogy of soul and city: the internally divided self is expressed, via a moral division of labour, in a divided social reality where the personal is equivalent to the life of an individual in society. However, parts of that social reality (some of its institutions) can be viewed as an institutional expression of the objective point of view. I shall discuss this key idea of a moral division of labour below.

Finally, one needs to be careful in assuming that the impartialist egalitarianism represented in *Equality and Partiality* is similar to Rawls's, given that its context is so different. Rawls is not, for example, a redistributive welfare state egalitarian. To the extent that Nagel's concerns are about how far we can move our existing, radically unequal, societies closer to an impartialist egalitarian ideal, he works within what Rawls would call "non-ideal" theory. But the major difference between the two views is that Nagel's paradox is generated by his impartialist egalitarianism being mandated by *the very same* standpoint within the individual that generates the objective component (part, but not the whole) of his hybrid ethical theory, as I shall now explain.

Nagel's paradox explained

My argument will focus on how Nagel conceives of the interface between the moral and the political. We knew, before reading *Equality and Partiality*, that how people lead their lives at an individual level can have an impact, through time, at the level of a collectivity made up of such individuals. Nor, for that matter, is Nagel the first person to argue that when it comes to the basic structure of society, our intuitive notion of responsibility hardly seems to apply. As I have already noted, because of his rejection of any pre-institutional notion of desert, Rawls does not allow responsibility to figure in any basic way in his account of the justification of distributive justice as a whole (Scheffler 2003). Anyone as influenced by Rawls as Nagel has been is bound to endorse the thought that we are as liable, politically, for what we fail to prevent as for that which we bring about.

The distinctive part of Nagel's view is that our commitment to strong impartial egalitarianism is not simply a commitment within our political principles. It is foreshadowed at the level of the ethics of individual conduct by the impartialist component of that view. It is this distinctive feature of the view (coupled with Nagel's analysis of the internally divided nature of persons) that forestalls a quick response that takes the form of a reminder that social space is made up of individual lives and that we simply have to choose. We have to choose between an ethical pluralism that gives significant scope to individual autonomy or a demanding egalitarianism that may prove burdensome at the level of the individual. If we build strong egalitarianism into the basic structure of society, and that frustrates the operation of a hybrid ethical theory at the individual level, then hybrid ethical theory ought not to be, on reflection, the theory we ought to endorse. If hybrid ethical theory is true and it frustrates the operation of strong egalitarianism, then we have the option of abandoning the latter, too. A more clear-eyed view simply insists that we face not paradox here, but a practical decision. I suspect this is, in fact, what the more orthodox Rawlsian ought to say; as I have already noted, one ground for political liberalism is a sensitivity to the "burdens of judgement" involved in determining a question as complex as the true reasonable comprehensive conception of the good, or even its general form (such as hybrid theory).

However, that response does not go to the heart of what is troubling Nagel. As he conceives of the problem, it is that the *same* impartial perspective that generates strong egalitarianism at the collective level is itself part of our hybrid theoretic ethical outlook. I noted, in the previous chapter, a circularity (not necessarily a vicious circularity) in the objective component of Nagel's hybrid view. The arguments of *Equality and Partiality* embed that circular justification in another, where what is justified is the hybrid view itself and the justifier is the higher-order political principle of impartiality. Nested structures like this are a potent source of paradox. Can we not insulate these two roles of the objective point of view, one in ethics, one in politics, to cancel out their mutual interference? I think we can and that there is an important advantage to be gained if we do so. We can then show that what Nagel takes to be his "second best", most feasible, egalitarianism is not a second best solution at all, but an attractive form of contemporary egalitarianism.

Contractualism and legitimacy

In Nagel's argument one is driven to a higher-order Kantian form of impartiality simply by the demands of legitimacy itself. However, if we are fundamentally torn between our impartial and our personal commitments, what will drive us to overcome this division at the level of political theory? In the case of ethics, Nagel argued that "the extent to which we should live without considering the objective point of view or even any reasons at all is itself determined largely from that point of view" (*VN*: 155). This is circular, but I noted earlier in discussing this point that not all circular justifications are vicious circles. But what is the basis for a similar self-ratification of the objective perspective by itself in political philosophy? That can seem, very plausibly, an area where we often "agree to differ" with those with whom we strongly disagree. We often conceive of politics itself as a matter of accommodating conflict (B. Williams 2005: 77).

Nagel has two responses: that we need to distinguish fundamental, constitutional questions from day-to-day politics, and that we do not want even the latter to be a matter of pure bargaining between special interest groups. Nagel assumes that however much citizens of a legitimate state may disagree over policy, they must share at a deep level a commitment to the legitimacy of the political process, perhaps expressed by a shared commitment to the fundamentals of a constitution. This need for unanimity is going to have to be reconciled with what Nagel takes to be our fragmented, dual nature.

I would argue that the problem with Nagel's contractualist model is not so much that a presupposition of agreement is being built into the operations of the model from the outset; the problem is, rather, the "thinness" of the contractualist model of agreement (non-divergence). Normally when we think of agreement and reasonable rejection, we appeal to a set of underlying considerations that are the grounds of such (dis)agreement. One might, for example, think that the correct normative ethical theory was the right one because of the values it incorporates. Therefore, no one could reasonably reject it because it was the correct account of those values. However, in the contractualist model, rightness just *is* being that set of principles that no one could reasonably reject. If a normative theory is correct by contractualist lights then there is no sensible question of the form "correct in virtue of what". There is no independent basis for correctness independently of the fact that it is the theory that no one can reasonably reject. To those sympathetic to contractualism, this line of objection is over familiar: it is *the* objection to contractualism as a moral theory and it has been much discussed.

A full consideration of this issue goes beyond the scope of this chapter, but I shall note a concern that contractualism does not fare better as a theory of political legitimacy, as opposed to a theory of rightness; indeed, it fares even worse. That is because of how one is to understand the concept of the political. In one of his last publications Bernard Williams argued that "political philosophy is not just applied moral philosophy, which is what in our culture it is often taken to be" (2005: 77). Political philosophy has a distinctive set of concepts, focused on the ideas of power and legitimation. Williams further argued that it has a distinctive notion of what constitutes a political disagreement; that it involves interpretation, but not in the limiting sense of determining what counts as particular instances of a political value; finally, that to make sense of politics you need to make sense of the idea of political opposition. Understanding how a certain kind of conflict is possible is integral to the concept of the political, as a concept allegedly distinct from the ethical (*ibid.*: 77ff.).

The main point that I want to take from Williams's insightful discussion is that making sense of the political involves making sense of conflict explained via the idea of political opposition. Conflicting political values are experienced as involving trade-offs and hence costs. If those costs are not to be resented by those who must bear them when they do not accept the justifications for them, a way must be found to accommodate this fundamental idea of political opposition. Legitimacy, here, is the acknowledgement of an authority that decides what will happen, but not, as Williams puts it, an authority that decides what will happen *rightly*, such that the opponents of the decision are revealed as merely intellectually confused all along. While originally directed at the liberalism of Ronald Dworkin, this argument seems to me to be applicable to Nagel's position in *Equality and Partiality*, too (*ibid.*: 84). If it is correct to connect the concept of the political to a certain kind of understanding of disagreement, then it is striking that in Nagel's version of a contractualist model of political legitimacy, the model itself presupposes convergence on agreement. It must be revised until that is precisely what it delivers. The problem of circularity transfers directly from the ethical case to the use of contractualism as a theory of political legitimacy.[10] But now a special, and different, problem emerges that is not only peculiar to the political, but tied to the very special conditions of responsibility that Nagel makes central to the political.

It is the contractualist view of political legitimacy that should, Nagel argues, lead us to reject the truth of strong egalitarianism. Strong egalitarianism may be a view forced on us by the impersonal perspective but that view proves to be too burdensome and demanding. (That is, after all, how the analogous argument would run within normative ethical theory.) But the special conditions of political responsibility, that is, an obliteration of any restricted notion of responsibility at the level of the basic structure of society, mean that *no view can be unduly burdensome*. If I am as responsible for that which I do not instruct the state to prevent as I am for that which the state brings about, then the already vague contractualist notion of unreasonable burdens becomes empty. The state is, after all, acting as our collective agent. That seems to me a serious problem for Nagel's contractualist model of legitimacy. It is distinct from the standard charge that contractualism is circular because it is motivated by Nagel's distinctive claims about the nature of political responsibility.

Is Nagel's "solution" only the second best?

It seems to me an important task to challenge some of Nagel's assumptions when his final position seems so plausible and attractive (at least to me) and yet it is overshadowed by the claim that the reasoning that endorses it is fatally marred by a paradox. Once again, Nagel's commitment to the ideal of authenticity is evident: we need to get on with the practical issues involved in living as justly as we can with our fellow citizens both within our political community and outside it. But living in the light of the truth also tells us that we have no coherent intellectual rationale even for our best current policy. It is important to realize that there are some very positive proposals in Nagel that, because of his view about the demands of strong egalitarianism, are presented by him as strictly "second best" solutions. I shall argue that not only has he precisely diagnosed forms of egalitarianism that are realistic and desirable normative goals, but that these goals are in no way compromised. They are made less attainable, however, by Nagel's theory of the person, and that theory has, therefore, to be amended.

It is only in the light of his claim that strong egalitarianism is morally demanded of us that Nagel presents us with two positions he sees as a failed "compromise". The first is a non-utopian extension of the form of egalitarianism that seems possible relative to current motivational structures. It is to be followed by a second, utopian commitment to a general disposition to be reluctant to have more than one's fellow citizens. My view is that the efficiency and aggregative considerations to which Nagel rightly draws our attention are, in fact, moral reasons for *not* aiming at the more utopian alternative, with the result that the first of his two options seems to me to be a feasible and attractive political ideal.

Realization of either or both of these goals would be considerably more difficult, however, if we acquiesced in Nagel's theory of the person. That theory is the major obstacle for taking Nagel's own egalitarian theory as a positive proposal of a feasible political theory for our contemporary circumstances. That theory is an abstract characterization of our "divided selves". I have already noted that abstracting is not idealizing: an abstract account of something leaves certain of its features out and does not attribute properties to it that it does not actually possess as an idealization does (O'Neill 1989). But one could argue that Nagel's account, abstract though it is, either leaves out important features of people that are just as abstract as those he identifies, or which are less abstract, but still a vital part of any solution to the problems Nagel considers. I shall argue that Nagel significantly under-describes our social nature. In addition, Nagel's theory of the person leads him to a distinctive conception of how we implement egalitarianism, namely, via the moral division of labour. This idea is as important as Nagel's theory of the nature of persons and both deserve a more extended critical analysis.

According to Nagel, it is because persons are fundamentally divided that we need to compensate for that fact in how we implement our egalitarianism. This strategy of implementation is expressed by the idea of a moral division of labour. Nagel appeals to this idea partly because Rawls's original egalitarian theory has been criticized for an allegedly myopic focus on institutions and structures as opposed to a focus on individuals. A philosopher whom Nagel has influenced and indeed with whom he has collaborated, Liam Murphy, has argued that Rawls is a "moral dualist" who applies different principles to institutions than to individuals. The moral monist believes, allegedly in opposition to Rawls, that the very same normative principles that apply to "institutional design" also apply to "the conduct of people" (Murphy 1998: 52). If these claims can be substantiated, then Rawls's egalitarianism can be criticized for being undemanding, either intentionally or unintentionally. It is not sufficiently demanding because its focus is too restricted. It is applied to the basic structure of society, but not directly applied to the motives of individuals.

How are Nagel's views placed *vis-à-vis* these well-known critiques of Rawls? In so far as Nagel sees us as committed to a demanding egalitarianism rooted in our recognition of the objective point of view, his view seems similar to Rawls's. But his recognition of the partial demands that arise from our divided nature is the most important countervailing impulse to this demanding egalitarianism. Nagel's account of the interface between the moral and the political, expressed by his "division of labour" metaphor, is a subtle one. (It does not, for example, fit neatly into the "moral monism" versus "moral dualism" dichotomy.) That is because Nagel argues that externalizing the demands of the objective point of view into institutions *still* corresponds to an objective motivation within the divided psychology of individuals. It represents an objective demand within the self. The implementation strategy of a moral division of labour aims to reconcile the tension between the objective and subjective motivation that tragically conflicts within individuals. The objective motivations are externalized into the design of a society's institutions.

In Nagel's version of Plato's analogy of city and soul, the distinction between individual and social is a counterpart of a motivational division within an individual (and not just one involving "supporting" an externalized institution). That is why it would be misleading to classify Nagel as either a moral monist or as a moral dualist. Applying justice to institutions is not incompatible, in his view, with inculcating the motivations of justice in individuals. Nagel seems, on the contrary, to imply that this is how we ought to proceed. That seems correct: it is implausible to argue that concern for one's fellow citizens in a particular political community can be fully externalized into institutions leaving only "the personal" untouched by the demands of justice. That which is externalized has a counterpart precisely in a desire to live justly on the part of the individual. There is certainly more to moral motivation than that, but there is at least that. It is a mistake to take the only motivation on the part of an individual to be that of "supporting" those institutions in which egalitarian justice has been externalized. This support only makes sense if, indeed, the individual has the motivation to be just in her dealings with others. Nagel seems to have finessed the distinction between moral monism and dualism in an appealing way.

The positive path forward, it seems to me, is to revise Nagel's account of the political to make his best ethical theory and his best political theory radically discontinuous. This was Rawls's own strategy in his political liberalism. The whole point of the transition, in his view, to political liberalism was not to put a theory of the self at the basis of his position, but to make the concept of citizenship central. Citizenship is simply a way in which we think about ourselves for the purpose of theorizing a distinctively political set of principles. Those principles are discontinuous with any particular reasonable comprehensive conception of the good life. There are reasons for suspecting that Rawls did not pursue his strategy of discontinuity far enough (B. Williams 2005; Thomas 2006b: 289–93). However, a more consistent application of this strategy would certainly offer a means of defusing Nagel's paradox. The idea would be that his conception of our divided selves, like any other liberal view that is based on an account of the fundamental nature of persons, needs to be replaced by the discontinuous strategy of political liberalism. In this justificatory strategy no metaphysical claim, including claims about the essential nature of persons, has a bearing on the justification of the principles of a strictly political conception of justice. What matters is how we reasonably think about ourselves for political purposes, not the truth of any particular philosophical anthropology, Nagel's included. The advantage of bringing about this structural change in Nagel's views is the insulation of the objective component of his hybrid ethical theory from the objective component in his egalitarianism, thereby reconciling the putative paradox. The result is that the egalitarianism defended in *Equality and Partiality* is no longer, as Nagel presents it, a second best solution. It is an independently appealing version of egalitarianism in its own right.

An egalitarian solution

Communitarianism is best viewed as a permanent corrective, within liberalism, to any tendency that liberalism may have to misrepresent our social nature as a compact between social atoms. We are rather, as Walzer (1990) puts it, "post-social" selves, most of whose associative obligations are not voluntarily undertaken, but who greatly value the option of breaking any particular associative bond. But communitarianism emphasized the importance of recognizing shared visions of the good in political life, as well as the recognition of rights, and the recognition of the connection between values and identity. One important strand of communitarian argument also emphasized traditional republican ideas such as the virtues of citizenship. It has seemed to some that developing an account of citizenship within the free associations characteristic of modern civil society is the best way forward in reconciling the claims of the individual and the social. It is not that Nagel is an atomist about persons: he is not. The social is a representative part of all of us. But the way that we are embedded in society seems mis-described in Nagel's argument. It is the whole person, not a part of us, that is fundamentally social.

If we are going to put identity at the heart of political philosophy, and if one does hope to develop ideas such as community being representative of shared values and serving as a locus of solidarity, Nagel's starting-point does not look hopeful. But his appeal to how our motivations can be taken up and transformed by the social is more promising. Communitarianism has its own dangers of presenting a utopian fantasy of communities structured by shared visions of the good that are strongly solidaristic, but still liberal in their relations to outsiders and to internal dissenters. It needs, as a corrective, Nagel's salutary emphasis on the claims of the personal. However, there are versions of communitarianism in which it is emphasized that we already have some forms of social life in which the individualism of one aspect of liberalism is balanced by the sociality of another aspect of liberalism, namely, its emphasis on free associations that are neither in the market or the state. This network of associations is civil society. These free associations are the venues for the development of the virtues of citizenship, which is the vital role in which the claims of the social and the claims of the individual are adjudicated within the individual.

The relevance of the related ideas of republicanism and civil society to our liberal egalitarian ideals has been much discussed (Thomas 2006b: ch. 12), and I do not want to minimize the difficulties facing a view of this kind. But my general aim is to draw attention to a sphere of social relations that is cooperative, not egoistic, and has a narrower scope than universal benevolence, but has a secure hold on the motivations of citizens by providing that which Walzer called "the setting of settings" (1992: 97–8). This is a "setting" that inculcates and develops the virtues of citizenship, including the duties of mutual civility and mutual restraint. It also seems to me to be the appropriate location for an ethos of mutual concern that would hinder unrestrained pursuit of economic profit if the cost is driving other citizens in one's society below a level at which they can lead decent lives free from institutionalized humiliation.

Any positive proposal of this kind tries to overcome the dichotomy between the individual and the social. From this perspective, Nagel's account of the self is under-described: we have conflicting commitments, but a recognition of the personal can be extended, via the duties and responsibilities of citizenship, to embrace the social as well. It is hard to see the possibility of a view of this kind if we see the impersonal standpoint within the agent as the internalized representative of the collectivity. If the personal spans both self-regarding actions and a legitimate ethical claim to self-realization and extends to things going well for those to whom one stands in a special relation (such as members of one's family, or friends), why cannot it extend to those with whom one shares a social life in a wider sense? This is the idea not that a political community should be modelled on a group of friends, but rather that co-citizenship could be extended on a basis analogous to friendship, for example, shared interests or values. If this is so, then the personal already contains within it the resources to represent a collectivity, and that idea should not be annexed and handed over to the "impersonal" standpoint.

I would argue that Nagel is unduly pessimistic about the prospects for the development of civic virtues in such a way that people can be motivated not to be content with a form of shared social life in which other members of their political community lead lives below a threshold of decency. He acknowledges that one way forward towards a more demanding egalitarianism would be a society in which people could work hard in their legitimate "personal" interests, but where they would feel guilty about being substantially better off than their fellow citizens. Nagel is pessimistic about such a transformation of motive, but perhaps we could be more optimistic about something less: the view that our society, with its particular shared values for us, is a collective enterprise and that it is a source of guilt if we see our fellow citizens, participants in that enterprise, leading lives that fall below a threshold of decency.

If Nagel has, in spite of his avowed pessimism, offered a positive way forward in the development of a more egalitarian conception of society, what is the source of the normative principle being advanced in this positive proposal? If Nagel generates theoretical paradox by taking the commitment to impartialism to feature both as a principle within his pluralist ethical theory and within his political egalitarianism, how is the paradox avoided? I would argue that it is by taking political egalitarianism to be precisely that: a political commitment discontinuous with our best reflective account of ethics. The idea of such a political, as opposed to moral or metaphysical, underpinning for political egalitarianism stems from Rawls's late work, although he goes on to explain exactly what he means by the politicization of his assumptions in such a way as largely to undercut his avowed intentions. Examining this controversial issue goes beyond the scope of this chapter, but it does suggest that in some ways Nagel's paradox is one that is representative of those views that take political principles to be moral principles simply occupying a different functional role (Thomas 2006b: 289–93).

I have been primarily concerned in this chapter with the paradoxicalness that Nagel diagnosed in an initially plausible set of assumptions. His claim went beyond the observation that pluralism in ethical theory may be difficult to reconcile with a political commitment to egalitarianism, or that that latter ideal may be compromised by the demands of efficiency and aggregative concerns. His paradox arose because the commitment to "strong egalitarianism" was tacitly part of our ethical outlook. It was a property both of the part and of the whole, but when it was applied to a whole society it was applied independently of any issues about responsibility.

I have attempted to defuse this whole line of argument. From within a pluralist ethical outlook, there is scope for recognizing a duty of universal beneficence. Politically, we may be committed to egalitarianisms of various different strengths. In the light of aggregative and efficiency considerations, we seek to reconcile these two demands. I have suggested that Nagel identifies a realistic goal for social democratic politics, namely, the cultivation of solidarity in such a way that these demands can be reconciled in a realistic way. But his theory of the person is an obstruction to this ideal, not of any assistance in its development. I have argued that we do not have to accept Nagel's further claim that this is a compromised ideal, expressive of an underlying paradox in our ethical and theoretical commitments. Positively, I have argued that a republican emphasis on the development of civic virtue, in the context of free associations, may be the best route to take in the direction of these uncompromised normative goals. However, those ideas are merely a complement to an attractive and feasible version of liberal egalitarianism developed by Nagel himself in a way contrary to his avowed intentions.

Conclusion

In this conclusion I would like to discuss issues that can only be appreciated at the end of this book with all the relevant evidence to hand. What kind of philosopher is Nagel? To what extent is he a systematic philosopher? Does his central distinction between the subjective and the objective retain a core meaning in all the different contexts in which he deploys it? Having traced Nagel's basic contrast between the subjective and the objective through all its specific articulations in the context of metaphysics and epistemology, the philosophy of mind, practical reason, normative ethics and political philosophy, it is evident that Nagel's distinctive philosophical achievement is the combination of a systematic impulse to philosophizing qualified by the detailed examination of particular problems.

We are now in a position to appreciate both the breadth of Nagel's application of the subjective versus objective contrast and the way in which its application is nuanced to respect the particularity of each topic. Here is a list of some of the main ways in which Nagel contrasts the subjective and the objective. Each contrast on the list has been described, at some point, in this book:

Subjective	**Objective**
Particular	General
Particular	Universal
Personal	Impersonal
Individual	Social or collective
Diversity, fragmentation	Totality, wholeness
Perspectival, subject-involving	Perspectival but detached or non-perspectival/absolute (Either:

	maximally independent of our perspective, or totally independent of our perspective)
Internal	External
First-personal	Third-personal
Inherently normative	Explanatory
Standpoint of agency	Actions as "mere" events
Agent-relative	Agent-neutral

Many of the criticisms I have suggested in this book have taken the form of arguing that one or other of these pairs of contrast misalign, or that they are only contraries, not contradictories, that can both be false together. (That is because they fail to capture one or more alternative descriptions of the topic to hand.)

However, the sheer range of these contrasts proves that Nagel is not a systematic philosopher who forces all philosophical problems into a Procrustean bed of his own system of categorization. He is a philosopher who is alert to the differences between problems that share an analogous form, but no more than that. He draws on a wide range of supplementary contrasts accurately to characterize particular cases. His philosophical instincts for finding a good solution to a philosophical problem, or rejecting a bad solution, or accepting that we are nowhere near a solution at all, take priority over systematic unity in Nagel's work. The unity of these issues is in the way they feature in his central philosophical ideal: living in the light of the truth. In that way he can be interpreted as respecting his own aims in philosophizing (as set out in Chapter 1).

The arguments of this book have demonstrated why the ideal of living reflectively in the light of the truth has a special emphasis in Nagel's work. The reason is that he believes that philosophers, above all, have tended to deny the reality of their own experience. They prioritize the solution of philosophical problems at the cost of plausibility in their own experience. When a philosopher constructs a theory too hastily, or confuses giving a good explanation with offering a global reduction of some area of thought or language, eliminating some of its key features, or supplying an objective surrogate for an irreducibly subjective feature, Nagel's response is always to return that philosopher to a careful description of the phenomena being denied.

This book has also demonstrated how, for Nagel, living in the light of the truth can involve living with irreducible conflicts rooted in our nature. Their inevitability and grounding in our human condition invites a description of such conflicts as tragic. Our human nature is fundamentally a composite. A central element in that composite, namely, our capacity for the detached use of reason via theory, conflicts with other parts of our nature. For such divided beings, living in the light of the truth often involves the acceptance of limitations in our thought. It can involve theoretical failures or failures to theorize some phenomena of which we wanted a theoretical explanation. Sometimes it involves aspiring to self-transcendence, an aspiration to using our powers of reason to view the world and our place in it from a maximally detached perspective. Yet in other cases this aspiration is shown not to be possible or to be desirable and as, indeed, a source of potential distortion or falsehood. Nagel's comprehensive philosophical ideal has been to map out, in different areas of philosophy, the balance to be found in each case between two ways of conceiving of the subject matter: subjective and objective ways. The working out of that ideal has been traced throughout this book.

In terms of historical influences, the fact that Nagel's first book was an exercise in transcendental argument and defended a neo-Kantian view of practical reasoning might suggest that Kant is the philosopher in the tradition who has most influenced Nagel's work. However, over the whole span of Nagel's philosophy, Descartes appears to exert an equal and complementary influence to that of Kant. Nagel's rationalism, foundationalism and realism about reason itself are all avowedly Cartesian. So is Nagel's realism, his appreciation of the depth and irrefutability of scepticism, and the way in which both realism and scepticism express an underlying truth about our own contingency and finitude.

Nagel believes that it is reason that makes us aspire to the ideal of self-transcendence. Furthermore, it is the origin of our impulse to integrate our view of the world into a unitary and substantial view. But the complementary aspect to Nagel's Cartesian commitment to the power of reason is his equal appreciation that this impulse to a unified worldview can lead us into philosophical error. This aspiration to self-transcendence can lead to the false objectification of that which cannot be objectified. Throughout this book it has been shown that objectification, for Nagel, is desirable in its proper place and when it is exercised to an appropriate extent. However, he believes that it is all too easy to fall victim to errors that are internal to our desire to be more objective about a particular topic. This recapitulates Kant's view of the powers and the pitfalls of possessing a faculty of pure reason conceived of as a distinct faculty separate from understanding and sensibility. Pure reason drives us on to think guided by its Ideas, but if we take these to be literal truths, as opposed to regulations for how we ought to think, we are precipitated into intellectual paradox as Kant demonstrated in the "Dialectic" of his *Critique of Pure Reason* ([1781/1783] 1929).[1] It is the working out of the creative tension generated by our capacity to reason that underlies all the disparate topics discussed in this book.

Nagel notes that objectivity is both undervalued and overvalued in contemporary philosophy: that remark was the guiding thread of Chapter 2. One way in which it is overvalued is in the form of scientism. Scientism takes its respect for the great cultural achievement represented by modern science too far. Those influenced by scientism seek to borrow the intellectual authority and cultural prestige of science when this is not warranted. They do so by mimicking its methods and styles of writing in areas where these are not appropriate. A great deal of academic philosophical writing, particularly in the school of analytic philosophy, is scientistic in style. It aims for an objectivized, impersonal style of writing intended to copy scientific writing. Nagel does not write like this: there is an intensely personal note to his work. That is one of the reasons, besides his gifts as a writer, why he is an excellent communicator who has shaped contemporary philosophical culture both through his own work and through his responses to the work of others.[2]

I have sometimes heard it said – although I have not seen this point committed to print – that Nagel is primarily a critic of the views of other philosophers and lacks a distinctive philosophical vision of his own. It is true that much of Nagel's work in philosophy is critical. However, it might reasonably be replied on his behalf that if other philosophers stopped producing falsely objectifying theories then he would have had less work to do pointing out this fact. The tradition of analytic philosophy, in particular, has an unfortunate tendency to have such confidence in its proprietary methods that, if they fail to yield a satisfactory treatment of a philosophical problem, it is the problem that is blamed rather than the methods. The problem is redefined to make it soluble using the three characteristic forms of false objectification: reductionism, eliminativism or the devising of an objective surrogate for the phenomenon that was to be explained. I think any impartial observer of contemporary philosophy would have no difficulty nominating approaches to philosophical problems that, unhappily, take these three forms. (This is particularly true in the philosophy of mind.)

In any case, the arguments of this book have demonstrated that Nagel is no mere chronicler of the errors of his peers, nor that his philosophy is simply that which remains standing when all around it has been demolished. The second point to be made in his defence is that his contributions to a central range of philosophical problems have changed the way in which they are discussed. This has happened in two ways: either directly, via the impact of Nagel's own work, or indirectly, via the impact of the work of those whom Nagel has strongly influenced. An incomplete list of the latter would include A. W. Moore, Colin McGinn, David Chalmers, Christine Korsgaard, Samuel Scheffler and Liam Murphy.

Finally, I think that those who undervalue Nagel's originality confuse not being fashionable with not being original. For a subject allegedly concerned with the eternal verities, philosophy is remarkably subject to rapidly changing approaches to its central problems. In that context, a defence of scientific realism, rationalism, foundationalism and formal principles immanent in practical reasoning will seem to many, for different reasons peculiar to each, as calculatedly unfashionable. Defending these views over a fifty-year period in a way that engages with the different forms taken by those who seek to challenge these commitments (internal realism, physicalism, ordinary-language philosophy) seems to me a remarkable and original achievement.[3] These judgements of originality and importance are for others to make; Nagel's overriding concern is simply to get things right.

Nagel frequently confesses that he finds philosophy hard. However, he also notes that he is not sick of the subject and does not want to be rid of it, unlike, for example, Wittgenstein, who combined philosophical genius with a suspicion that there was something deeply pathological about the activity itself (*VN*: 11). If Nagel's philosophy is ultimately grounded on a philosophical anthropology that sees us as tragically divided between our capacities for both an objective and a subjective point of view, then he shows the truth of this claim by the example of his own philosophical work. The demands of truthfulness and intellectual responsibility are for each of us to work out from our first-personal point of view. That is the case even if Nagel is as robustly realist about the impersonal guidance from norms that ought to govern our thinking as any philosopher has ever been. However, if each of us has to find our own way out of Plato's cave to the sunlight on our own, then we could do a lot worse than to follow the path that Nagel has, over five decades, mapped out for each of us with exemplary clarity, imagination and insight.

Notes

Preface

1. Page references to *The Possibility of Altruism* are to the paperback edition published in 1978 by Princeton University Press.
2. In particular I regret not being able to discuss either Colin McGinn's *The Subjective View: Secondary Qualities and Indexical Thoughts* (Oxford: Oxford University Press, 1983) or A. W. Moore's *Points of View* (Oxford: Oxford University Press, 1997), two important contributions to contemporary metaphysics, both of which, in different ways, reflect Nagel's influence.

Chapter 1: Subjective and objective

1. I shall, in this chapter and throughout this book, replace Nagel's terminology of the "subjective" and the "objective" in the case of his account of realism, with the terminology of "perspectival" versus "non-perspectival" or "absolute" representations. See § "Representation and perspective". This is primarily in the interests of clarity. The "Conclusion" reviews the multiplicity of uses to which Nagel puts his subjective–objective distinction and I disambiguate this distinction for particular topics where possible.
2. For a development of this important point see Moore, *Points of View*, ch. 4, §3.
3. This is a broad characterization of idealism intended to cover both views that see the world as constituted of mental items and views that see the world as constitutively dependent on the mind.
4. I shall note some necessary qualifications in Chapter 3 to deal with the most basic case of all: a subject of experience's acquaintance with his or her own mind. In this case the "point of view" metaphor does seem strained for reasons that I shall discuss in that chapter.
5. This issue is discussed by Dancy in "Contemplating One's Nagel", *Philosophical Books* **29**(1) (1988), 7–8. My reasons for dissenting from his pessimistic verdict are set out in Chapter 2, § "Cartesian absolutism".
6. A comparison with Hegel is apposite because when, in his version of philosophical dialectic, thesis and antithesis are reconciled at a higher level of

reflection, Hegel claims that the tension between them is both overcome and *preserved*.

7. I am indebted to Dancy's careful account of the two models of objectification in "Contemplating One's Nagel", 4–7.
8. This connection between Cartesian objectification and treating the human condition as a constitutive source of error is noted in Dancy, "Contemplating One's Nagel", 7. I discuss it in more detail in Chapter 2, § "Knowledge and the shadow of scepticism".
9. An example of a philosophical view that might seem committed to the idea of a perspectival fact is Nelson Goodman's "irrealism", expressed in *Ways of Worldmaking* (Indiana, IN: Hackett, 1978). But Goodman's views are very subtle: he is as pluralist about the meta-level philosophical question as to how many perspectives there are as he is about the first-order perspectives themselves.

    > As intimated by William James's equivocal title *A Pluralistic Universe*, the issue between monism and pluralism tends to evaporate under analysis. If there is but one world, it embraces a multiplicity of contrasting aspects; if there are many worlds, the collection of them all is one. The one world may be taken as many, or the many worlds taken as one; whether one or many depends on the way of taking. (*Ibid.*: 2)

10. For an account of Pauli's use of this phrase see P. Woit, *Not Even Wrong: The Failure of String Theory and the Search for Unity in Physical Law* (New York: Basic Books, 2007), xii.

Chapter 2: Understanding, knowledge and reason

1. This kind of scepticism about science claims that scientific representations of the world are not what they seem. They purport to be objective but in fact they are subjective in a damaging way that needs (the critic argues) debunking. There is no such thing as the disinterested search for truth; any putative example of disinterestedness is a prior interest furthering itself by disguising itself, in a way that calls for a certain kind of "unmasking". The so-called "strong programme" in the sociology of science represents a view of this kind. For views of this kind see, for example, B. Barnes, "Realism, Relativism and Finitism", in *Cognitive Relativism and Social Science*, D. Raven, L. van Vucht Tijssen & J. de Wolf (eds), 131–47 (Piscataway, NJ: Transaction, 1992) or A. Pickering, *Constructing Quarks: A Sociological History of Particle Physics* (Chicago, IL: University of Chicago Press, 1984).
2. Nagel states that "there is an excellent account of this idea in Williams" (*VN*: 15 n.1).
3. If this interpretation is correct then how do I explain Nagel's title "*The View from Nowhere*"? A distinguished philosopher and historian of science, Lorraine Daston, calls this title a "brilliant oxymoron" ("Objectivity and the Escape from Perspective", *Social Studies of Science* **22**[4] [1992], 599). I think authors should be granted a degree of poetic licence!
4. The word "anyway" is precisely the one Bernard Williams chose to use in describing our intuitive realism and the concept of knowledge that he associated with it in his book on Descartes). Our knowledge is of a world that exists anyway (*Descartes: The Project of Pure Enquiry* [Harmondsworth: Penguin, 1978], 64).

5. In a later "Replies" to some of his critics Williams noted that "I do accept that some formulations of the idea [of an absolute conception] have implied a poorly considered causal theory of knowledge. I believe that the general idea is independent of such a theory" ("Replies", in *World, Mind and Ethics: Essays on the Ethical Philosophy of Bernard Williams*, J. E. J. Altham & T. R. Harrison [eds], 185–224 [Cambridge: Cambridge University Press, 1995], 209).
6. A similar misrepresentation is offered by the physicalist who develops a parallel critique of Nagel and Williams to that developed by Putnam.
7. I have, for ease of exposition, focused solely on Putnam's critique of the absolute conception. However, parallel arguments have been developed by Richard Rorty, John McDowell, Jane Heal and Warren Quinn. For further references see my *Value and Context: The Nature of Moral and Political Knowledge* (Oxford: Oxford University Press, 2006), 135–44.
8. How, then, can I explain away the phrase that concludes this sentence:

    > The question is how limited beings like ourselves can alter their conception of the world so that it is no longer just the view from where they are but in a sense a view from nowhere, which includes and comprehends the fact that the world appears to them as it does prior to the formation of that conception ... and *explains how they can arrive at that conception itself.* (*VN*: 70, emphasis added)

    I explain it in this way: it involves no commitment to explaining the absolute conception using concepts directly vindicated solely by that conception itself. I believe the same is true of the later discussion (*VN*: 74). Nagel there refers to a "self-referential understanding" but simply means that our final worldview will refer to itself – something that need not operate under the stringent constraints of the physicalist. For further evidence on this point: our capacity for objectivity is described as a "complete mystery" and inexplicable in terms of "anything more basic" (*VN:* 78); later, an ideally reflexive account of the absolute conception is described as "just a dream" (*VN*: 85). So Nagel is not committed to it.
9. See Chapter 3, § "Nagel's anti-objectivist arguments", for a discussion of Nagel's anti-objectivism in the philosophy of mind.
10. And, to a lesser extent, the views of Peter Strawson (see *VN*: 99–105). I will not discuss the arguments of this section of *The View from Nowhere* as, for the reasons Nagel himself notes, there seems to me much less distance between Nagel's views and Strawson's than between Nagel and Wittgenstein and Davidson.
11. For a very helpful overall discussion of Davidson's views see S. Evnine, *Donald Davidson* (Stanford, CA: Stanford University Press, 1991).
12. Charles Taylor applies this idea, developed via an appeal to the parallel notion of a "fusion of horizons" taken from the German philosophers Hans-Georg Gadamer, to the theory of interpretation in "Interpretation and the Sciences of Man", in his *Philosophical Papers, Volume 2: Philosophy and the Human Sciences*, 15–57 (Cambridge: Cambridge University Press, 1985).
13. In particular, I have omitted for reasons of space Hurley's very interesting discussion of Davidson's externalism in the philosophy of mind and the role that causation plays in the formation of thought contents. Externalism is the view that the identity and the individuation of mental states can depend on the relations in which such states stand to the physical and social environment. Hurley argues that it is a neglect of that aspect of Davidson's views that lends Nagel's critique a false credibility.

14. An interesting comparison to Hurley's views is the straightforwardly verificationist "extension" of Davidson's argument offered by Richard Rorty:

    If we can never find a translation, why should we think we are faced with language users at all? It is, of course, possible to imagine humanoid organisms making sounds of great variety at one another in very various circumstances with what appear to be various effects upon the interlocutors' behaviour. But suppose that repeated attempts systematically to correlate these sounds with the organisms' environment and behavior fail ... Once we imagine different ways of carving up the world, nothing could stop us attributing "untranslatable languages" to *anything* that emits a variety of signals. But, so this verificationist argument concludes, this degree of open-endedness shows us that the purported notion of an untranslatable language is as fanciful as that of an invisible color.

    (*Consequences of Pragmatism* [Minneapolis, MN: Minnesota University Press, 1982], 6)

15. This interpretation of Wittgenstein is developed in Michael Luntley, *Wittgenstein: Meaning and Judgement* (Oxford: Blackwell, 2003).
16. Nagel studied as a postgraduate student at Oxford University: certainly aspects of his views seem to be a counter-reaction to the dominant tradition of "ordinary language" philosophy at Oxford (*VN*: 71), on the understanding that it takes a very wide understanding of that phrase to include J. L. Austin, Peter Strawson and Paul Grice under one description.
17. I say "can represent" as someone committed to the Cartesian model could acknowledge the role played by our human nature without viewing that negatively as constitutively involving an error as Nagel seems to. Nagel seems to concede this alternative view is possible: "The pure idea of realism ... implies nothing specific about the relation between the appearances and reality, except that we and our inner lives are part of reality" (*VN*: 70). For a cogent observation on the damaging role of this concession for Nagel's claim that realism necessarily commits one to the irrefutability of scepticism, see Michael Williams, *Unnatural Doubts* (Oxford: Blackwell, 1991), 250.
18. Is there not, however, still a problem? Even if Nagel is running together two models of objectivity it is simply intellectually troubling that a vindication of our worldview will never be complete as it presupposes the nature of the epistemic subject. No, because this incompletability is not, as Nagel implies, a concession that scepticism is true: "This may show that the quest for objective knowledge will never terminate ... but it will not show that objective knowledge undermines itself, that objective knowledge is impossible" (M. Williams, *Unnatural Doubts*, 250).
19. An example of heroic epistemologizing is Ayer's original discussion: having identified the gaps between various different classes of evidence and the knowledge claims that they putatively support Ayer's response is to carry on with our knowledge-acquiring practices in a way that acknowledges this under-determination but does not resolve it (*The Problem of Knowledge* [Harmondsworth: Penguin, 1956]).
20. One might take issue with this aspect of Nagel's view too. As Dancy notes "there is a suggestion that appearances are intrinsically unreliable ... But this ... is not part of either sense of objectification" ("Contemplating One's Nagel", 9). See also Michael Williams, *Unnatural Doubts*, 249, and the incisive discussion in Edward Craig, *Knowledge and the State of Nature: An Essay in Conceptual Synthesis* (Oxford: Clarendon Press, 1990), 125–9.

Chapter 3: Placing the mind in the physical world

1. There are various problems in interpreting this metaphor of a point of view when it comes to mentality. It would seem to be a very basic case, fundamental to understanding what points of view are. But I shall argue that, on the contrary, it is the basic nature of the case that generates the puzzle. The mind's self-acquaintance is foundational to how we think about the mental but for that reason it is difficult to come up with a convincing metaphor for *it*. Subjects of experience do not occupy a point of view in virtue of which they have experiences with mental aspects; it is less misleading, but still awkward in ordinary language, to say that they are points of view, to which non-mental things are disclosed. For an exploration of this idea of the mind's self-acquaintance see the subtle account in D. Zahavi, *Subjectivity and Selfhood* (Cambridge, MA: MIT Press, 2006).
2. That explains what may seem otherwise puzzling, namely, why his account of the fundamental datum an approach to the mind needs to explain is presented alongside speculation about the mental lives of bats. This detour can seem unmotivated: I have heard of an exasperated psychologist who remarked of Nagel's topic that "not even a bat knows what it is like to be a bat"! For a criticism of Nagel's argument strategy see Owen Flanagan, *Consciousness Reconsidered* (Cambridge, MA: MIT Press, 1992), ch. 5. For a sympathetic defence of Nagel's argument from Flanagan's critique see T. Alter, "Nagel On Imagination and Physicalism", *Journal of Philosophical Research* **27** (2002), 143–58.
3. I noted in the previous chapter the influence on his work of Peter Strawson's *Individuals: An Essay in Descriptive Metaphysics* (London: Methuen, 1959). In that work, which describes the most fundamental concepts and categories in how we think of the world, persons are a fundamental category. They have the feature that they are the subject of the ascription of both mental and physical predicates. That view, and the similar view of the later Wittgenstein, seems to me to lie behind Nagel's insistence that our concept of the mind is, from the outset, a general one. On that basis Nagel thinks we can give short shrift to an orthodox scepticism about how we know about other minds. That sceptical approach takes it for granted that we understand what it is to ascribe mentality to others but then asks what justification we have for doing so? Nagel's enquiries are deeper. He is concerned with how, given the characteristic ways in which mental concepts are acquired and used, there can be so much as an understanding of the candidate for knowledge, whether true or false. His problem of other minds is a conceptual one (A. Avramides, *Other Minds* [London: Routledge, 2001], 257ff.).
4. This assumption is central to the argument of *The Possibility of Altruism*. In her interesting discussion of Nagel's views in connection with other minds, Anita Avramides argues that his presentation is ambivalent between an attempt to reconstruct an intersubjective general concept of mentality from a conceptually solipsistic perspective via the imagination and a different view that takes the generality of our concept of mind as given (*Other Minds*, 259–60). I think, in fact, we can take Nagel as clearly committed to the latter (not least because Avramides shows some of the serious problems with the former view; *ibid.*, 263–4). But she goes on to offer an interesting interpretation of Nagel's entitlement simply to assume generality in the concept of mind, pointing to those passages of *The View from Nowhere* where Nagel concludes that "the conditions of objectivity

that I have been defending lead to the conclusion that the basis of most real knowledge must be a priori and drawn from within ourselves" (*VN*: 83–4). For a contrasting view that Nagel fails to motivate these "conditions of objectivity" for both first personal and third personal mental ascriptions see K. Wider, "Overtones of Solipsism in Thomas Nagel's 'What is it Like to be a Bat?' and *The View from Nowhere*", *Philosophy and Phenomenological Research* **50**(3) (1990), 481–99.

5. This work is discussed in Janet Levin's "Nagel versus Nagel on the Nature of Phenomenal Concepts", *Ratio* **20**(3) (2007), 293–307, an excellent paper to which I am much indebted.
6. One way to put this is that Nagel has devised a theory of error for those intuitions that stem from the nature of our concepts alone, showing that they are an unreliable source of intuitions when they are so dependent on our imagination. This is the conclusion of Christopher Hill and Brian McLaughlin ("There Are Fewer Things In Reality than are Dreamt of in Chalmers's Philosophy", *Philosophy and Phenomenological Research* **59**[2] [1999], 445–54). In his later work, described below, Nagel steps back and takes this theory of error to be true of our current stock of mental concepts, suggesting we need a new and better stock (PN: 218). (The same conclusion is true, he believes, for physical concepts too.)
7. I have referred throughout this chapter to a particular interpretation of the idea of a perspectival fact in the philosophy of mind, namely, the idea that there are ineffable subjective facts known only by the thinker concerned. Such facts are essentially first personal and revealed to each person's point of view. In the course of establishing whether Nagel holds such a view Biro finds it clearly expressed by John Searle (J. Biro, "Consciousness and Subjectivity", in *Consciousness: Philosophical Issues*, E. Villanueva [ed.], 113–33 [Atascadero, CA: Ridgeview, 1991], 129). Biro quotes extensively from an early version of the material that became Chapter 1 of J. Searle, *The Rediscovery of the Mind* (Cambridge, MA: MIT Press, 1992). The relevant passages are:

   > It is essential to see that in consequence of its subjectivity, the pain is not equally accessible to any observer. Its existence, we might say, is a first-person existence. For it to be a pain it must be somebody's pain; and this in a much stronger sense than the sense in which a leg must be somebody's leg ... what is true of pains is true of conscious states generally ... Subjectivity has the further consequence that all of my conscious forms of intentionality that give me information about the world independent of myself are always from a special point of view. The world itself has no point of view, but my access to the world through my conscious states is always perspectival, always from my point of view. (*Ibid*., 94–5)

   However, this evidence seems to me merely to highlight the fact that, throughout Biro's fair-minded discussion, he can find no equivalent to these claims in Nagel's work.
8. For the record, Biro argues that the fixed–portable distinction is not best explained in terms of the token–type distinction but that is not essential to the exposition of his views here (J. Biro, "A Point of View on Points of View", *Philosophical Psychology* **19**[1] [2006], 6–7).
9. I say "for" a self not "to" a self as I do not believe that this claim necessarily implies, as Daniel Dennett has argued, that anyone holding this kind of view is committed to a "Cartesian Theatre". That would be a unitary location in the mind where the self surveys its entire disparate mental goings on a stage

laid out before it (D. C. Dennett, *Consciousness Explained* [Boston, MA: Back Bay Books, 1991], 107). "Self-hood" here is more akin to a unifying *function*, as it is, ironically, in Dennett's own positive view. For the latter interpretation of Dennett see David Carr, "Phenomenology and Fiction in Dennett", *International Journal of Philosophical Studies* **6**(3) (1998), 331–44.

10. I here follow the convention of referring to concepts, as opposed to the words that express them, in bold typeface.
11. A further idea is that a contingent truth is actually true, which is for it to be true in the possible world that is the actual world. On that basis modal logicians construe the word "actually" as working like an indexical.
12. There is no prospect here of reducing this "causal–historical" theory of referring to causes alone as it depends essentially on what each speaker in the chain intends to do in using the name, namely, preserve the connection established in the initial act of baptism.
13. That is my interpretation of the relevant texts; Nagel is asking for an analogous level of rational intelligibility not the same level of rational intelligibility. But he does use the word "transparent".
14. A. W. Moore discusses this passage, and the wider issue, very insightfully in "Review of Thomas Nagel, *The View from Nowhere*", *Philosophical Quarterly* **37**(148) (1987), 325–6.
15. A caveat: anyone referring back to Tim Crane's discussion in "Subjective Facts", in *Real Metaphysics*, H. Lillehammer & G. Rodriguez-Pereyra (eds), 68–83 (London: Routledge, 2003) should note that he and Nagel mean slightly different things by the word "objectivism".
16. This idea looks ahead to the discussion of ethics in Chapter 6. I shall there canvas this issue of whether, in spite of the importance to ethics of the fact that we can develop such an objective conception of ourselves, it is always ethically important to attach supreme authority to the objective point of view. See also my "Reasonable Partiality and the Agent's Personal Point of View", *Ethical Theory and Moral Practice* **8**(1–2) (2005), 25–43.
17. This suggests that Nagel could have developed his argument here by appealing to Wittgenstein's distinction between saying and showing; *Tractatus Logico-Philosophicus*, D. Pears & B. F. McGuinness (trans.) (London: Routledge, 1961), §§4.121, 4.122. See the fascinating discussion of this distinction in A. W. Moore's "On Saying and Showing", *Philosophy* **62**(292) (1987), 473–97.

Chapter 4: The possibility of altruism

1. You might describe transcendental argumentation as philosophy's form of "reverse engineering".
2. This priority of a formal account of good reasoning to a material account is questioned by, *inter alia*, R. Brandom, "Action, Norms, and Practical Reasoning", *Noûs* **32**, *Supplement: Philosophical Perspectives, 12, Language Mind and Ontology* (1998), 127–39.
3. This is not, in my view, the most helpful way to think of why we use such arguments: for a convincing alternative see G. Buchdahl, "Realism and Realization in a Kantian Light", in *Reading Kant*, E. Schaper & W. Vossenkuhl (eds), 217–49 (Oxford: Blackwell, 1989) and P. Strawson, *Scepticism and Naturalism: Some Varieties* (London: Methuen, 1985), 13.
4. As discussed above in Chapter 2.

5. This argument once again reflects the influence of Strawson's *Individuals*. Strictly speaking, in this book Strawson's aim was simply descriptive. Scepticism, like other revisionary proposals, was simply neutrally recorded as proposing revisions to our ordinary conceptual scheme. By the time of Strawson's later *Scepticism and Naturalism*, such descriptions were at the service of a comprehensive philosophical naturalism that undercut the sceptic. There is an excellent discussion of responses of this kind in M. Bell & M. McGinn, "Naturalism and Scepticism", *Philosophy* **65**(254) (1990), 399–418.
6. There is considerable controversy as to whether any philosopher has ever held the simple motivational view. It is sometimes suggested that Hume did, but apart from the question of whether Hume held any theory of normative reasons at all, there is reason to question this attribution. See E. Millgram, "Was Hume a Humean?", *Hume Studies* **21**(1) (1995), 75–93; I. Persson, "Hume – Not a 'Humean' about Motivation", *History of Philosophy Quarterly* **14**(2) (1997), 189–206. Another candidate is Hobbes, but on that attribution, see Bernard Gert's "Review of Thomas Nagel, *The Possibility of Altruism*", *Journal of Philosophy* **69**(12) (1972), 340–44, in the course of which he shows that it cannot possibly be correct either. Perhaps the best route to take is to claim that the simple motivational view represents a cluster of commitments, some of which have been definitely held by particular philosophers, even if the whole cluster has only ever been attributed by some philosophers to others (in the course of rejecting it). For related, but far more sophisticated, versions of simple motivational theory see D. Parfit, *Reasons and Persons* (Oxford: Oxford University Press, 1984) and M. Smith, "The Humean Theory of Motivation", *Mind*, new series, **96**(381) (1987), 36–61.
7. This is worth stressing as at least one informed commentator, Jonathan Dancy, at one time took Nagel (and by extension John McDowell) to be committed to an unstable hybrid view that deployed the concept of desire in two incompatible roles when desires are interpreted as motivated or unmotivated. That led Dancy in the direction of a purely cognitivist view in which beliefs motivate alone (*Moral Reasons* [Oxford: Blackwell, 1993]). Whatever the merits of that view I simply note that it would be a very radical departure from anything in *The Possibility of Altruism*.
8. This distinction has been attributed to G. E. M. Anscombe, *Intention* (Oxford: Blackwell, 1957), but strictly speaking that work only defines one direction of fit. The extension of the view from giving an account of how descriptions fit the world is in J. Searle, *Intentionality* (Cambridge: Cambridge University Press, 1992).
9. I say "in some way involves" as one sophisticated version of this view treats such involvement of desire in practical reasoning presuppositionally. See P. Pettit & M. Smith, "Backgrounding Desire", *Philosophical Review* **99**(4) (1990), 565–92.
10. For historical background to this crucial distinction in *The Possibility of Altruism*, see N. Dent, *The Moral Psychology of the Virtues* (Cambridge: Cambridge University Press, 1984).
11. By "simply given" here I mean to bring out the analogies, in the case of action, for those merely given mental states that ground our perceptual experience in a way criticized by W. Sellars, *Empiricism and the Philosophy of Mind* (Cambridge, MA: Harvard University Press, 1997) and J. McDowell, *Mind and World* (Cambridge, MA: Harvard University Press, 1994).
12. For the placing of this form of judgement internalism among the varieties of internalisms, see the helpful discussion in D. Brink, *Moral Realism and*

the Foundations of Ethics (Cambridge: Cambridge University Press, 1989).

13. The terminology was introduced by W. Frankena, "Obligation and Motivation in Recent Moral Philosophy", in *Essays in Moral Philosophy*, A. I. Melden (ed.), 40–81 (Seattle, WA: University of Washington Press, 1958) and W. D. Falk, "'Ought' and Motiviation", reprinted in his *Ought, Reason and Morality* (Ithaca, NY: Cornell University Press, 1986).
14. So I think *The Possibility of Altruism* is not really a criticism of an inadequate moral psychology, but a deeper rejection of the idea of the "merely given" in the theory of motivation. See also J. McDowell, "Are Moral Requirements Hypothetical Imperatives?", *Proceedings of the Aristotelian Society Supplementary Volume* **52** (1978), 13–29.
15. That is, no atomistically conceived state could discharge the role that our folk-psychological notion of a motivation plays in the formal structures of practical reasoning that the argument of *The Possibility of Altruism* identifies.
16. For the idea of a *prima facie* reason, see W. D. Ross, *The Right and the Good* (Oxford: Oxford University Press, 1930), 20.
17. I insert the rider "in a non-alienated way" given that, as Pink emphasizes, you might choose to control your future actions in a way that is alienated from your capacity for action control, such as when you do not trust yourself and put mechanisms in place to override your future capacity for rational decision (such as placing the alarm clock out of reach); T. Pink, *The Psychology of Freedom* (Cambridge: Cambridge University Press, 1996).
18. For a development of this idea as a solution to the traditional problem of diachronic identity, see the competing arguments of C. Korsgaard, "Personal Identity and the Unity of Agency: A Kantian Response to Parfit", in her *Creating the Kingdom of Ends*, 363–98 (Cambridge: Cambridge University Press, 1996) and S. Blackburn, "Has Kant Refuted Parfit?", in *Reading Parfit*, J. Dancy (ed.), 180–201 (Oxford: Blackwell, 1997).
19. This line of argument is analysed in a fascinating way by Luca Ferrero; see, as representative, "Decisions, Division of Deliberative Labor and Diachronic Autonomy", unpublished manuscript.
20. As argued by S. Blackburn, "Practical Tortoise Raising", *Mind* **104**(416) (1995), 695–711, and P. Railton, "On the Hypothetical and Non-hypothetical in Reasoning about Action", in *Ethics and Practical Reason*, G. Cullity & B. Gaut (eds), 53–79 (Oxford: Oxford University Press, 1997).
21. There is no need, for example, to postulate a faculty of sympathy understood as disposed to supply particular desire-based motivation when triggered on a particular occasion.
22. The latter, epistemological, problem takes the idea of other people having minds for granted and asks how we have knowledge of them. See Chapter 3, notes 2 and 3.
23. Are we allowed to talk about values at all? *The Possibility of Altruism* stated that all its analyses were going to be "merely formal". Classifying the different kinds of values in the way that Nagel does, does not seem to be a "merely formal" exercise. This is another vulnerable point in Nagel's overall argument.

Chapter 5: Practical objectivity, freedom and a realistic autonomy

1. What, then, exactly is Nagel's relation to Strawson, given that in Chapter 2 I also described Strawson as one of the "New Humeans" to be bracketed with

Nagel? The explanation of this apparent inconsistency is that Strawson's *Individuals* simply described our existing conceptual scheme and treated the sceptic as a person who made poorly motivated suggested revisions to that scheme. But in his later work, notably *Scepticism and Naturalism*, ch. 1, Strawson changed tack. Scepticism is now strictly speaking rationally irrefutable, but unable to make any headway against that which we simply naturally believe.

2. For the terminology of epistemic defeaters see J. L. Pollock, *Contemporary Theories of Knowledge* (Totowa, NJ: Rowman & Littlefield, 1986).

Chapter 6: Normative ethics: Nagel's hybrid ethical theory

1. The main difference between these three views is over their relationship to naturalism (Brink is an ethical naturalist, Shafer-Landau a non-naturalist and I am a naturalist of "second nature" of the kind defended in McDowell, *Mind and World*.) and over the word "independence". Brink and Shafer-Landau treat moral properties as mind-independent in an unqualified way; following the lead of Wiggins and McDowell, my approach attempts to qualify what can be meant by "independence" in this context. All three views contrast with Nagel's. The distinction between moral realism and cognitivism is that the latter is the claim that in its primary dimension of assessment, a core of ethical judgements express knowledge and belief. Realism is an explanation of why this is so, but one that may be nuanced according to the relevant standards of what it is to be a realist in different domains: a realist about ethics does not, for example, have to be a realist about mathematics in exactly the same way.
2. To be precise, the claim is that there is an asymmetric dependence here without reductionism, a claim that can also be expressed using the idea of supervenience. For the claim that supervenience need not involve reduction see Donald Davidson, "Mental Events", in his *Essays on Actions and Events*, 207–27 (Oxford: Oxford University Press, 1980). For a well-known scepticism as to whether this position is ultimately tenable see J. Kim, "Supervenience, Determination, and Reduction", *Journal of Philosophy* **82**(11) (1985), 616–18.
3. For helpful discussion of this general kind of view see J. Skorupski, "Buck-passing about Goodness", in *Hommage à Wlodek: Philosophical Papers Dedicated to Wlodek Rabinowicz*, T. Rønnow-Rasmussen, B. Petersson, J. Josefsson & D. Egonsson (eds). http://www.fil.lu.se/hommageawlodek/ (2007).
4. As previously noted either Millgram, "Was Hume a Humean?", or Persson, "Hume – Not a 'Humean' about Motivation", contain helpful discussions of Hume's views.
5. Again, this is a restatement of the generality constraint of *The Possibility of Altruism*; Nagel has never been particularly friendly to the idea known as moral particularism, in which the nature of reasons is interpreted as ruling out any substantive role in ethical judgement for ethical principles. For an insightful recent discussion of the latter view, see J. Dancy, *Ethics Without Principles* (Oxford: Oxford University Press, 2004).
6. For an independent assessment of Parfit's view see B. Hooker, "Parfit's Arguments for the Present-aim Theory", *Australasian Journal of Philosophy* **70**(1) (1992), 61–75.

7. "The relation between agent-relative and agent-neutral reasons is probably the central question of ethical theory" (*VN*: 159).
8. Given the immense literature on this subject, I omit many necessary qualifications. Applied to token actions, the view is an act consequentialism; applied to types of action, the view is a form of rule consequentialism. The contrast between maximizing and "satisificing" is the contrast between a view that asks the agent to bring about as much value in outcomes as possible, as opposed to meeting a reasonable threshold constraint (adapting an idea of Herb Simon, "A Behavioural Model of Rational Choice", *Quarterly Journal of Economics* **69**[1] [1955], 99–118).
9. The most well-known form of consequentialism, utilitarianism, is related to the former as species to genus. Consequentialism tells you what rightness is for action tokens or types while presupposing a value. Different species of the genus define that value, or not, as the case may be; so G. E. Moore, for example, was a consequentialist who did not think the relevant value (goodness) was definable. Utilitarians believe goodness can be defined in terms of utility but there is wide variation in the different accounts of utility.
10. Like so much else in philosophy, this taxonomy is not uncontroversial. For some caveats, see J. Dreier, "Structures of Normative Theories", *The Monist* **76**(1) (1993), 22–40, where it is argued that a better classification scheme would return to Parfit's use of an agent-neutral–agent-centred distinction, explained in terms of the aims that theories give to agents.
11. A further qualification is that an important footnote in *The View from Nowhere* notes that Scanlon and Hare are both partly right in trying to develop an impartialist model of some of these notions: "I shall not try to show that these reductions of the agent-relative to the agent-neutral fail, since I believe they are partly correct" (*VN*: 166 n.).
12. For criticism see C. M. Korsgaard, "The Reasons We Can Share", *Social Philosophy and Policy* **10**(1) (1993), 24–51.
13. Interestingly, in the paragraph following the one quoted, Nagel does suggest another way in which agent-relative values may be represented indirectly at the objective level. What you can do, at that level, is recognize such values "vicariously", going via "the perspective of the person who has chosen it" (*VN*: 168). But I am not sure about the details of how this works given that at that level one thinks of everyone as "no one in particular". Does not some individual in particular need to be picked out so as to ground even this indirect identification of agent-relative values?
14. It is worth bearing in mind, in assessing this point, that Nagel has already declared the kind of Platonism about value that denies that value is distinctively anthropocentric is wholly misguided.

Chapter 7: Justice, equality and partiality

1. This chapter supersedes my earlier discussion of Nagel's views in "Nagel's Paradox of Equality and Partiality", *Res Publica* **2**(3) (2003), 257–84.
2. Rawls was Nagel's thesis supervisor; over the course of his career Nagel has produced several highly regarded papers interpreting Rawls's views ranging from "Rawls on Justice", *Philosophical Review* **82**(2) (1973), 220–34, to "Rawls and Liberalism", in *The Cambridge Companion to Rawls*, S. Freeman (ed.), 62–85 (Cambridge: Cambridge University Press, 2003).
3. Given that Rawls is constructing a model of justice, he is free to adjust the

model to produce the results he wants. For example, since the parties do not know who they are they cannot choose on the basis of their own preferences, so they have to choose from a list of primary goods.

4. Thus they do not choose the principles they select as "just"; they do not select them under that description. (That would be a very unenlightening theory of justice.) That which models justice in conditions of full knowledge is the completely specified model: the original position, the individuals in that position with their motivations and the veil of ignorance itself.
5. For interpretation of this principle see A. Williams, "The Revisionist Difference Principle", *Canadian Journal of Philosophy* **25** (1995), 257–82 or P. Van Parijs, "Difference Principles", in *The Cambridge Companion to Rawls*, 200–240.
6. I say "oddly" as Rawls's lexically prior principles to the difference principle are also radically egalitarian.
7. I assume it would be unduly costly to leave economic life as a whole, so Rawls's principles do cover one's decisions to market one's labour.
8. Rawls was not, however, a welfare state egalitarian for the reasons given in R. Krouse & M. Macpherson, "Capitalism, 'Property Owning Democracy' and the Welfare State", in *Democracy and the Welfare State*, A. Gutmann, 78–105 (Princeton, NJ: Princeton University Press, 1998).
9. This claim has proved highly controversial. One prominent strand in the so-called "communitarian" critique of liberalism argued that Rawls's views were internally inconsistent. The demandingness of the egalitarianism that Rawls derived requires a society that exhibits strong ties of mutual solidarity. Yet Rawls's use of rational decision theory showed that he was committed to an implicit theory of what people are: atomistic choosers whose identity does not depend on their cultural or social identity. This argument, developed by Michael Sandel in his *Liberalism and the Limits of Justice* (Cambridge: Cambridge University Press, 1982) has been extensively discussed. Rawls denied that his use of rational decision theory committed him to any theory of the person (*Political Liberalism* [New York: Columbia University Press, 1993], 27). One of the most helpful contributions to this argument was Nagel's observation that, to have any justificatory force, in identifying with a party in the original position you have to think of yourself as taking up a certain role (Nagel, "Rawls on Justice"). But it is a large and unmotivated further step to take that role to be the essence of your identity or express any theory of the nature of persons.
10. When it comes to the actual procedure by which Nagel hopes to generate assent to such principles, his own preferred account of the ethical suggests that no principled solution can be found. Rather than acquiesce in this result, however, Nagel concludes that the very failure to come up with principles that no one can reasonably reject is itself a basis for revising the relevant standards of reasonableness. It appears that when we fail to derive the outcome we want, we are given another attempt at laundering our initial position until it gives us the right outcome. This is clearly not going to give us much by way of independent justification.

Conclusion

1. This was Kant's interpretation of Plato's Ideas. Our capacity to reason suggests these ideals to us but they are not literally truths about how we ought to think.

2. This is particularly so in the case of Nagel's book reviews. He has, over the course of his career, reviewed a great deal and some of the most important of these reviews form most of the text of both *Other Minds: Critical Essays, 1969–1994* (Oxford: Oxford University Press, 1995) and *Concealment and Exposure and Other Essays* (Oxford: Oxford University Press, 2002).
3. I say "fifty years" as Nagel's first publications, remarkably, appeared in 1959 when he was twenty-two years old.

Bibliography

Major works by Thomas Nagel

This is a *selective* list of those works that are, in my view, Nagel's major publications. A comprehensive list is available from Nagel's webpage at New York University (http://philosophy.fas.nyu.edu/object/thomasnagel).

Nagel, T. 1959a. "Hobbes's Concept of Obligation". *Philosophical Review* **68**(1): 68–83.

Nagel, T. 1965. "Physicalism". *Philosophical Review* **74**(3): 339–56.

Nagel, T. 1969a. "Sexual Perversion". *Journal of Philosophy* **66**(1): 5–17.

Nagel, T. 1969b. "The Boundaries of Inner Space". *Journal of Philosophy* **66**(14): 452–8.

Nagel, T. 1970a. *The Possibility of Altruism*. Oxford: Oxford University Press. Reprinted (Princeton, NJ: Princeton University Press, 1978).

Nagel, T. 1970b. "Death. *Noûs* **4**(1): 73–80.

Nagel, T. 1970c. "Armstrong on the Mind". *Philosophical Review* **79**(3): 394–403.

Nagel, T. 1971a. "Brain Bisection and the Unity of Consciousness". *Synthese* **22**(3–4): 396–413.

Nagel, T. 1971b. "The Absurd". *Journal of Philosophy* **68**(20): 716–27.

Nagel, T. 1972a. "War and Massacre". *Philosophy and Public Affairs* **1**(2): 123–44.

Nagel, T. 1972b. "Aristotle on Eudaimonia". *Phronesis* **17**(3): 252–9.

Nagel, T. 1973a. "Rawls on Justice". *Philosophical Review* **82**(2): 220–34.

Nagel, T. 1973b. "Equal Treatment and Compensatory Discrimination". *Philosophy and Public Affairs* **2**(4): 348–62.

Nagel, T. 1974a. "Freud's Anthropomorphism". In *Freud*, R. Wollheim (ed.), 11–24. New York: Doubleday.

Nagel, T. 1974b. "What is it Like to be a Bat?" *Philosophical Review* **83**(4): 435–50.

Nagel, T. 1975. "Libertarianism without Foundations". *Yale Law Journal* **85**(1): 136–49.

Nagel, T. 1976. "Moral Luck". *Proceedings of the Aristotelian Society Supplementary Volume* **50**: 137–55.

Nagel, T. 1977a. "The Fragmentation of Value". In *Knowledge, Value and Belief*, D. Callahan & H. T. Engelhardt Jr, (eds), 279–94. Hastings-on-the-Hudson, NY: Institute of Society, Ethics and the Life Sciences.

Nagel, T. 1977b. "Poverty and Food: Why Charity is Not Enough". In *Food Policy*, P. G. Brown & H. Shue (eds), 54–62. New York: Free Press.

Nagel, T. 1978a. "Ethics as an Autonomous Theoretical Subject". In *Morality as a Biological Phenomenon*, G. S. Stent (ed.), 221–32. Berlin: Dahlem Workshop.

Nagel, T. 1978b. "The Justification of Equality". *Critica* **10**(28): 3–27.

Nagel, T. 1978c. "Ruthlessness in Public Life". In *Public and Private Morality*, S. Hampshire (ed.), 75–91. Cambridge: Cambridge University Press.

Nagel, T. 1979a. *Mortal Questions*. Cambridge: Cambridge University Press.

Nagel, T. 1979b. "The Meaning of Equality". *Washington University Law Quarterly* **25**: 25–31.

Nagel, T. 1979c. "Subjective and Objective". In his *Mortal Questions*, 196–214. Cambridge: Cambridge University Press.

Nagel, T. 1980. "The Limits of Objectivity". In *The Tanner Lectures on Human Values, Volume I*, S. McMurrin (ed.), 75–139. Cambridge: Cambridge University Press.

Nagel, T. 1983a. "The Objective Self". In *Knowledge and Mind*, C. Ginet & S. Shoemaker (eds), 211–32. Oxford: Oxford University Press.

Nagel, T. 1983b. "In the Mind's Eye: Review of Colin McGinn, *The Subjective View*". *Times Literary Supplement*, 18 November: 1283.

Nagel, T. 1986. *The View from Nowhere*. Oxford: Oxford University Press.

Nagel, T. 1987a. *What Does It All Mean? A Very Short Introduction to Philosophy*. Oxford: Oxford University Press.

Nagel, T. 1987b. "Moral Conflict and Political Legitimacy". *Philosophy and Public Affairs* **16**(3): 215–40.

Nagel, T. 1988. "The Foundations of Impartiality". In *Hare and His Critics*, N. Fotion & D. Seanor (eds), 101–12. Oxford: Oxford University Press.

Nagel, T. 1989. "What Makes a Political Theory Utopian?". *Social Research* **56**(4): 903–20.

Nagel, T. 1991. *Equality and Partiality*. Oxford: Oxford University Press.

Nagel, T. 1994a. "La Valeur de l'inviolabilité". *Revue de Métaphysique et de Morale* **99**(2): 149–66.

Nagel, T. 1994b. "Consciousness and Objective Reality". In *The Mind–Body Problem*, R. Warner & T. Szubka (eds), 63–8. Oxford: Blackwell.

Nagel, T. 1995a. *Other Minds: Critical Essays, 1969–1994*. Oxford: Oxford University Press.

Nagel, T. 1995b. "Moral Epistemology". In *Society's Choices: Social and Ethical Decision Making in Biomedicine*, R. E. Bulger, E. M. Bobby & H. V. Fineberg (eds), 201–14. Washington, D.C.: National Academy Press.

Nagel, T. 1995c. "Personal Rights and Public Space". *Philosophy and Public Affairs* **24**(2): 83–107.

Nagel, T. 1997a. *The Last Word*. Oxford: Oxford University Press.

Nagel, T. 1997b. "Justice and Nature". *Oxford Journal of Legal Studies* **17**(2): 303–21.

Nagel, T. (with Ronald Dworkin, Robert Nozick, John Rawls, Thomas Scanlon, and Judith Jarvis Thomson) 1997c. "Assisted Suicide: The Philosophers' Brief". *New York Review of Books*, 27 March.

Nagel, T. 1998a. "Reductionism and Antireductionism". In *The Limits of Reductionism in Biology*, G. R. Bock & J. A. Goode (eds), 3–10. New York: John Wiley.

Nagel, T. 1998b "Concealment and Exposure". *Philosophy and Public Affairs* **27**(1): 3–30.

Nagel, T. 1998c. "Conceiving the Impossible and the Mind–Body Problem". *Philosophy* **73**(285): 337–52.

Nagel, T. 1999. "Davidson's New Cogito". In *The Philosophy of Donald Davidson*, L. Hahn (ed.), 195–206. Chicago, IL: Open Court.

Nagel, T. 2000. "The Psychophysical Nexus". In *New Essays on the A Priori*, P. Boghossian & C. Peacocke (eds), 432–71. Oxford: Clarendon Press.

Nagel, T. 2001. "Pluralism and Coherence". In *The Legacy of Isaiah Berlin*, R. Dworkin, M. Lilla & R. B. Silvers (eds), 105–11. New York: New York Review of Books Publications.

Nagel, T. & L. Murphy 2001. "Taxes, Redistribution, and Public Provision". *Philosophy and Public Affairs* **30**(1): 53–71.

Nagel, T. 2002. *Concealment and Exposure and Other Essays*. Oxford: Oxford University Press.

Nagel, T. & L. Murphy 2002. *The Myth of Ownership: Taxes and Justice*. Oxford: Oxford University Press.

Nagel, T. 2003a. "Rawls and Liberalism". In *The Cambridge Companion to Rawls*, S. Freeman (ed.), 62–85. Cambridge: Cambridge University Press.

Nagel, T. 2003b. "John Rawls and Affirmative Action". *Journal of Blacks in Higher Education* **39**: 82–4.

Nagel, T. 2004. "Comments: Individual Versus Collective Responsibility". *Fordham Law Review* **72**: 2015–20.

Nagel, T. 2005 "The Problem of Global Justice". *Philosophy and Public Affairs* **33**(2): 113–47.

Bibliography of other works

Adams, R. M. 1979. "Primitive Thisness and Primitive Identity". *Journal of Philosophy* **76**(1): 5–26.

Almog, J., J. Perry & H. Wettstein (eds) 1989. *Themes from Kaplan*. Oxford: Oxford University Press.

Alter, T. 2002. "Nagel On Imagination and Physicalism". *Journal of Philosophical Research* **27**: 143–58.

Altham, J. E. J. & T. R. Harrison (eds) 1995. *World, Mind and Ethics: Essays on the Ethical Philosophy of Bernard Williams*. Cambridge: Cambridge University Press.

Anscombe, G. E. M. 1957. *Intention*. Oxford: Blackwell.

Anscombe, G. E. M. 1967. *An Introduction to Wittgenstein's Tractatus*. London: Hutchinson.

Austin, J. L. 1961a. *Philosophical Papers*. Oxford: Oxford University Press.

Austin, J. L. 1961b. "Other Minds". See Austin (1961a), 76–116.

Austin, J. L. 1961c. "A Plea for Excuses". See Austin (1961a), 175–204.

Austin, J. L. 1961d. "Three Ways of Spilling Ink". See Austin (1961a), 272–87.

Avramides, A. 2001. *Other Minds*. London: Routledge.

Ayer, A. J. 1956. *The Problem of Knowledge*. Harmondsworth: Penguin.

Ayer, A. J. (ed.) 1959. *Logical Positivism*. New York: Free Press.

Barnes, B. 1992. "Realism, Relativism and Finitism". In *Cognitive Relativism and Social Science*, D. Raven, L. van Vucht Tijssen & J. de Wolf (eds), 131–47. Piscataway, NJ: Transaction.

Bell, M. & M. McGinn 1990. "Naturalism and Scepticism". *Philosophy* **65**(254): 399–418.

Biro, J. 1991. "Consciousness and Subjectivity". In *Consciousness: Philosophical Issues*, E. Villanueva (ed.), 113–33. Atascadero, CA: Ridgeview.

Biro, J. 1993. "Consciousness and Objectivity". In *Consciousness*, M. Davies & G. W. Humphreys (eds), 178–96. Oxford: Blackwell.

Biro, J. 2006. "A Point of View on Points of View". *Philosophical Psychology* **19**(1): 3–12.

Blackburn, S. 1995. "Practical Tortoise Raising". *Mind* **104**(416): 695–711.

Blackburn, S. 1997. "Has Kant Refuted Parfit?". In *Reading Parfit*, J. Dancy (ed.), 180–201. Oxford: Blackwell.

Blackburn, S. 1998. "Review of Thomas Nagel, *The Last Word*". *Philosophical Review* **107**(4): 653–6.

Block, N. (ed.) 1980. *Readings in the Philosophy of Psychology*, vol. 1. Cambridge, MA: Harvard University Press.

Block, N. (ed.) 1981. *Readings in the Philosophy of Psychology*, vol. 2. Cambridge, MA: Harvard University Press.

Block, N., O. Flanagan & G. Guzeldere (eds) 1997. *The Nature of Consciousness: Philosophical Debates*. Cambridge, MA: MIT Press.

Bock, G. R. & J. A. Goode (eds) 1998. *The Limits of Reductionism in Biology*. New York: John Wiley.

Boghossian, P. & C. Peacocke (eds) 2000. *New Essays on the A Priori*. Oxford: Clarendon Press.

Bradley, F. H. 1999. "My Station and Its Duties". In his *Ethical Studies*, 145–92. Bristol: Thoemmes Press.

Brand, M. & D. Walton (eds) 1976. *Action Theory*. Dordrecht: Reidel.

Brandom, R. 1994. *Making it Explicit*. Cambridge, MA: Harvard University Press.

Brandom, R. 1998. "Action, Norms, and Practical Reasoning". *Noûs* **32**, *Supplement: Philosophical Perspectives, 12, Language Mind and Ontology*: 127–39.

Bratman, M. 1999. *Intentions, Plans and Practical Reasoning*. Cambridge: Cambridge University Press.

Brink, D. 1989. *Moral Realism and the Foundations of Ethics*. Cambridge: Cambridge University Press.

Brink, D. 1992. "Sidgwick and the Rationale for Ethical Egoism". In *Essays on Henry Sidgwick*, B. Schultz (ed.), 199–240. Cambridge: Cambridge University Press.

Brink, D. 1997. "Kantian Rationalism: Inescapability, Authority, and Supremacy". In *Ethics and Practical Reason*, G. Cullity & B. Gaut (eds), 255–91. Oxford: Oxford University Press.

Brook, R. 1991. "Agency and Morality". *Journal of Philosophy* **88**(4): 190–212.

Brown, P. G. & H. Shue (eds) 1977. *Food Policy*. New York: Free Press.

Buchdahl, G. 1989 "Realism and Realization in a Kantian Light". In *Reading Kant*, E. Schaper & W. Vossenkuhl (eds), 217–49. Oxford: Blackwell.

Bulger, R. E., E. M. Bobby & H. V. Fineberg (eds) 1995. *Society's Choices: Social and Ethical Decision Making in Biomedicine*. Washington, D.C.: National Academy Press.

Burnyeat, M. (ed.) 1983a. *The Skeptical Tradition*. Berkeley, CA: University of California Press.

Burnyeat, M. 1983b. "Can The Skeptic Live His Skepticism?". In his *The Skeptical Tradition*, 117–48. Berkeley, CA: University of California Press.

Butler, J. 2000. "The Analogy of Religion". In *The Works of Joseph Butler*, Elibron Classics facsimile edition. Boston, MA: Adamant Media Corporation.
Callahan, D. & H. T. Engelhardt Jr (eds) 1997. *Knowledge, Value and Belief*. Hastings-on-the-Hudson, NY: Institute of Society, Ethics and the Life Sciences.
Carr, D. 1998. "Phenomenology and Fiction in Dennett". *International Journal of Philosophical Studies* **6**(3): 331–44.
Cavell, S. 1999. *The Claim of Reason*. Oxford: Oxford University Press.
Chalmers, D. 1995. "Facing Up to the Problem of Consciousness". *Journal of Consciousness Studies* **2**(3): 200–219.
Chalmers, D. 1997. *The Conscious Mind*. Oxford: Oxford University Press.
Chappell, T. J. (ed.) forthcoming. *Ethical Demandingness*. Basingstoke: Palgrave Macmillan.
Charles, D. & W. Child (eds) 2001. *Wittgensteinian Themes*. Oxford: Oxford University Press.
Chisholm, R. M. 1976. "The Agent as Cause". In *Action Theory*, M. Brand & D. Walton (eds), 199–211. Dordrecht: Reidel.
Chomsky, N. 1995. "Language and Nature". *Mind* **104**(413): 1–61.
Clark, M. 1990. *Nietzsche on Truth and Philosophy*. Cambridge: Cambridge University Press.
Clarke, T. 1972. "The Legacy of Scepticism". *Journal of Philosophy* **69**(20): 754–69.
Cottingham, J., B. Feltham & P. Stratton-Lake (eds) forthcoming. *Impartiality and Partiality in Ethics: Volume II*. Oxford: Oxford University Press.
Craig, E. 1990. *Knowledge and the State of Nature: An Essay in Conceptual Synthesis*. Oxford: Clarendon Press.
Crane, T. 2003. "Subjective Facts". In *Real Metaphysics*, H. Lillehammer & G. Rodriguez-Pereyra (eds), 68–83. London: Routledge.
Cullity, G. & B. Gaut (eds) 1997. *Ethics and Practical Reason*. Oxford: Oxford University Press.
Curley, E. 1972. "Locke, Boyle, and the Distinction between Primary and Secondary Qualities". *Philosophical Review* **8**(4): 438–64.
Dancy, J. 1988. "Contemplating One's Nagel". *Philosophical Books* **29**(1): 1–16.
Dancy, J. 1993. *Moral Reasons*. Oxford: Blackwell.
Dancy, J. (ed.) 1997. *Reading Parfit*. Oxford: Blackwell.
Dancy, J. 2004. *Ethics Without Principles*. Oxford: Oxford University Press.
Darwall, S. 1983. *Impartial Reason*. Ithaca, NY: Cornell University Press.
Darwall, S. 1986. "Agent-Centered Restrictions from the Inside Out". *Philosophical Studies* **50**(3): 291–319.
Daston, L. 1992. "Objectivity and the Escape from Perspective". *Social Studies of Science* **22**(4): 597–618.
Davidson, D. 1980a. *Essays on Actions and Events*. Oxford: Oxford University Press.
Davidson, D. 1980b. "Actions, Reasons and Causes". See Davidson (1980a), 3–19.
Davidson, D. 1980c. "Mental Events". See Davidson (1980a), 207–27.
Davidson, D. 1984a. *Inquiries into Truth and Interpretation*. Oxford: Oxford University Press.
Davidson, D. 1984b. "Truth and Meaning". See Davidson (1984a), 17–36.
Davidson, D. 1984c. "Radical Interpretation". See Davidson (1984a), 125–39.
Davidson, D. 1984d. "On the Very Idea of a Conceptual Scheme". See Davidson (1984a), 183–98.

Davidson, D. 1984e. "The Method of Truth in Metaphysics". See Davidson (1984a), 199–214.
Davies, M. & G. W. Humphreys (eds) 1993. *Consciousness*. Oxford: Blackwell.
Dennett, D. C. 1991. *Consciousness Explained*. Boston, MA: Back Bay Books.
Dent, N. 1984. *The Moral Psychology of the Virtues*. Cambridge: Cambridge University Press.
DeRose, K. 1995. "Solving the Skeptical Problem". *Philosophical Review* **104**(1): 1–52.
Donagan, A. 1987. *Choice: The Essential Element in Human Action*. London: Routledge.
Dreier, J. 1993. "Structures of Normative Theories". *The Monist* **76**(1): 22–40.
Dworkin, R., M. Lilla & R. B. Silvers (eds) 2001. *The Legacy of Isaiah Berlin*. New York: New York Review of Books Publications.
Eilan, N. 2001. "The Reality of Consciousness". In *Wittgensteinian Themes*, D. Charles & W. Child, 163–94. Oxford: Oxford University Press.
Eilan, N. forthcoming. *The Reality of Consciousness*. Oxford: Oxford University Press.
Evnine, S. 1991. *Donald Davidson*. Stanford, CA: Stanford University Press.
Falk, W. D. 1986. "'Ought' and Motivation". In his *Oughts, Reasons and Morality*, 21–41. Ithaca, NY: Cornell University Press.
Ferrero, L. n.d. "Decisions, Division of Deliberative Labor and Diachronic Autonomy". Unpublished ms.
Field, H. 1972. "Tarski's Theory of Truth". *Journal of Philosophy* **69**(13): 347–75.
Field, H. 1981. "Mental Representation". In *Readings in the Philosophy of Psychology*, vol. 2, N. Block (ed.), 78–114. Cambridge, MA: Harvard University Press..
Flanagan, O. 1992. *Consciousness Reconsidered*. Cambridge, MA: MIT Press.
Foot, P. 1985. "Utilitarianism and the Virtues". *Mind* **94**(374): 196–209.
Foster, J. & H. Robinson (eds) 1985. *Essays on Berkeley*. Oxford: Oxford University Press.
Fotion N. & D. Seanor (eds) 1988. *Hare and His Critics*. Oxford: Oxford University Press.
Frankena, W. 1958. "Obligation and Motivation in Recent Moral Philosophy". In *Essays in Moral Philosophy*, A. I. Melden (ed.), 40–81. Seattle, WA: University of Washington Press.
Freeman, S. (ed.) 2003. *The Cambridge Companion to Rawls*. Cambridge: Cambridge University Press.
Frege, G. 1948. "On Sense and Reference", M. Black (trans.). *Philosophical Review* **57**(3): 207–30.
Fried, C. 1978. *Right and Wrong*. Cambridge, MA: Harvard University Press.
Gaut, B. 1999. "Ragbags, Hard Cases, and Moral Pluralism". *Utilitas* **11**(1): 37–48.
Gert, B. 1972. "Review of Thomas Nagel, *The Possibility of Altruism*". *Journal of Philosophy* **69**(12): 340–44.
Ginet, C. & S. Shoemaker (eds) 1983. *Knowledge and Mind*. Oxford: Oxford University Press.
Goodman, N. 1978. *Ways of Worldmaking*. Indiana, IN: Hackett.
Gutmann, A. (ed.) 1998. *Democracy and the Welfare State*. Princeton, NJ: Princeton University Press
Hahn, L. (ed.) 1999. *The Philosophy of Donald Davidson*. Chicago, IL: Open Court.

Haksar, V. 1981. "Nagel on Subjective and Objective". *Inquiry* **24**(1): 105–14.
Hampshire, S. (ed.) 1978. *Public and Private Morality*. Cambridge: Cambridge University Press.
Hare, R. M. 1982. *Moral Thinking: Its Levels, Methods and Point*. Oxford: Oxford University Press.
Harman, G. 1977. *The Nature of Morality*. Oxford: Oxford University Press.
Harrison, R. (ed.) 1979. *Rational Action*. Cambridge: Cambridge University Press.
Hill, C. 1996. "Imaginability, Conceivability, Possibility and the Mind/Body Problem". *Philosophical Studies* **87**(1): 61–85.
Hill, C. & B. McLaughlin 1999. "There Are Fewer Things In Reality than are Dreamt of in Chalmers's Philosophy". *Philosophy and Phenomenological Research* **59**(2): 445–54.
Honderich, T. 1996. "Consequentialism, Moralities of Concern, and Selfishness". *Philosophy* **71**(278): 499–520.
Hooker, B. 1992. "Parfit's Arguments for the Present-aim Theory". *Australasian Journal of Philosophy* **70**(1): 61–75.
Hurley, P. 1997. "Agent-centered Restrictions: Clearing the Air of Paradox". *Ethics* **108**(1): 120–46.
Hurley, S. 1992. "Intelligibility, Imperialism and Conceptual Schemes". *Midwest Studies in Philosophy* **17**: 89–108.
Jackson, F. 1982. "Epiphenomenal Qualia". *Philosophical Quarterly* **32**(127): 127–36.
Jackson, F. 1986. "What Mary Didn't Know". *Journal of Philosophy* **83**(5): 291–5.
Jackson, F. 1998. "Postscript on Qualia". In his *Mind, Method and Conditionals*, 76–9. London: Routledge.
James, W. [1907] 1988. "What Pragmatism Means", lecture II of *Pragmatism*. Reprinted in *William James: Works 1902–1910*. New York: Library of America.
Kant, I. [1781/1783] 1929. *Critique of Pure Reason*, N. Kemp Smith (trans.). London: Macmillan.
Kaplan, D. 1989. "Demonstratives". In *Themes from Kaplan*, J. Almog, J. Perry & H. Wettstein (eds), 481–563. Oxford: Oxford University Press.
Kim, J. 1985. "Supervenience, Determination, and Reduction". *Journal of Philosophy* **82**(11): 616–18.
Korsgaard, C. M. 1993. "The Reasons We Can Share". *Social Philosophy and Policy* **10**(1): 24–51.
Korsgaard, C. M. 1996a. *The Sources of Normativity*. Cambridge: Cambridge University Press.
Korsgaard, C. M. 1996b. *Creating the Kingdom of Ends*. Cambridge: Cambridge University Press.
Korsgaard, C. 1996c. "Personal Identity and the Unity of Agency: A Kantian Response to Parfit". In her *Creating the Kingdom of Ends*, 363–98. Cambridge: Cambridge University Press.
Kripke, S. 1980. *Naming and Necessity*. Cambridge, MA: Harvard University Press.
Krouse, R. & M. Macpherson 1998. "Capitalism, 'Property Owning Democracy' and the Welfare State". In *Democracy and the Welfare State*, A. Gutmann, 78–105. Princeton, NJ: Princeton University Press.
Langton, R. 2007. "Objective and Unconditioned Value". *Philosophical Review* **116**(2): 157–85.
Larmore, C. 1990. "Political Liberalism". *Political Theory* **18**(3): 339–60.

Levin, J. 2007. "Nagel versus Nagel on the Nature of Phenomenal Concepts". *Ratio* **20**(3): 293–307.
Levine, J. 1983. "Materialism and Qualia: the Explanatory Gap". *Pacific Philosophical Quarterly* **64** (October): 354–61.
Levine, J. 2001. *Purple Haze: The Puzzle of Consciousness*. Oxford: Oxford University Press.
Lewis, D. 1990. "What Experience Teaches". In *Mind and Cognition: A Reader*, W. H. Lycan (ed.), 499–519. Oxford: Blackwell.
Lillehammer, H. & G. Rodriguez-Pereyra (eds) 2003. *Real Metaphysics*. London: Routledge.
Loar, B. 1997. "Phenomenal States (Second Version)". In *The Nature of Consciousness: Philosophical Debates*, N. Block, O. Flanagan & G. Guzeldere (eds), 597–616. Cambridge, MA: MIT Press.
Lucas, J. R. 1993. *Responsibility*. Oxford: Oxford University Press.
Luntley, M. 2003. *Wittgenstein: Meaning and Judgement*. Oxford: Blackwell.
Lycan, W. H. (ed.) 1990. *Mind and Cognition: A Reader*. Oxford: Blackwell.
Mackie, J. L. 1977. *Ethics: Inventing Right and Wrong*. Harmondsworth: Penguin.
Madell, G. 1983. *The Identity of the Self*. Edinburgh: Edinburgh University Press.
McDowell, J. 1978. "Are Moral Requirements Hypothetical Imperatives?". *Proceedings of the Aristotelian Society Supplementary Volume* **52**: 13–29.
McDowell, J. 1986. "Critical Notice: *Ethics and the Limits of Philosophy*". *Mind* **95**(379): 377–86.
McDowell, J. 1994. *Mind and World*. Cambridge, MA: Harvard University Press.
McDowell, J. 2001. *Mind, Value and Reality*. Cambridge, MA: Harvard University Press.
McGinn, C. 1980. "Anomalous Monism and Kripke's Cartesian Intuitions". Reprinted in *Readings in the Philosophy of Psychology*, vol. 1, N. Block (ed.), 156–8. Cambridge, MA: Harvard University Press.
McGinn, C. 1983. *The Subjective View: Secondary Qualities and Indexical Thoughts*. Oxford: Oxford University Press.
McGinn, C. 1987. "Review of Thomas Nagel, *The View from Nowhere*". *Mind* **96**(382): 263–72.
McGinn, C. 1991a. *The Problem of Consciousness*, Oxford: Blackwell.
McGinn, C. 1991b. "Can We Solve the Mind–Body Problem?". In his *The Problem of Consciousness*, 1–22. Oxford: Blackwell.
McGinn, C. 1991c. "The Hidden Structure of Consciousness". In his *The Problem of Consciousness*, 89–125. Oxford: Blackwell.
McGinn, C. 1995. "Consciousness and Space". *Journal of Consciousness Studies* **2**(3): 220–30.
McMahon, C. 1991. "The Paradox of Deontology". *Philosophy and Public Affairs* **20**(4): 350–77.
McMurrin, S. (ed.) 1980. *The Tanner Lectures on Human Values, Volume I*. Cambridge: Cambridge University Press.
McNaughton, D. & P. Rawling 1995. "Value and Agent-Relative Reasons". *Utilitas* **7**(1): 31–47.
Melden, A. I. (ed.) 1958. *Essays in Moral Philosophy*. Seattle, WA: University of Washington Press.
Mellor, D. H. 1989. "I and Now". *Proceedings of the Aristotelian Society* **89**: 79–94.

Mellor, D. H. 1991a. *Matters of Metaphysics*. Cambridge: Cambridge University Press.

Mellor, D. H. 1991b "Analytic Philosophy and the Self". Reprinted in his *Matters of Metaphysics*, 1–16. Cambridge: Cambridge University Press.

Mellor, D. H. 1992–3. "Nothing Like Experience". *Proceedings of the Aristotelian Society* **93**: 1–16.

Mellor, D. H. 1998. *Real Time II*. London: Routledge.

Michael, M. & J. O'Leary-Hawthorne (eds) 1984. *Philosophy in Mind*. Dordrecht: Kluwer.

Mill, J. S. 1843. *A System of Logic*. London: John W. Parker.

Mill, J. S. 1969. *Utilitarianism*. Belmont, CA: Wadsworth.

Millgram, E. 1995. "Was Hume a Humean?", *Hume Studies* **21**(1): 75–93.

Moore, A. W. 1987a. "Review of Thomas Nagel, *The View from Nowhere*". *Philosophical Quarterly* **37**(148): 323–7.

Moore, A. W. 1987b. "Points of View". *Philosophical Quarterly* **37**(146): 1–20.

Moore, A. W. 1987c. "On Saying and Showing". *Philosophy* **62**(292): 473–97.

Moore, A. W. 1997. *Points of View*. Oxford: Oxford University Press.

Moore, A. W. 1999. "One or Two Dogmas of Objectivism: A Critical Notice of Thomas Nagel, *The Last Word*". *Mind* **108**(130): 381–93.

Moore, A. W. 2007. "Realism and the Absolute Conception". In *Bernard Williams*, A. Thomas (ed.), 24–46. Cambridge: Cambridge University Press.

Moran, R. 1994. "The Expression of Feeling in Imagination". *Philosophical Review* **103**(1): 75–106.

Mouffe, C. (ed.) 1992. *Dimensions of Radical Democracy: Citizenship, Pluralism, Community*. London: Verso.

Murphy, L. 1998. "Institutions and the Demands of Justice". *Philosophy and Public Affairs* **27**(4): 251–91.

Nemirow, L. 1980. "Review of Thomas Nagel's *Mortal Questions*". *Philosophical Review* **89**(3): 473–7.

Nemirow, L. 1990. "Physicalism and the Cognitive Role of Acquaintance". In *Mind and Cognition: A Reader*, W. H. Lycan (ed.), 490–99. Oxford: Blackwell.

Neurath, O. 1959. "Protocol Sentences". In *Logical Positivism*, A. J. Ayer (ed.), 199–208. New York: Free Press.

Oddie, G. 2005. *Value, Reality and Desire*. Oxford: Oxford University Press.

O'Neill, O. 1989. "Constructivisms in Ethics". In her *Constructions of Reason: Explorations of Kant's Practical Philosophy*, 206–18. Cambridge: Cambridge University Press.

O'Shaughnessy, B. 1980. *The Will: A Double Aspect Theory*, 2 vols. Cambridge: Cambridge University Press.

Papineau, D. 1993. *Philosophical Naturalism*. Oxford: Blackwell.

Parfit, D. 1973. "Later Selves and Moral Principles". In *Philosophy and Personal Relations*, A. Montefiore (ed.), 139–42. London: Routledge.

Parfit, D. 1984. *Reasons and Persons*. Oxford: Oxford University Press.

Parfit, D. 1995. "The Unimportance of Identity". In *Identity: Essays Based on Herbert Spencer Lectures given in the University of Oxford*, H. Harris (ed.), 13–45. Oxford: Clarendon Press.

Parfit, D. 1999. "Experiences, Subjects, and Conceptual Schemes". *Philosophical Topics* **26**(1–2): 217–70.

Peacocke, C. 1985. "Imagination, Experience and Possibility: A Berkeleian View Defended". In *Essays on Berkeley*, J. Foster & H. Robinson (eds), 19–35. Oxford: Oxford University Press.

Peacocke, C. 1989. "No Resting Place: A Critical Notice of Thomas Nagel, *The View from Nowhere*". *Philosophical Review* **98**(1): 65–82.
Percival, P. 1994. "Absolute Truth". *Proceedings of the Aristotelian Society* **94**: 189–213.
Persson, I. 1997. "Hume – Not a 'Humean' about Motivation". *History of Philosophy Quarterly* **14**(2): 189–206.
Pettit, P. & M. Smith 1990. "Backgrounding Desire". *Philosophical Review* **99**(4): 565–92.
Pickering, A. 1984. *Constructing Quarks: A Sociological History of Particle Physics*. Chicago, IL: University of Chicago Press.
Pink, T. 1996. *The Psychology of Freedom*. Cambridge: Cambridge University Press.
Pippin, R. B. 1987. "Kant on the Spontaneity of Mind". *Canadian Journal of Philosophy* **17**(2): 449–75.
Pippin, R. B. 1991. *Modernism as a Philosophical Problem*. Oxford: Blackwell.
Pippin, R. B. 1999. *Modernism as a Philosophical Problem*, 2nd edn. Cambridge: Cambridge University Press.
Place, U. T. 1956. "Is Consciousness a Brain Process?". *British Journal of Psychology* **47**: 44–50.
Pollock, J. L. 1986. *Contemporary Theories of Knowledge*. Totowa, NJ: Rowman & Littlefield.
Priest, S. 2000. *The Subject in Question*. London: Routledge.
Prior, A. N. 1976. "Thank Goodness That's Over". In his *Papers in Logic and Ethics*, 78–84. London: Duckworth.
Putnam, H. 1981. *Reason, Truth and History*. Cambridge: Cambridge University Press
Putnam, H. 1992. *Realism with a Human Face*. Cambridge, MA: Harvard University Press.
Putnam, H. 1995a. *Renewing Philosophy*. Cambridge, MA: Harvard University Press.
Putnam, H. 1995b. "Bernard Williams and the Absolute Conception of the World". In his *Renewing Philosophy*, 80–107. Cambridge, MA: Harvard University Press.
Quinn, W. 1994a. *Morality and Action*. Cambridge: Cambridge University Press.
Quinn, W. 1994b "Reflection and the Loss of Moral Knowledge: Williams on Objectivity". See Quinn (1994a), 134–48.
Quinn, W. 1994c. "Actions, Intentions and Consequences: The Doctrine of Doing and Allowing". See Quinn (1994a), 149–74.
Quinn, W. 1994d. "Actions, Intentions and Consequences: The Doctrine of Double Effect". See Quinn (1994a), 175–93.
Railton, P. 1997. "On the Hypothetical and Non-hypothetical in Reasoning about Action". In *Ethics and Practical Reason*, G. Cullity & B. Gaut (eds), 53–79. Oxford: Oxford University Press.
Ratcliffe M. 2002. "Husserl and Nagel on Subjectivity and the Limits of Physical Objectivity". *Continental Philosophy Review* **35**(4): 353–77.
Raven, D., L. van Vucht Tijssen & J. de Wolf (eds) 1992. *Cognitive Relativism and Social Science*. Piscataway, NJ: Transaction.
Rawls, J. 1971. *A Theory of Justice*. Cambridge, MA: Harvard University Press.
Rawls, J. 1993. *Political Liberalism*. New York: Columbia University Press.
Rawls, J. 1999a. *Collected Papers*. Cambridge, MA: Harvard University Press.

Rawls, J. 1999b. *The Law of Peoples*. Cambridge, MA: Harvard University Press.

Rawls, J. 2001. *Justice as Fairness: A Restatement*. Cambridge, MA: Harvard University Press.

Reid, T. 2002. *Essays on the Intellectual Powers of Man*, D. R. Brocker & K. Haakonssen (eds). Edinburgh: Edinburgh University Press.

Rønnow-Rasmussen, T., B. Petersson, J. Josefsson & D. Egonsson (eds) 2007. *Hommage à Wlodek. Philosophical Papers Dedicated to Wlodek Rabinowicz*. http://www.fil.lu.se/hommageawlodek/

Rorty, A. O. (ed.) 1986. *Essays on Descartes' Meditations*. Berkeley, CA: University of California Press.

Rorty, R. 1982. *Consequences of Pragmatism*. Minneapolis, MN: Minnesota University Press.

Rosen, G. 1984. "Objectivity and Modern Idealism". In *Philosophy in Mind*, M. Michael & J. O'Leary-Hawthorne (eds), 277–319. Dordrecht: Kluwer.

Ross, W. D. 1930. *The Right and the Good*. Oxford: Oxford University Press.

Rousseau, J.-J. 1997. *The Social Contract and Other Later Political Writings*. Cambridge: Cambridge University Press.

Sacks, M. 1989. *The World We Found*. London: Duckworth.

Sandel, M. 1982. *Liberalism and the Limits of Justice*. Cambridge: Cambridge University Press.

Sartre, J.-P. 1960. *The Transcendence of the Ego: An Existentialist Theory of Consciousness*, F. Williams & R. Kirkpatrick (trans.). New York: Hill & Wang.

Scanlon, T. 1998. *What We Owe to Each Other*. Cambridge, MA: Harvard University Press.

Schaper E. & W. Vossenkuhl (eds) 1989. *Reading Kant*. Oxford: Blackwell.

Scheffler, S. 1994. *The Rejection of Consequentialism*, 2nd edn. Oxford: Oxford University Press.

Scheffler, S. 2003. "Justice and Desert in Liberal Theory". In his *Boundaries and Allegiances: Problems of Justice and Responsibility in Liberal Theory*, 173–96. Oxford: Oxford University Press.

Schultz, B. (ed.) 1992. *Essays on Henry Sidgwick*. Cambridge: Cambridge University Press.

Searle, J. 1992a. *Intentionality*. Cambridge: Cambridge University Press.

Searle, J. 1992b. *The Rediscovery of the Mind*. Cambridge, MA: MIT Press.

Sellars, W. 1997. *Empiricism and the Philosophy of Mind*. Cambridge, MA: Harvard University Press.

Sen, A. 1979. "Informational Analysis of Moral Principles". In *Rational Action*, R. Harrison (ed.), 115–32. Cambridge: Cambridge University Press.

Sen, A. 1983 "Evaluator Relativity and Consequential Evaluation". *Philosophy and Public Affairs* **12**(2): 113–32.

Shafer-Landau, R. 2005. *Moral Realism: A Defence*. Oxford: Oxford University Press.

Sidgwick, H. 1981. *The Methods of Ethics*. Indianapolis, IN: Hackett.

Siewert, C. 1998. *The Significance of Consciousness*. Princeton, NJ: Princeton University Press.

Sie, M. 2005. *Justifying Blame*. Amsterdam: Rodopi.

Simon, H. 1955. "A Behavioural Model of Rational Choice". *Quarterly Journal of Economics* **69**(1): 99–118.

Skorupski, J. 2007. "Buckpassing about Goodness". In *Hommage à Wlodek: Philosophical Papers Dedicated to Wlodek Rabinowicz*, T. Rønnow-Rasmussen, B. Petersson, J. Josefsson & D. Egonsson (eds). http://www.fil.lu.se/hommageawlodek/

Smith, M. 1987. "The Humean Theory of Motivation". *Mind*, new series, **96**(381): 36–61.
Stalnaker, R. 2003a. *Ways a World Might Be*. Oxford: Oxford University Press.
Stalnaker, R. 2003b. "Thomas Nagel's Objective Self". In his *Ways a World Might Be*, 253–87.
Stent, G. S. (ed.) 1978. *Morality as a Biological Phenomenon*. Berlin: Dahlem Workshop.
Strawson, P. 1959. *Individuals: An Essay in Descriptive Metaphysics*. London: Methuen.
Strawson, P. 1974a. *Freedom and Resentment and Other Essays*. London: Methuen.
Strawson, P. 1974b. "Freedom and Resentment". In his *Freedom and Resentment and Other Essays*, 1–25. London: Methuen.
Strawson, P. 1974c. "Social Morality and Individual Ideal". In his *Freedom and Resentment and Other Essays*, 26–44. London: Methuen.
Strawson, P. 1985. *Scepticism and Naturalism: Some Varieties*. London: Methuen.
Stroud, B. 1984. *The Significance of Philosophical Scepticism*. Oxford: Oxford University Press.
Stroud, B. 1999. *The Quest for Reality*. Oxford: Oxford University Press.
Stroud, B. 2000. "Practical Reasoning". In *Reasoning Practically*, E. Ullmann-Margalit (ed.), 27–38. Oxford: Oxford University Press.
Sturgeon, N. 1974. "Altruism, Solipsism and the Objectivity of Reasons". *Philosophical Review* **83**(3): 374–402.
Taylor, C. n.d. "Justice After Virtue". Unpublished ms.
Taylor, C. 1985. "Interpretation and the Sciences of Man". In his *Philosophical Papers, Volume 2: Philosophy and the Human Sciences*, 15–57. Cambridge: Cambridge University Press.
Tenenbaum, S. 2006. *Appearances of the Good*. Cambridge: Cambridge University Press.
Tenenbaum, S. (ed.) 2007a. *New Trends in Philosophy: Moral Psychology*. Amsterdam: Rodopi.
Tenenbaum, S. 2007b. "The Conclusion of Practical Reason". In his *New Trends in Philosophy: Moral Psychology*, 323–43. Amsterdam: Rodopi.
Thomas, A. 1997. "Kant, McDowell and the Theory of Consciousness". *European Journal of Philosophy* **5**(3): 283–305.
Thomas, A. 2003a. "Nagel's Paradox of Equality and Partiality". *Res Publica* **2**(3): 257–84.
Thomas, A. 2003b. "An Adverbial Theory of Consciousness". *Phenomenology and the Cognitive Sciences* **2**(3): 161–85.
Thomas, A. 2005. "Reasonable Partiality and the Agent's Personal Point of View". *Ethical Theory and Moral Practice* **8**(1–2): 25–43.
Thomas, A. 2006a. "Reconciling Conscious Absorption and the Ubiquity of Self-Awareness". Paper presented to the tenth conference of the Association for the Scientific Study of Consciousness, 23–6 June 2006, Oxford.
Thomas, A. 2006b. *Value and Context: The Nature of Moral and Political Knowledge*. Oxford: Oxford University Press.
Thomas, A. (ed.) 2007. *Bernard Williams*, Cambridge: Cambridge University Press.
Thomas, A. forthcoming (a). "Is Practical Reasoning Essentially First Personal?". In *Impartiality and Partiality in Ethics: Volume I*, J. Cottingham, B. Feltham & P. Stratton-Lake (eds). Oxford: Oxford University Press.

Thomas, A. forthcoming (b). "Consequentialism, Integrity and Demandingness". In *Ethical Demandingness*, T. J. Chappell (ed.). Basingstoke: Palgrave Macmillan.
Tollefsen, C. 1999. "Sidgwickian Objectivity and Ordinary Morality". *Journal of Value Inquiry* **3**(1): 57–70.
Ullmann-Margalit, E. (ed.) 2000. *Reasoning Practically*. Oxford: Oxford University Press.
Urmson, J. 1974/5. "A Defence of Intuitionism". *Proceedings of the Aristotelian Society* **25**: 111–19.
Van Gulick, R. 1997. "Understanding the Phenomenal Mind". In *The Nature of Consciousness: Philosophical Debates*, N. Block, O. Flanagan & G. Guzeldere (eds), 559–66. Cambridge, MA: MIT Press.
Van Parijs, P. 2003. "Difference Principles". In *The Cambridge Companion to Rawls*, S. Freeman (ed.), 200–240. Cambridge: Cambridge University Press.
Villanueva, E. (ed.) 1991. *Consciousness: Philosophical Issues*. Atascadero, CA: Ridgeview.
Wallace, R. J. 2007. "The Argument from Resentment". *Proceedings of the Aristotelian Society* **107**: 295–318.
Walzer, M. 1990. "The Communitarian Critique of Liberalism". *Political Theory* (February) **18**(1): 6–23.
Walzer, M. 1992. "The Civil Society Argument". In *Dimensions of Radical Democracy: Citizenship, Pluralism, Community*, C. Mouffe (ed.), 89–107. London: Verso.
Warner, R. & T. Szubka (eds) 1994. *The Mind–Body Problem*. Oxford: Blackwell.
Wider, K. 1990. "Overtones of Solipsism in Thomas Nagel's 'What is it Like to be a Bat?' and *The View from Nowhere*". *Philosophy and Phenomenological Research* **50**(3): 481–99.
Wiggins, D. 1968. "On Being in the Same Place at the Same Time". *Philosophical Review* **77**(1): 90–95.
Wiggins, D. 2000a. *Needs, Values, Truth: Essays in the Philosophy of Value*. Oxford: Oxford University Press.
Wiggins, D. 2000b. "Towards a Reasonable Libertarianism". In his *Needs, Values, Truth: Essays in the Philosophy of Value*, 269–302. Oxford: Oxford University Press.
Wiggins, D. 2001. *Sameness and Substance Renewed*. Cambridge: Cambridge University Press.
Williams, A. 1995. "The Revisionist Difference Principle". *Canadian Journal of Philosophy* **25**: 257–82.
Williams, B. with J. J. C. Smart 1973. *Utilitarianism: For and Against*. Cambridge: Cambridge University Press.
Williams, B. 1978. *Descartes: The Project of Pure Enquiry*. Harmondsworth: Penguin.
Williams, B. 1981a. *Moral Luck*. Cambridge: Cambridge University Press.
Williams, B. 1981b. "Wittgenstein and Idealism". In his *Moral Luck*, 144–63. Cambridge: Cambridge University Press.
Williams, B. 1985. *Ethics and the Limits of Philosophy*. London: Fontana.
Williams, B. 1990 "The Need to Be Sceptical". *Times Literary Supplement* **16–22** (February): 163–4.
Williams, B. 1991. "Terrestrial Thoughts, Extraterrestrial Science: Review of Hilary Putnam, *Realism with a Human Face*". *London Review of Books* (7 February): 12–13.

Williams, B. 1995. "Replies". In *World, Mind and Ethics: Essays on the Ethical Philosophy of Bernard Williams*, J. E. J. Altham & T. R. Harrison (eds), 185–224. Cambridge: Cambridge University Press.
Williams, B. 1997a. *Making Sense of Humanity*. Cambridge: Cambridge University Press.
Williams, B. 1997b. "What Does Intuitionism Imply?". In his *Making Sense of Humanity*, 182–91. Cambridge: Cambridge University Press.
Williams, B. 1997c. "The Point of View of the Universe: Sidgwick and the Ambitions of Ethics". In his *Making Sense of Humanity*, 153–71. Cambridge: Cambridge University Press.
Williams, B. 1998. "The End of Explanation?: Review of Thomas Nagel, *The Last Word*". *New York Review of Books* **45**(18) (19 November): 40–42.
Williams, B. 2002. *Truth and Truthfulness: An Essay on Genealogy*. Princeton, NJ: Princeton University Press.
Williams, B. 2005. "From Freedom to Liberty: The Construction of a Political Value". In *In the Beginning was the Deed*, G. Hawthorn (ed.), 75–96. Princeton, NJ: Princeton University Press.
Williams, M. 1986. "Descartes and the Metaphysics of Doubt". In *Essays on Descartes' Meditations*, A. O. Rorty (ed.), 117–39. Berkeley, CA: University of California Press.
Williams, M. 1991. *Unnatural Doubts*. Oxford: Blackwell.
Williams, M. 2001. *Problems of Knowledge*. Oxford: Oxford University Press.
Wittgenstein, L. 1961. *Tractatus Logico-Philosophicus*, D. Pears & B. F. McGuinness (trans.). London: Routledge.
Wittgenstein, L. 2001. *Philosophical Investigations*, G. E. M. Anscombe (trans.). Oxford: Blackwell.
Woit, P. 2007. *Not Even Wrong: The Failure of String Theory and the Search for Unity in Physical Law*. New York: Basic Books.
Wollheim, R. (ed.) 1974. *Freud*. New York: Doubleday.
Wright, C. 1992. *Truth and Objectivity*. Cambridge, MA: Harvard University Press.
Zahavi, D. 2006. *Subjectivity and Selfhood*. Cambridge, MA: MIT Press.

Index